John Charles Thomas

John Charles Thomas

Beloved Baritone of American Opera and Popular Music

Michael J. Maher

McFarland & Company, Inc., Publishers
Jefferson, North Carolina, and London

Frontispiece: A studio portrait of John Charles Thomas, c. 1930.

[Library of Congress Online Catalog]

Maher, Michael J.
    John Charles Thomas : beloved baritone of American opera and
popular music / Michael J. Maher.
      p.   cm.
    Includes bibliographical references and index.

    ISBN-13: 978-0-7864-2668-3
    ISBN-10: 0-7864-2668-3 (softcover : 50# alkaline paper)

    1. Thomas, John Charles, 1891–1960.   2. Baritones (Singers)—
United States— Biography.   I. Title
ML420.T455 M34   2006

                                   2006020493

British Library cataloguing data are available

On the cover: John Charles Thomas, 1947 (Photograph courtesy
Leigh Martinet).

Manufactured in the United States of America

McFarland & Company, Inc., Publishers
  Box 611, Jefferson, North Carolina 28640
  www.mcfarlandpub.com

For Carl J. Burlage, S.J.
Teacher, philosopher, lover of great singing

Table of Contents

Preface

It is difficult to describe the place that John Charles Thomas once had in American music, as a singer who could make an audience feel at home with an operatic aria, an art song, a pop favorite, or a hymn; an artist who introduced many to serious music who would not have gone to a concert of any other classical singer. At the peak of his popularity, from 1934 to 1946, he was one of the best known names in American music sought out by composers like Jerome Kern and Vincent Youmans as a man who could make their songs hits. No one has filled the place he once held in American music, yet he is all but forgotten among both operatic and popular audiences.

It is not uncommon for operatic or classically trained singers to venture into popular music. Amelita Galli-Curci recorded songs by Victor Herbert, and Mario Lanza had a successful Hollywood career. It is rare, however, for such artists to be equally at home in both worlds. Thomas was. As Virgil Thomson wrote of him, "Thomas pleases everyone. Perhaps not with every song, but at some point in his concert, every member of the audience hears the music he likes."[1]

Today it seems quite natural for symphony orchestras and classical artists to offer "pop" concerts. Yet in his time, it was Thomas's determination to include popular material in his concerts that made him a kind of pariah with many critics. That reputation as a popular singer rather than a serious artist has pursued him ever since.

The sheer vitality of John Charles Thomas, and the fascinating course of his life, would be sufficient reason for a biography. A novelist could not invent a character who was more at the center of the good life in the twentieth century than John Charles Thomas. From 1915 to 1922, he lived the high life of a Broadway star in New York. In the Roaring Twenties he lived a transatlantic life, with bases in Paris, Brussels, London, New York, and Palm Beach. During the thirties, when he became the only Broadway star

1

ever to make a career at the Metropolitan Opera, he settled in New York and on Maryland's Eastern Shore. In the 1940s, he moved to Los Angeles, a city full of energy and change during the war years.

Thomas lived with more gusto and enthusiasm than any of his contemporaries in the musical world, taking all he could from life in some of the hardest years of the nation's history. Thomas's interests ran from golf, yachting, speedboat racing, and deep-sea fishing to pig farming and chicken ranching. These were not hobbies in which he dabbled, but real enthusiasms, and his enthusiasm was infectious. It was this irrepressible buoyancy in his personality in the midst of Depression and War that made his operatic performances—complete with whistles and cartwheels—as well as his concerts and radio broadcasts, great audience favorites.

Yet there was a dark side to this artist as well. Longtime friends and professional acquaintances who remembered him as a generous, loyal friend and a great gentleman also knew him to be hot-tempered, even cruel. Many who had brief encounters with him found him arrogant and self-important. He broke with his accompanist of twelve years, the highly respected Carrol Hollister, over trivial political differences. His practical jokes could be heavy-handed and tasteless. Though not an alcoholic, he was a heavy drinker, and a womanizer.

All of these characteristics, even paradoxes—the humble beginnings, the brash self-confidence, eventual affluence, the great appetite for life — find expression in Thomas's singing. How could someone who sang French art songs and operatic arias so elegantly make "Home on the Range" a signature song? If you understand that the man who lived on yachts and in fine homes, who ate gourmet meals and loved fine wine, was still the boy who had run through fields and hunted squirrels in his childhood, his breadth as an artist begins to make sense. He was Peter Pan with an appreciation for good music and the good life.

While Thomas had a spectacularly successful career, he has paid a high price for his attempt to straddle the worlds of serious and popular music. Other popular singers of his generation, Nelson Eddy, Paul Robeson, even Al Jolson, are still well known to a general musical audience today, as the names of Rosa Ponselle and Lawrence Tibbett are well known to classical listeners. Their recordings are still found in classical CD bins, their faces even appear on US postage stamps. Thomas tends to be remembered, if at all, as a singer of cute "character" songs like "The Green Eyed Dragon" and "Lord Randall." Yet in his day, composers wrote material for Thomas because he could make their songs popular as few others could. For three successive years during the Second World War, Thomas was voted the most popular classical singer in America. How does one explain a singer who was once so popular, but whose name is now largely forgotten, and whose place in the world of American music has been left unfilled?

Thomas ascribed his neglect by critics to his commitment to include serious works by American composers in all of his concerts. He championed the work of composers like Ernest Charles, Henry Burleigh, Sydney King Russell, Pearl Curran, Beatrice Fenner and many others. And who ever sang their work better? Only Richard Crooks approached Thomas's elegant diction in English, French, Italian and Latin. Thomas's vocal range ran from the bass clef to tenor regions, from the softest half voice to a stirring, full-throated fortissimo. The voice itself was extraordinary. Perfectly placed, unforced, with true bel canto production, it had a manly American sound that was, as one critic described it, "like the average person would like to sound if they could sing opera."

Thomas had two special qualities that distinguished him as a concert artist: he could invest his personality in his singing — whether a hymn, a child's song, a sea shanty, or an aria — and he could deliver a show-stopping, rafter-rattling performance. Yet he was also a subtle and gifted musician. Thomas's real métier was in the rare and difficult repertoire of the French high baritone — operas of Massenet: *Thais, Herodiade, Le Roi de Lahore*; or Italian operas like *Zaza, Don Carlos*, and *La Favorita*. Unfortunately, despite a French wing at the Metropolitan Opera that included Lilly Pons, Bidu Sayao, Helen Jepson, Georges Thill and Richard Crooks during the years in which Thomas was a member of the company, the Met confined itself to conventional offerings of Faust and the occasional rolling out of a much cut version of Donizetti's *Daughter of the Regiment* as a vehicle for Pons. Parts that seemed written for Thomas, such as Wrestling Bradford in *Merry Mount*, or the *Emperor Jones*, were given instead to Lawrence Tibbett. Thomas was even denied the opportunity to sing Escamillio in *Carmen*. That role went to Ezio Pinza, a great singer, but not a man at home with the French language.

All his life, John Charles Thomas was an extraordinarily competitive man. It is one of the best keys to understanding his personality. He was a competitive athlete in school, where he held a record for a high jump at 5'10". He was competitive as a singer. Not content with the easy money that was his as a Broadway matinee idol, he went to Paris and Brussels to perfect his French, study repertoire under the legendary tenor Jean de Reszke, and acquire operatic training and experience. He successfully broke into the Metropolitan Opera despite the management's bias against American singers. He defied the critics and presented concerts and radio shows that reached out to a broad public. He tried very hard to make hit records— million sellers— during the Depression, when single records were not only very expensive — the equivalent of a good concert seat or a week's worth of lunches—but had been replaced by radio as the public's favorite entertainment medium. His goal seemed to be to command the heights of both the operatic world and the world of popular music, to be both the Caruso and the Jolson of his generation. Unfortunately, his time did not offer sufficient outlets for the full range of his talent. At some point, probably by the early 1940s, he simply gave up trying to extend his art, and sang what the audiences came to hear.

It is not uncommon for a singer to outlive his popularity. It is the norm. In Thomas's case, there is little reason for disappointment. By most standards, he had a hugely successful career. His gradual retirement in the early 1950s came when he was in his early sixties and had performed before the public for over forty years. His voice was not yet showing the ravages that often affect fine voices at that stage of life. If his vibrato had begun to widen, and the flexibility of the voice was no longer what it had once been, the color and tone of the voice were wholly intact. Yet the end came abruptly for all that. There was no great farewell tour, no gala celebration of his long career; he simply faded into the background as musical tastes changed.

Other popular music fashions of his era were also waning: Big Band music and Swing gave way to sentimental "top 40" ballads and then to rock and roll. It was a change of taste that Thomas could not understand and dismissed with contempt. While interest in Big Bands and Swing has revived in recent years, the revolution in musical taste has run diametrically opposite the ground Thomas commanded. All the music which was regarded as distinctly lowbrow in the 1930s and '40s— black gospel music, rhythm and blues, and folk songs— are now the focus of much critical interest, while the standard of singing that Thomas represented survives, if at all, only among classical singers.

Such changes in fashion are common enough in the entertainment world, and certainly warrant no tragic coloring in the case of Thomas's career. If there is tragedy, it is in the man himself, and his reaction to his artistic fortunes. In many ways, beneath the bonhomie and zest of the Thomas persona, there was a deeper disappointment: disappointment with the banality of the operatic standards of the day, disappointment with colleagues, with impresarios, and ultimately disappointment with himself.

It is easy to assign responsibility for the anemic standards of taste and performance at the Metropolitan or at RCA to economic conditions during the Depression and the Second World War. These organizations did what they could, given their resources and the market. Yet Thomas's response to this banality was to plumb deeper depths. From "Annie Laurie" he moved to "Lord Randall"; from the Barber of Seville he went to the "Barber of Turin"; from Negro spirituals he turned to imitation spirituals like "Ev'ry Time I Feel de Spirit." It was easy to do, but it took a toll on artist and audience. One event is representative of this trend in Thomas's later career. At a 1946 concert in Cleveland for the musically literate audience at Oberlin College, a low groan went through the audience when Thomas announced his next selection, some trifle like so many composed especially for him by Blanche Seaver or others. "I don't care whether you like it or not," he said, "I'm going to sing it anyway." Would that he had taken that attitude with a finer quality of song. Instead, he pursued a career that paid well, and used the money to support the lifestyle to which he had been accustomed since his early years on Broadway.

At least his attachment to popular music was an honest one. At the peak of his career, in 1938 and 1939, he appeared in operettas like *Apple Blossoms* and *The Gypsy Baron* for two-week engagements, and toured with a troupe in *HMS Pinafore*, all for high fees. He enjoyed appearing at the Covered Wagon Days in Salt Lake City, and, at the end of his career, spent weeks recording scores of hymns in the hope of selling packaged programs to radio stations around the country. Such projects might be fun, but they resulted in so much less than the legacy he might have left.

This was the beginning of the era of magnetic tape and LPs. He could have chosen to record French and Italian art songs, or rare operatic arias, or recruited great voices among his contemporaries to join him in the studio to produce extended recordings of material that might challenge the musicianship of all participants. Alas for him and for us, he did not. For the most part, his sole interest in recording was financial. Thomas chose to make his reputation in popular music, and to a great extent abandoned that portion of his audience who admired his singing of opera and classical works. His reputation has never overcome that choice.

Yet, his distinctive repertoire provides another reason for this biography. History often focuses on pioneers of movements that assume greater importance at a later time. Thomas represents the opposite: a moment. His career peaked at the end of the 1930s and during the Second World War. The musical styles and standards of that era, the rich, extravagant Hollywood sound of his best recordings, seem in retrospect like a great flowering that bloomed for a moment and then simply died. It was not high art. It was a mixture of commercial values and classical influences produced by the many émigré musicians who found refuge in the United States in the 1930s and '40s. Commercial success was very nearly its sole reason for being, and the reason for its failure to leave a legacy. Nevertheless, the art was so integral with the manners of the times that the two define an era of classic American culture. John Charles Thomas, too, was an American classic who lived in and for that moment.

A word on sources for this biography. Merle Armitage, an agent for sopranos Amelita Galli-Curci and Rosa Ponselle, and later a book designer, "discovered" John Charles Thomas at a matinee of The Highwayman on a rainy day in Boston in 1917, and eventually persuaded him to make a career as a concert artist. For several years, Armitage managed Thomas, and remained a lifelong friend. With Thomas's cooperation and encouragement, he began a biography in the late 1950s, producing a draft of seven or eight chapters that found their way into the John Charles Thomas Papers at the Peabody Conservatory after Thomas's death. Armitage knew Thomas longer and better than anyone but Thomas's boyhood friend Charlie Parker. As a manager of other great singers, Armitage also knew the world of classical music. He knew Thomas's voice from the very beginning of his professional career. The changes in the voice are obvious from recordings, yet Armitage tells us nothing about this artistic transformation, or the artistic choice to emphasize popular music in Thomas's repertoire. Armitage's chapters were little more than the outline of a celebrity bio. He did touch on Thomas's temper, but said little of his character, his early training, or his years in Europe.

The manuscript of a more ambitious biography was completed by Ken Darby, a successful Academy Award–winning musical director who first met Thomas when he led the King's Men quartet and a fifteen-member male chorus on the Westinghouse Show during World War II.[2] Darby was Boswell to Thomas's Johnson, an unabashed admirer whose study is full of personal detail, particularly of Thomas's last years, that would be impossible to uncover today. Alas, however, Darby was too uncritical to be a great biographer. It is clear from hints in his manuscript that he knew as much as anyone about the flaws in his hero, but he would not bring himself to write what he knew, or even speak it in telephone interviews.

Even with their faults, the works of Armitage and Darby must be the core of any researcher's efforts at biography. Their portrait of Thomas as a hearty, likeable, life-loving personality must be respected as touching the essence of the man.

There are relatively few reminiscences of Thomas in the memoirs of his contemporaries. Where he is mentioned, it is with affection, and then a dismissive barb that echoes the misgivings critics had about Thomas in his prime. Rosa Ponselle's autobiography contains a brief mention of Thomas making his debut with her at the Metropolitan, then reports that "eventually, radio and phonograph records, rather than the Metropolitan, made him a household name...."[3] In fact, Thomas had already established quite a name for himself in those fields before his Met debut.

Biographers of Lawrence Tibbett do not mention the friendship between the most famous baritones of their time, or the circumstances of the rupture of that friendship in later years. Robert Merrill recalled Thomas's cheerful encouragement to younger singers not to be nervous on the stage, remembered him as a heavy drinker, and suggests, as does Jerome Hines, that he was better suited to the popular stage than opera.[4]

One of the great pleasures of researching Thomas's life was the opportunity it offered to meet and interview those who knew and worked with him. To speak on the phone, or meet in person, a few of the great singers of his era was to live a little in that time. Who could ever forget a description, from one who was there, of Melchior, Flagstad, and Crooks playing cards and drinking beer backstage on the Metropolitan tours? It was equally rewarding to talk with members of the Victor Young Orchestra who supported Thomas on his weekly Westinghouse radio program from 1943 to 1946. Their recollections of the rehearsals, and their enduring devotion to Victor Young, are reminders of the very high quality of Thomas's artistic colleagues. Their evocative image of that smaller, wartime Los Angeles, with its uncluttered coastline and groves of orange and date trees, is poignant to recall. Victor Young's Papers are divided between the Archives of Brandeis University and the Music Department of the Boston Public Library. The latter holds scores for and indexes to the music performed on the Westinghouse program.

Apart from his commercial recordings, perhaps the best recorded example of Thomas's art is compiled in the Armed Forces Radio transcriptions of the Westinghouse program. In many respects, the Westinghouse years were the high point of Thomas's career. Whatever the show's artistic shortcomings, those recordings present weekly snapshots of Thomas's voice just past its peak, with the support of a sixty-two piece orchestra under the direction of Victor Young, and choral forces under the direction of Ken Darby. The Westinghouse show embodied all the elements that led to Thomas's artistic decline: a big production that paid well, with unambitious artistic standards in a seductive southern California setting. These were exactly the temptations that lured great composers such as Arnold Schoenberg, writers such as Faulkner and Fitzgerald, and an army of aspiring actors to Hollywood. Very few were able to walk away from those temptations, and Thomas was no exception.

John Charles Thomas began his career on the Broadway stage. The Shubert Archives in New York still holds many of his early contracts, newspaper clippings, and some important correspondence with the formidable brothers who dominated the world of light opera, Lee and J.J. Shubert. The staff of the Archives made working there a pleasure.

No one can research the career of a popular American musical entertainer without recourse at some point to the Rodgers and Hammerstein collection of the New York Public Library. That collection provided much useful information about Thomas's early career.

Information about Thomas's years at La Monnaie opera in Brussels came by chance just as this book was being completed. Richard T. Soper, author of a definitive volume, Belgian Opera Houses and Singers, had valuable information on the operatic traditions in Belgium, the operatic scene in the 1920s (of which Thomas was part), and colleagues with whom he performed at La Monnaie.[5] He was able to put the author in contact with Jacques Fievez, a student of the career of the bass Lucien Van Obbergh (1887–1959), who was a close friend of John Charles and Dorothy Thomas. M. Fievez shared with the author his detailed list of Thomas performances at La Monnaie (see Appendix B), as well as photographs and correspondence of Thomas and Van Obbergh.

Although the author was unable to interview contemporaries who knew Thomas in Palm Beach, a visit to the Palm Beach County Historical Society provided valuable information about the lifestyle of that resort during the Roaring Twenties.

The Archives of RCA (now BMG) have also been consulted, though these are surprisingly incomplete when one considers the musical history which they hold.

Finally, there are the Papers of John Charles Thomas, which were left to the Peabody Institute in Baltimore by Dorothy Thomas in the early 1960s, and were organized to archival standards in 1990. The author first saw the Thomas Papers in the early 1980s, still packed in the same boxes in which they had been shipped from Apple Valley. It was a sobering experience. The residue of a career of one of the most famous voices of his age lay in a half-dozen shipping boxes. Costumes had been handed on to the wardrobe unit of the Peabody for use in school performances. Some of the sheet music had been filed with the general music collection in the Peabody music library.

The Papers themselves contain important insights into the man and his career. Thomas was a meticulous and methodical archivist, something rather rare in performers. His papers consist, first of all, of his music collection: thousands of copies of sheet music and operatic scores that comprised his repertoire. These were arranged alphabetically by composer, with smaller thematic sections for seasonal music, patriotic songs, cowboy songs and sea shanties. Then there is a nearly complete collection of Thomas's concert programs, from an early recital at the Peabody to his final appearances in Apple Valley. There is a notebook of handwritten concert programs from the late 1930s, with notations on pieces that were being performed for the first time, and the key in which they were sung. These notes were used as a guide to what the artist could offer as fresh concert material in a city that he may have visited many times previously on concert tours. A similar list of selections performed on each of his radio appearances saved him from a too-frequent repetition of the same material.

Unlike many performers, Thomas did not use a single program (or even two) during a concert season. His repertoire was famously large. He might have four or five programs that he could vary in each city, and often used concerts in smaller towns to try out material that might later be presented to sophisticated metropolitan audiences. At a 1938 concert in Ottumwa, Iowa, for example, which the local press reported drew an audience from as much as sixty miles away, Thomas offered a program that began unexpectedly with a series of German lieder before continuing with his more conventional concert favorites.

The Papers also include many photographs of Thomas at different stages in his career, with other musicians and celebrities, in performance and recital, in rehearsals for radio broadcasts, and in retirement. A small portion of those photos comprise the majority of the photos in this volume. Needless to say, this book could not have been completed without the complete access to the Papers given to the author by Elizabeth Schaaf, the Peabody Archivist, and her countless hours of advice and discussion about Thomas's career. Noticeably missing from the Papers is documentation of Thomas's Broadway career and his engagements in Europe between 1922 and 1930.

The author is also grateful to a small circle of Thomas enthusiasts in Baltimore, particularly Mr. Leigh Martinet and Andrew Pope, who have reviewed this work and advised on its writing over several years.

With all this, there is still much that remains elusive about Thomas. The bon vivant personality is amply documented. The serious artist is harder to find. It is as though the artist, finally defeated by the pop singer's publicity, settled for that identity. Thomas attributed many of the key decisions in his life to chance: the toss of a coin decided him on a singing career; another coin toss settled his decision about leaving Broadway for the concert stage; and a chance encounter led him to audition for an operatic contract at La Monnaie in Brussels. In the end he seems to have shown the same diffidence toward his reputation in history.

1

A Preacher's Son

Standard biographical material distributed by John Charles Thomas during his career gave his date of birth as September 6, 1891, in Meyersdale, Pennsylvania, and named Dora and Milson Thomas as his parents. His parents were first and second generation Americans, of German and Welsh heritage respectively. Milson was the son of Charles and Harriet Thomas. His father had begun life working in the Cardiff mines, but became a tinker or tool repairer when he married. Milson was born in Gloucestershire, England, February 7, 1865, and took passage to America with his parents in 1867. Henry and Elizabeth Schnaeble had crossed the Atlantic three years earlier, in 1864. Their daughter Dora was born September 13, 1867.[1] Both families settled in the mining region of Western Pennsylvania.

Milson attended Cumberland Academy in Cumberland, Maryland, and then enrolled in Duff's College in Pittsburgh, expecting to prepare himself for work in some business. Soon after his arrival, however, he had a religious experience and decided that his true calling was the ministry. It must have been a disappointment to his parents, who had struggled to escape the world of mining, when their son, with his good education, took up the life of a miner in order to pursue his vocation as an itinerant preacher. For many years, Milson's choice of careers required traveling from one mining settlement to another, frequently staying overnight in the homes of congregants. On the day before his 24th birthday, February 6, 1889, he married Dora in a Lutheran church ceremony.

Life was a struggle for the couple. They had very little money, and Milson's calling required frequent travel to revival camp meetings, and several moves to new homes before he finally settled in a vicarage in Towson, Maryland (rhymes with "how sun"), immediately north of Baltimore. The picture that emerges of Milson Thomas is that of a man struggling with life's demons: strict, unbending, what we would today call a "controlling personality." In contrast, "Mother" Thomas emerges from most accounts as a much simpler, supportive, and indulgent parent.

Thomas's parentage was much questioned during his lifetime, when it was widely, if privately, assumed that he was adopted by the kindly Thomas family. With his large head and broad face, he certainly did not look Welsh, though there was a strong resemblance between mother and son. The uncertainty on this point was sufficiently strong to make Ken Darby and others search for John Charles' birth certificate. These efforts turned up a marriage license that gave Thomas's year of birth as 1889 rather than the 1891 date that the singer used in his publicity releases. Thomas had hinted at a discrepancy between his publicized birth date and his true age during his lifetime, when he told Darby that placing himself in the 1890's rather than the 1880's made him seem less of an antique.[2]

Thomas would not have been the first performer to bend dates in this way. At the least, the earlier birth date suggests that Thomas was born seven months after his parents' marriage, which seems inconsistent with what we know of Milson's stern morality. It would not have been uncommon, however, for a new birth certificate to be issued to the adoptive parents of a foundling. In a characteristically indulgent gesture, Ken Darby decided to set Thomas's date of birth just a year earlier than the official date, in September 1890, thus restoring the reputation of Milson and Dora, while allowing John Charles to start life in the last decade of the nineteenth century.

Whatever the exact nature of his heritage, it is amusing to find all the characteristics of the adult Thomas evident from early youth. He was a stubborn, willful, self-assured, and vibrant personality with a strong competitive streak. His self-confidence was fostered by a doting mother who dressed him in Little Lord Fauntleroy costumes for his boyhood singing appearances.[3] Thomas spent his life —from a very early age — staking out his own values, setting his own goals, defying convention, and flaunting his delight in what others looked down on, whether cowboy music or pig farming. He was not given to introspection or reflection. From his youth, his personality was that of an individual who seized what he wanted. These are qualities that are essential in a solo artist, such as Thomas became.

Fading photographs survive showing Thomas, aged twelve or thirteen, posing with playmates around a sled on a snowy day. His favorite pastimes seemed to be fishing and fighting. A boyhood companion recalled youthful outings roaming the hills of Western Maryland and south central Pennsylvania in the spring to gather sassafras blossoms to dry for tea, or in the autumn to gather nuts and hunt squirrels and rabbits.

Given his parents' financial struggles, Thomas did not have an easy childhood, nor always a happy one. When Merle Armitage was working on his biography of Thomas in the early 1960s, Dorothy Thomas cautioned him against making her husband's childhood sound too ideal. There was a lot from those years that stung for a long time. Despite the buoyant persona he presented to the world, the childhood memories he recounted for Ken Darby when the singer was in his late fifties and early sixties reveal a man who still held on to grievances with a tenacity remarkable in someone who had enjoyed so much success in life. Yet that tenacity fed his ambition. The success he enjoyed as a result of following those ambitions led him to be most comfortable around other "self-made" men.

In high school, Thomas recalled liking English best and Latin least.[4] He joined several athletic teams, from swimming to baseball, though Darby hints that he was not particularly popular among his teammates. He played football at one point against a team from a school for Native Americans that included Jim Thorpe, and recalled that when he tackled Thorpe, it was like hitting a brick wall. The sport in which he excelled, however, was track. In 1910, Thomas ran a mile in five minutes, and his high jump of 5'10" remained an impressive record for those years.

He also found time for music. At his father's many camp meetings, Thomas regularly sang sentimental fare like "Where Is My Wandering Boy Tonight," and received his first vocal training at age eleven in Mt. Savage, Maryland, from a Catholic nun who also gave him piano lessons. In high school, he joined in and even led impromptu choral sessions in the school's boiler room. He never lost his appreciation for choral singing and the power of leading a hundred voices.

As Dorothy had hinted to Merle Armitage, life in the Thomas household was not without its strains. Thomas was frank to say that he did not always get along well with his father, a strict disciplinarian who disapproved of the boy's fighting, among other things. One crisis came about when, at age 15, John Charles brought home a dog. When his father said he could not keep the dog — the suggestion being that the family could scarcely feed themselves, much less a dog — John Charles ran away. He returned to his parents when an employee of a nearby railroad station detained the boy for the night and contacted the Thomases, who traveled twenty-five miles to collect their son. Milson Thomas frequently punished his son the old fashioned way, with a belt. When he was 16, John Charles announced that he would no longer submit to such discipline. Within a few years, he had moved out of the family home, and though he visited his parents during holidays, from about the age of nineteen he made his own way in the world.

In his youth, John Charles's chores consisted of cleaning his father's church, dusting the pews, sweeping the carpets, painting walls, and helping with church building when Milson was called to a new congregation. The family moved often. From 1891 to 1894 they lived in Meyersdale. During the next four years, they resided in Paw Paw, Maryland; from 1900 to 1903 in Mt. Savage, Maryland. In John Charles' early high school years, 1904–1906, the family resided in Carlisle, Pennsylvania, and, after 1907, settled in Towson.

At school, the young Thomas was something of a daredevil. While taking a test one day, he crawled out the window and along a ledge to the adjacent classroom to ask another boy how he was doing on the test. His purpose was simply to shock the other students with his bravado. He recalled the exact moment when his voice changed. It was during a discussion with a teacher over whether John Charles had or had not used the same answer as his friend Charlie Parker on a classroom quiz. The beginning of the sentence was spoken in a boy's treble, the end in an adult baritone.[5]

Thomas as a young man. (Courtesy of the Archives of the Peabody Institute of The Johns Hopkins University)

As a boy, Thomas had a strapping build, good looks, and wavy blond hair. Work on a farm during his teens developed his physique and his tan to a point where girls at school the following Autumn began to take more notice of him. His good looks would stay with him into his thirties, and were an important advantage in his Broadway career, as well as in his relations with women.

One of the most intriguing details of John Charles Thomas's life was his long-term friendship with a neighbor and classmate, Charlie Parker. As boys they fished, played, argued and fought together — and tried to sing louder than each other at Sunday services. When the Thomas family moved to another town, John Charles would travel to visit Charlie on weekends. The two families eventually found themselves living in the same town again in Cumberland, Maryland, where both boys attended Cumberland Academy. When John Charles went to Baltimore to study medicine after high school, and then transferred to the Peabody Conservatory, and thence to New York, the tie was broken. During a visit to his parents in Towson one Christmas after he had begun to make his mark on Broadway, Thomas looked up Charlie, who suggested that his friend employ him as a general factotum. Thomas agreed, and for the next four decades Charlie Parker remained in his friend's employ.[6]

In their senior year prophecies, Thomas's classmates were close to the mark in predicting that his future lay in acting. His father, however, urged the young man to consider the ministry for his career. Instead, after graduating from the Cumberland Academy, a prep school for Dickinson College in Carlisle, Pennsylvania, Thomas enrolled in the Mount Street School for Homeopathy in Baltimore. He had long shown an interest in medicine, even setting a broken arm for a classmate in high school. There are suggestions that he might have been offered a scholarship to Colgate University, and that he took courses at Dickinson College. For the rest of his life, he retained an interest in medicine. He once was able to keep a man alive who had been electrocuted by high voltage wires until the arrival of a doctor. Later he concocted a mouth rinse that he felt helped to relax his vocal chords. Despite his leanings toward medicine, however, he had retained his interest in singing too, and when he learned of an audition for a scholarship at the Peabody Conservatory, he walked in one Saturday to pit his talent against that of other contestants.

If vocal competitions in 1909 were anything like those of today, there were probably six or seven female contestants for each male, and two or three tenors for every baritone. Each contestant was asked to sing Handel's "Care selva," and after listening to a few of the early contestants, Thomas took a walk. Singers were heard alphabetically, so he knew he would not be scheduled until the afternoon.

"Care selva" is an interesting selection for an audition piece. It requires only a modest range, little dramatic effort or vocal acrobatics beyond a trill the singer may choose to insert. The primary requirement of the piece is good breath control and an even vocal production for fairly long phrases. It is an effective test of trained or untrained voices for professional careers, but an ordeal for judges sentenced to listen over and over to the same steady line.

Late in the afternoon, Thomas returned to the Peabody, took his place on stage, sang the piece, and was greeted with a storm of applause. Declared the winner of the competition, he was offered a full scholarship at the Peabody for the following year. Should he take the scholarship, or continue his medical studies? Milson, a strict Methodist, opposed the idea of his son singing professionally, particularly on the musical stage. After several days of consideration, it was decided to flip a coin to decide. Heads for music, tails for medicine. The coin came up heads, and Thomas's course in life was set.

This story is one of the pillars of what might be called the canon of Thomas mythology, like that of his playing football opposite Jim Thorpe. We shall meet other parts of the canon in later chapters, many of them rather dubious. This story has two versions. In the late teens, when Thomas was a Broadway star, one journalist reported that Thomas had, in fact, come in second the first year he tried out for the scholarship, and had only won the audition on his second attempt. This is more consistent with his age in 1909. At nineteen, he would have been one year out of high school. If we accept his date of birth as 1889, he could have been twenty.

Even so, for a nineteen-year-old lad from the coalfields of central Pennsylvania and western Maryland, whose chief singing experience was hymns sung at church services, to know and easily perform a classical aria such as "Care selva" would have required more than simple vocal talent. He must have known beforehand what aria was to be sung for the audition, and had a few weeks to practice it. It certainly required stage presence, ease with an unfamiliar accompanist, vocal projection, and, perhaps the real secret of the aria, dynamics, knowledge of when to swell the sound and then diminish it, how to rise to a middle high note at the ending, but in a soft voice. None of this suggests a casual dropping in to an audition. We know that Thomas had been considering a musical career at Cumberland Academy, and was encouraged to pursue music by one of his teachers, "Docky Hutch" Hutchinson. The story of a casual decision to walk in to a Peabody audition sounds as contrived as the one told of his audition for La Monnaie opera in Brussels, where a friend is said to have urged him to take the train from Paris to Brussels to try out for an audition. In fact, Thomas had been talking of going to Europe to study and perform in opera since 1917, and his teacher at Peabody, Adelin Fermin (the "friend" in the story), a native of Holland, would certainly have had contacts in Brussels who could have arranged this audition.

The strict facts of these stories, however, are less important than their underlying truth. John Charles Thomas had very great natural talent combined with an ambition to make his way in the world. What Thomas brought to the Peabody was brash self-confidence and a personality that was accustomed to receiving attention. The Peabody would reinforce all those personality characteristics while offering a disciplined training that brought out all his musical potential that, at age nineteen, was little more than raw talent. At the same time, from what we can tell, Thomas saw music as a career, a job. It is difficult to say that he ever fully appreciated his gift as art.

The aspiring vocal student showed many of the characteristics that would emerge more clearly in later years. He was boyish, full of high spirits, and a prankster. There was also a willful, rebellious streak in his character that might have derived from his complicated relationship with his father. He certainly did not share his father's strict morality. But he loved to sing hymns, and would quickly turn on the tub-thumping revival preacher's voice and style when show business programming called for something in that vein. It can be heard in his Johnny Appleseed show on the Westinghouse program in the 1940s, or in his recording of "Ev'ry Time I Feel de Spirit." In the 1940s he launched Preacher's Night at the Bohemian Club's semi-annual encampments when he discovered that many of the Club's members were also sons of ministers.

Thomas's career as an itinerant concert singer had many points in common with his father's career as an itinerant preacher. Both professions involved a kind of theater, where the preacher/artist employs tested material to warm up the audience, tries out new material, holds an audience in the palm of his hand, playing on their emotions, giving them a glimpse of a spiritual world, basking in the audience's appreciation until the big finish. While his father may have left town with little more than enough to cover his expenses, John Charles regularly earned more in one night on a concert tour than the average man in the audience would earn in a year. Like his father, Thomas was a solo act. He kept his own counsel, he took advice on his career and art from very few associates, and paid little attention to reviews, whether favorable or critical.

Thomas grew increasingly self-motivated as his career advanced. When he entered the Peabody, however, he was nearly a blank slate musically. He would find two teachers there who transformed him into one of the finest artists of his generation.

2

Finding His Voice

In 1909, the Peabody Conservatory was one of the premier musical schools in the United States. It had been established in 1857 with an endowment from George Peabody, who had made his fortune in railroads and other investments. Located at the southeast corner of Mount Vernon Square in Baltimore, one block east of the home of John Garrett, President of the Baltimore and Ohio Railroad, the Peabody was in the center of Baltimore's most prestigious residential neighborhood. Wealthy families like the Garretts had country houses just a few miles north of the Peabody, where the town began to fade away into a series of large plantation-like southern estates extending north from the city to the Pennsylvania line. Directly across the street from the Peabody, William and Henry Walters, father and son whiskey merchants, railroad magnates, investors, and art collectors, maintained a private art collection which they opened to the public each year in the Spring.

In 1910, Baltimore was still a major if somewhat fading commercial center of the mid–Atlantic, with a population of just over half a million. It was the home of H. L. Mencken, whose critical assessment of the rest of America was shared by the rest of the population. Baltimore was a southern city with a monument to the women of the Confederacy, but it had the same scorn for what Mencken called the "booboisie" of the South as it did for the inhabitants of the "federal village" fifty miles south. It considered itself a more gracious sister of the great commercial centers of Philadelphia and New York. The Peabody Institute was one expression of that graciousness.

The Peabody offered a four-year course of training in voice or instrument. In 1909, the conservatory enrolled 1200 students, divided into two or three categories. There were well-bred young ladies who sought musical training to complete their command of the social graces. There were also pianists and organists who trained at the Peabody to become music teachers and church organists in the community. It may have been one of these graduates who guided Thomas to the scholarship competition. Then there were the talented performers on whom the professors focused most of their attention in order to transform musical potential into professional talent. It was in this latter group that John Charles took his place.

The Peabody curriculum included Harmony, Sight Reading, Vocal Instruction, Solfagio, Ear Training, Elements of Music, the History of Music, Musical Appreciation, and language study in English, French, German, and Italian. Music Theory held an important place in the curriculum, because the Directors of the Conservatory were composers. Classes were surprisingly small — seldom more than eight, and often just two or three.

In his first year, Thomas studied under Blanche Sylvania Blackman, a student of the great Mathilde Marchesi, perhaps the leading trainer of soprano voices in her age.[1] According to Blackman's reports, and his own later admission, Thomas had little or no musical knowledge. He lacked a full scale, did not know how to breathe properly, or how to give his singing resonance. But he did have that voice, which his teacher slowly trained to a high professional standard.

In 1910, as Thomas began his second year of study, the Peabody hired 43-year-old Adelin Fermin as the Conservatory's principal voice professor. In the Spring of that year, Fermin happened by Blackman's room while she was giving Thomas a lesson. He stepped into the room, asked Thomas to repeat what he had just sung, and then announced that henceforward Thomas would be his student. Blackman resigned from the Peabody that year, perhaps because she was unwilling to continue under Fermin's shadow, but Thomas never failed to give both teachers credit for training his voice.

Fermin, a Dutch-born baritone of French parentage, had graduated from high school in Maastricht in 1884, then attended conservatories in Liege and Amsterdam, graduating from the latter in 1892. He made his operatic debut in Antwerp and also performed in The Hague. Although he had a fine baritone voice, he was uncomfortable singing before an audience, and found it much more congenial to sing with the Amsterdam *a cappella* choir, with which he toured between 1892 and 1895. He recalled the choir as one of the finest in Europe. They rehearsed four times a week, and each singer had to be able to sing their part solo without losing pitch. At various times, he had also conducted the Maastricht choir. Fermin had sung before the Prince of Wales in London in May, 1894, as well as for Queen Wilhelmina of Holland. However, he was so uneasy about giving the recitals usually expected of voice teachers that he was overjoyed when the Peabody released him from that obligation in his 1914 contract. Fermin was also a composer in a modest way, and had published six small collections of lieder by the time he came to the Peabody.

Fermin emphasized "color" in training a voice, and taught Thomas to sing each language in its particular style.[2] Growing up as he did in Holland, surrounded by different languages, Fermin would be particularly sensitive to the variations in national tongues. He classified English as a nasal language, French as a chest language, German as guttural, while Italian was produced with head tones.

Thomas got along very well with Fermin, and invariably praised his teacher in later years when the subject of his vocal training arose. For his part, Fermin spent many hours working with Thomas beyond the requirements of routine vocal coaching. Thomas spent one summer taking lessons with Fermin at his home. They may even have spent one summer in Holland in the last years before the First World War.[3] The only other description of Fermin's training technique we have is Thomas's recollection that his teacher found the best tone in his voice, then worked to bring all the other notes in balance with it. This sounds simpler than it is. Great singers must have a seamless color and tone in their voice throughout its range, along with flawless breathing technique. When they have that, it goes completely unnoticed, but it is instantly clear when singers have not achieved that level of vocal control. In later years Thomas practiced a vocalise that came from his days at the Peabody, starting with Aa, then Ee, back to Aa, then to Oh, back to Aa, then OO, Aa, Ah, Aa and so forth until all the vowel sounds were in harmony[4]. Eventually, he would develop a range of a little over two octaves, from F to high A, just two notes below high C.

Aldelin Fermin (1884–1941), Thomas's principal teacher at the Peabody Conservatory. (Courtesy of the Archives of the Peabody Institute of The Johns Hopkins University)

Fermin remained in contact with Thomas long

after they both left the Peabody, continuing to offer vocal coaching and professional advice to his star student. Thomas might have been luckier than he knew in finding Fermin, for there could have been few vocal teachers in the United States competent to train him in the basics of the French style of singing that was so suitable for his voice. More than color and tone in the voice, what Thomas acquired from Fermin and the Peabody was a distinctive bel canto vocal style characterized by a long, smooth, unforced line of singing, in contrast to the more explosive bursts of singing in the "verismo" style. Thomas could certainly sing dramatic parts, but he was probably at his best in long lyrical passages like "Nemico della patria" from *Andrea Chenier*.

With a full scholarship, some money to cover living costs, and ready income from weekend engagements in Baltimore churches, Thomas probably had as good an income as any student in the Conservatory. He took a position as director of choral singing at a Methodist camp one summer to earn extra income. He retained a love for singing with large choral groups all his life. In the summer of 1911, he worked at an auto dealership, demonstrating Oldsmobiles, probably up the street from the Peabody near the Pennsylvania Station, which was then auto row in Baltimore. There he developed his love of fine motorcars, particularly the Packard. By his third year at the Peabody, he claimed to be the highest paid church singer in Baltimore. Essentially, John Charles Thomas was self-supporting from age nineteen. This would not have been uncommon at the time, when young men were expected to make their own livelihood by their early twenties. Many would have been earning some sort of a living from their mid-teens. For an aspiring singer, however, then as now, it was not so easy to make a living from art.

Thomas made friends at the Peabody, and returned throughout his career to offer concerts at the school at reduced fees, and welcome scores of old friends who would crowd into his dressing room after a performance. Yet a number of Peabody students found him a little roughhewn for their taste. For them, he was simply "that man who likes cowboy music," or "hillbilly" music to others. Roughhewn though he was, and would remain, Thomas had learned something about popular music at his father's revival meetings that his fellow students may not have understood. He knew that music brought people into churches in large numbers, and stirred them to make generous offerings at collection time.

Thomas acquired all the skills he needed at the Peabody to succeed as a professional singer. These included the techniques of vocal production, musicianship, how to approach and study a role, and the mundane but important matter of record keeping. He had also acquired a mentor in the person of Adelin Fermin, who would continue to help him develop both his voice and his career over the next twenty years.

In the Spring semester of 1912, Thomas's third year at the Peabody, Fermin scheduled him in the annual Exhibition Concert at which the Peabody showed off its best students. Thomas sang an aria from *Martha*, and the "Toreador Song" from *Carmen*. George W. Chadwick, a professor at the New England Conservatory of music and collaborator with Walter Browne in the musical play *Everywoman*, was in the audience. He was impressed with the voice, and arranged for Thomas to tour with the *Everywoman* company in the role of Passion. The manager of the company, Henry Savage, quipped that his only reservation in hiring Thomas was that he was a church singer, and stage performers had to take care not to sully their reputations by such associations! But there was a bit of Elmer Gantry in this preacher's son, and Thomas would soon make a reputation among the ladies who swooned for matinee idols.

After touring with the *Everywoman* company for seventy performances, the young baritone was offered the lead in *The Adventurer* in London, Ontario, in the autumn of 1912; and from that point on in his career he was never hired for anything but leading roles. This particular role, however, soon ended, and Thomas was once again looking for work. It was still an open question whether he could make a living from his art. For a time, he trudged the sidewalks of New York with three friends looking for work and surviving on free lunches in the metropolis's many saloons. For the price of a beer, the friends could manage at least one good meal a day if they were careful not to go to the same bar more than once a week.

Thomas made the rounds of agents' offices in New York, with little success. His predicament is familiar to every young performer: producers wanted singers with experience, but how was a young man to get experience unless someone hired him? Fermin came along once again to restart Thomas's career. He wrote a letter of introduction for his protégé to Thomas de Koven, a leading member of a Gilbert and Sullivan company in New York. This led to an audition for the manager of the company, an appropriately named Mr. Savoyard. Thomas had sung the role of the Judge in a Peabody production of *Trial by Jury*, and would sing the lead roles in the *Mikado*, the *Gondoliers*, and *H.M.S. Pinafore* with de Koven's troupe. Later in his career, he would sometimes perform the "Tit Willow" song from the *Mikado* in the manner of de Koven.[5]

The star of the company was DeWolf Hopper, famed for his recitation of "Casey at the Bat."[6] What Thomas learned from Hopper and Gilbert and Sullivan that perhaps no other musical experience could teach so well was

On tour as "Passion" in *Everywoman*, his first professional engagement, in Sioux City, Iowa, 1912. (Courtesy of the Archives of the Peabody Institute of The Johns Hopkins University)

meticulous diction. The whole success of Gilbert and Sullivan performances hinges on clearly articulated and often rapidly sung phrases that add just the right portion of Victorian propriety to the cardboard characters that populate the world of Gilbert and Sullivan. It was a skill that Thomas retained throughout his career. His diction was polished, precise, even elegant, without being pretentious or stilted. It had its idiosyncrasies—the broad 'a's, the expansive diphthongs such as "heaart," or "deahr," the clipped prepositions and stress on the final consonant in a word—that are as inimitably a part of Thomas as the delicious brogue that belonged to John McCormack. He also took to heart Fermin's advice as he pushed his discouraged student back into the world of the New York stage. "There is no standing still in music, you must always move forward." He added, perhaps reflecting on his student's stiffness in performance, that there can be no art without passion.[7]

We do not know what kind of a career Thomas intended to make for himself when he left the Peabody. He may not have expected to settle in musical theater, but a brief taste whetted his appetite. Once he had achieved some success, however, he was quick to express his interest in pursuing a career as a concert or operatic artist. Whatever his discontents with theatrical life, at age 22 or 23, Thomas, with wavy blond hair and the profile of an Arrow shirt man, was ideally suited for the musical stage. The stage had much to teach the young man about singing for the public that he could never learn at a conservatory or an opera house.

New York was just going vertical when Thomas arrived. The stories he later told of his early years in New York suggested a hard struggle against adversity to climb to success, but they are not convincing. In the first place, he had sufficient means to marry a young singer, Ruby Rothnour, who had played the role of Modesty to John Charles' Passion in *Everywoman*, and whom he may have known at the Peabody. They were married on October 12, 1913, in a ceremony in Baltimore at which Milson officiated.

Here again is one of the mysteries of Thomas's life. Over the years, there were suggestions that the couple had a child, but this cannot be documented. Darby mentions a man who took the name of John Charles Thomas Jr., who was born in 1911. This would suggest a reason for Thomas's somewhat premature departure from the Peabody after only three years of study, and his pressing need for steady work. Thomas never acknowledged having a child, and was firmly set against having children in his second marriage. It is not even clear when the first marriage ended. Darby cites February 4, 1916, as the date of the divorce in Reno, Nevada, but the usual date given is 1923 or '24, prior to Thomas's marriage to Dorothy Kaehler. Dorothy was quick to insist that she had not been responsible for the breakup of the first marriage, that it was over long before she came on the scene. If Thomas really had been divorced in 1916, however, it would hardly have been a sensitive subject for Dorothy, who married Thomas nine years later, in 1925. More decisive evidence of Thomas's marital state may be found in his contracts with the Shubert organization,

John Charles Thomas and his first wife, Ruby Rothnaur, in a production of *Every-woman*. (Courtesy of the Archives of the Peabody Institute of The Johns Hopkins University)

which as late as 1919 stipulated that the Shuberts were to pay for first class travel accommodations for Thomas, his wife, and his valet, presumably Charlie Parker.

Despite this, the marriage was clearly finished in all but name by 1917. None of the early publicity stories about the rising baritone mention Ruby, and there is no indication that Thomas spoke about this marriage to Merle Armitage, who first met him in the summer of 1917. Although he was one of Thomas's closest friends for the last sixteen years of the singer's life, Ken Darby knew nothing of Ruby until he began researching the singer's life after Thomas's death.

Apart from the evidence this marriage provides of Thomas's solvency, the record shows fairly steady employment in the New York theatrical world. The two men responsible for Thomas's success were the Shubert brothers, Lee (1873?–1953) and Jake, or J.J. (1879–1963). The Shuberts were already Broadway powerbrokers in 1913. Their older brother, Sam Shubert (1875?–1905), had launched the family in the theatrical world when he bought the New England touring rights to a play called *A Texas Steer*. The success of the play enabled him to move to New York City and acquire the Herald Square Theater, the first of many properties in what eventually became a great theatrical empire.

From the outset, each of the brothers seemed to gravitate toward their specialty. Sam Shubert was the energetic creative force, whose winning personality and drive made him an irresistible power in the theater world. Lee, who was sometimes called the cigar store Indian for his quiet ways and artificially maintained tan, managed the finances and properties of the business, while J.J. managed the out of town productions, and took a special interest in operettas. In May of 1905, Sam died in a freak railway accident when the passenger train he was riding in collided with a train carrying explosives.

Lee and J.J. Shubert made Thomas's career when they signed him to appear as Baron Bolo Baransky in *The Peasant Girl*, which opened at the 44th St. Theater on March 2, 1913, to enthusiastic reviews for Thomas's singing. That summer, Thomas was employed with the Edward Temple Opera Company performing nightly at Olympic Park in Newark, New Jersey. He was put in the company to get stage experience and learn the grind of Broadway rehearsals. The troupe rehearsed from 9 to 5 Tuesday through Friday for a new opera starting the following week, while performing nightly in the current week's offering. In late July, Thomas took a role, or rather three, in the Shubert Brothers review *Passing Show of 1913*, the second year of that long-running variety show. He appeared again in the *Passing Show of 1915*, and on October 14, 1915, in *Alone at Last*, an operetta by

Lehar which opened a run of 180 performances at the Shubert Theatre. The role of Sandor the Gypsy leader in Victor Herbert's *The Fortune Teller* was Thomas's third operetta role in New York, and on May 29, 1916, he appeared as Charles Chickering in *Step This Way* for the first of 88 performances.

It is easy to look down on the simplistic plot lines of these operettas, their sentimentality and predictable outcomes. Yet music historians have pointed out that they played an important role in educating their audiences, many of whom were immigrants, to American life and values while holding on to a warm image of the old European world. *Alone at Last*, by Franz Lehar, is a good model of the type. A beautiful young American girl is on holiday in the Austrian Alps and sets out with a ski instructor for an outing on the slopes. They are caught in a snowstorm and return to the Lodge to find that her American beau has jilted her. The ski guide, however, asks her to marry him and reveals that he is actually a prince. Sigmund Romberg's great hit *The Student Prince* follows a similar pattern. In *Maytime*, the lovers cannot cross the social bar in their generation, but their grandchildren do. The pattern is always the same. In the United States, social class is no barrier to love and happiness.

At this point, at age 27, Thomas was earning $350 a week, and his contract stipulated increases in successive years to $400 and $450. That was $10–14,000 a year at a time when the average worker might make $1,000 a year or less. One of the entertainers Thomas befriended in these years was the young comedian Ed Wynn. The two men would remain friends throughout their lives, and, remarkably enough, would stay fairly well matched in earning power. The Shubert records show Ed Wynn's earnings in 1916 totaled $16,000. Thomas's salary would grow as his star power grew brighter, so that in the four years between 1917 and 1921, Thomas's earnings probably exceeded in buying power that of any other period of his life.

Thomas always complained of boredom with these musicals, however, citing the tedium of having to run through the same role, the same lines, the same songs night after night. In 1913 he took up golf to give himself some exercise and diversion from the dull routine of the musical stage. The record of his appearances, however, suggests that he would have been lucky to learn one role before he was offered another. Six months after launching *Step This Way* in May, 1916, Thomas was playing Alain Tenure in *Her Soldier Boy*, a topical production on the European War that opened December 6, 1916, and ran for 198 performances. The best known song from the play was "Pack Up Your Troubles in Your Old Kit Bag," but Thomas would revive "Mother's Song" from this play on his radio broadcasts during the next war.

On January 17, 1917, little more than a month later, Thomas walked out on the play after the first act. Two letters in the Shubert files give a dramatic picture of the day. The first, from J.J., begins, "Dear Sir: I hardly know how to begin this letter to you as your actions this afternoon are beyond words." It goes on for a page and a quarter of single spaced typing to complain about Thomas's walking out after the first act of *Her Soldier Boy* when it was too late to call back his understudy. J.J notes that while he complained of ill health, "you were able to argue with Mr. Simmons and every one in the company ... but you were *not* able to finish the performance." The letter concludes with a threat: "If it is your intention to use methods of this kind in order to breach your contract, we assure you that your project will fail."

But a notation at the top of the letter reports simply "not sent." Adjoining it in the file is a three-sentence, hand-written note from Thomas that begins: "Dear Mr. Lee — It was unfortunate that I was compelled to leave the theater today during the matinee, but I could not have gone on the stage again if my life depended on it. I hope this will not cause you or the company any embarrassment. I have been ordered to bed for a rest by Dr. LaVigne and this is what I have been fighting against for some weeks. Very sincerely yours."

There is no record of further discussions after this incident, but something was afoot. A month later, on February 9, an article appeared in the *New York Herald* reporting that Thomas planned to travel to The Hague in Holland in early Spring with his vocal teacher, Adelin Fermin, to pursue a career in opera, as Enrico Caruso, the Metropolitan's leading tenor, had encouraged him to do. If this was a ploy to get a better salary from the Shuberts, his timing could not have been worse. Germany declared unrestricted submarine warfare a week earlier, and by April 6 — early Spring, just when Thomas was hoping to travel to Europe — the United States would be at war. There would be no Atlantic crossings for the duration.

Yet on March 19, 1917, two months after walking out on *Her Soldier Boy,* Thomas came to terms with the Shuberts, who gave him a new contract, raising his pay from $325 per week to $500 a week starting April 15, 1917, through October 1, and then $600 a week after October 1 for 30 weeks per year. He would make even more in the next few years. Another clause in this contract stipulated that Thomas would not be required to perform at the Winter Garden Theatre. The most likely explanation for this is that

Opposite: In costume as an alpine ski guide in *Alone at Last,* 1915. (Courtesy of the Archives of the Peabody Institute of The Johns Hopkins University)

the Winter Garden was the site of the very popular Passing Show, which, like the Ziegfeld Follies, was famous for its scantily clad beauties. Thomas may have considered any association with the theater inappropriate for an artist aspiring to establish a career as a more serious performer.

In May 1917, he became Dick Fitzgerald for 22 performances in a revival of Reginald de Koven's 1897 musical *The Highwayman*, and subsequently journeyed with the show to Boston. As a twenty-seven or twenty-eight-year-old, Thomas might have been liable for the draft when the United States entered the First World War in April, 1917. He registered for the draft, but was not called to service, and continued performing on Broadway. On November 26, 1917, he took the role of Arthur Howard in *The Star Gazer* at the Plymouth Theatre. Notwithstanding a score by Lehar, the show closed after just eight performances. The setting, as with so many musicals, was Austria, and after the American entry into the War, that proved an unpopular locale even for a fictional musical.

By 1918, Thomas's contract guaranteed him 10 percent of the House's gross at every performance, with a guaranteed base of $650 a week for thirty weeks. He was to be the only featured member of the cast, and each show in which he appeared was to have a 25-piece orchestra. The Shuberts were to pay the salary of his valet, and pay rail and steamship transport for his wife and valet in parlor car and sleeping car accommodations, but dressing room or state room accommodations when available. He was not to perform more than eight times a week, and he could not be replaced by a substitute. Any income from movies or recordings was to be split with the Shuberts. This contract was cancelled September 9, 1918, when Thomas had exceeded his thirty week obligation under his previous contract, but was engaged to perform in the final five weeks of *Maytime* at the Broadhurst Theater, and then take it on the road. We do not know the terms of his new contract, but we do know that by the time he left Broadway in 1922 he was a millionaire — and lived like one.

Maytime, the great Sigmund Romberg hit, opened in New York on August 16, 1917, with Charles Percell as the leading man at the Shubert Theater. It was so successful that a second company was added, with Thomas taking the lead in a run at the Studebaker Theatre in Chicago starting January 8, 1918, before opening at the 44th Street Theater in New York on February 18, 1918. Thomas moved with it to the Broadhurst Theatre on April 1, then to the smaller Lyric Theatre on August 5 for the slow

Opposite: Thomas on tour with an unknown companion as a young Broadway performer. (Courtesy of the Archives of the Peabody Institute of The Johns Hopkins University)

part of the summer season, and ultimately returned to the Broadhurst September 9, where it finally closed after a total New York run of 492 performances. Thomas and the "Chicago" cast of the show then took it on the road to Philadelphia from October 30 to January 4, and subsequently to the Jefferson Theatre in St. Louis.

Thomas appears to have finally traveled to Europe at this time, though it was just two months after the Armistice, for he did not appear on Broadway again until October 7, 1919, when Fritz Kreisler's *Apple Blossoms* opened at the Globe Theatre after a one-week trial run at Ford's Theatre in Baltimore. It ran for 256 performances, until May 1920. Besides Thomas, the cast included Fred and Adele Astaire. While Kreisler composed most of the score, the two biggest hits in the play, "You Are Free" and "Little Girls Goodbye," were written by Victor Jacobi. Thomas would continue to perform these numbers throughout his career. A revival of Victor Herbert's *Naughty Marietta* followed, and then an appearance as Philip Delma in *The Love Letter* on October 4, 1921, again with the Astaires.[8] *Love Letter*, with a score by Victor Jacobi, was another Viennese musical, set, for variety, in Hungary. It ran only four weeks, and Jacobi died shortly after, at the age of thirty-seven, some said from shock at the failure of his last work.

Thomas enjoyed critical acclaim as well as box-office success. The eminent critic James Gibbon Hunecker wrote in a 1919 review, "Watch young Thomas. He has the most striking voice of any American singer thus far." Despite his popularity and success on Broadway, however, Thomas never became a good actor, and was surprisingly stiff for a man so clearly at ease in his singing. Three Vitaphone films, early talking pictures with separately recorded soundtracks, made in April 1927, confirm what contemporary reviewers reported about his acting skills.[9] He also had his share of professional disappointments. Sigmund Romberg wrote *Blossom Time* with Thomas in mind for the lead as Franz Schubert. Contractual commitments, however, obligated the show's producers to cast Howard March in the lead when it opened September 29, 1921, and Thomas would have to wait until 1938 to perform the role.

Thomas found other employment outside of Broadway. As early as August 1914 he made a test recording for the Edison Company, "By the Dreamy Susquehana." Edison liked the voice and instructed his executives to give him a contract. "This man has a good voice, you better make arrangements with him. He is good for us, voice very steady and timbre pleasing." This endorsement notwithstanding, Thomas was paid $25 for the recording, but it was never released. The company subsequently employed him to introduce arias recorded by other artists, for which he was paid $15 per job. Thomas's voice in this debut recording is that of a young conservatory-trained singer trying perhaps to sound a little older. The production qualities of the Edison cylinders are quite good, and Thomas is accompanied by a chorus during the four-minute recording. The voice sounds stiff, but not unpleasant. The most noticeable characteristic familiar from later Thomas recordings is the distinctive pronunciation of his broad vowels and a tendency to hold onto some of the notes for effect. What he does not yet display is his later mastery of the musical line of the song, the ability to make the material his own.

In the 1915 recording of "Thy Heart My Prize" from *The Peasant Girl* for Rex records, we hear a Broadway voice with as much stage tenor in it as operatic baritone, but one strong enough, even through a scratchy acoustic recording, to deliver a showstopper number. The following year he sang the "Solenne in quest 'ora" duet from *Forza del Destino*, with Mario Chamlee, for the Lyric Company. Both performers used pseudonyms. Thomas was "Enrico Martini," while Chamlee was "Mario Rodolfi." The record was probably an effort to cash in on the public appetite for the Victor version of this aria recorded by Enrico Caruso and Antonio Scotti, where it was difficult to tell whether the baritone or tenor sang the opening line. In 1920, Thomas signed his first long-term recording contract with the Vocalion label.[10]

Both as a recording artist and a Broadway performer, and, by the mid–1920s, as a radio performer, Thomas was among the pioneers. It is worth considering what that meant in both fields, for it explains an attitude Thomas maintained toward important commercial aspects of the entertainment business.

The theatrical world which Thomas entered in 1913 was divided into Vaudeville and Broadway. Vaudeville consisted of fifteen- or twenty-minute variety acts in a hierarchy that ranged from cheap ticket theaters in small towns to major acts that played at the premier theaters in the largest cities. The Broadway stage presented musical plays and operettas. Just as they are today, these plays were tried out in various East Coast cities prior to opening in New York, and touring companies would present the shows around the country after a Broadway success, though rarely with the leading performers who had performed on Broadway. The Keith-Albee Orpheum syndicate controlled vaudeville theaters throughout the country, with some competition from the Sullivan & Considine circuit. The Shubert Brothers may not have had a monopoly on Broadway productions, but they were one of the major powers in the legitimate theater.

Both systems, vaudeville and musical theater, were hierarchical, and effectively monopolies that gave the theater owners enormous power over who performed, who was designated a star, and how much performers were paid. While stars were very well paid, supporting players in both sectors were not. It was in the interest of the theater owners to maintain control of the cost of their performers, but it was also in their interest to create stars and pamper them with very high salaries. Satisfied stars showed up for performances and had a shared interest in the show's success. But there was never a shortage of talent to take their place. Without question, Broadway was the pinnacle of the American entertainment industry. Hollywood was only beginning to make movies, and while Mary Pickford and Charlie Chaplain were well-paid superstars, the financial potential of the movies was just beginning to be appreciated.[11]

There was resistance to these entertainment monopolies. In June of 1900, a "White Rats" movement of Vaudeville players attempted to break the Keith monopoly by organizing their own companies and performing in theaters not owned by Keith. They objected not only to the total control over performers' careers exercised by the theater owners, but the 5 percent commission they exacted for acts they booked into their own theaters. The plan of the White Rats was that the actors' organization itself would collect the 5 percent commission, but be in a position to make theaters bid for the services of the performers, then raise their salaries. When the Keith Circuit dropped its commission charge early in the following year, performers returned to the old Syndicates and the White Rats movement collapsed. Once Keith had consolidated his position, he once again imposed the commission.

As an aspiring young performer, Thomas was lucky, with his good looks and vocal talent, to be put on a path to stardom and even groomed by the Shuberts—in the manner of the later Hollywood studio system — with experience and training to improve his theatrical skills, particularly his acting. While his success with the Broadway side of the business is well known, it is less well known that he was under contract in Vaudeville too. Thomas relished the chance to play vaudeville, and made two national tours on the vaudeville circuit. He did a good imitation of dancer Harry Ender's double shuffle, and a twenty-minute stint of popular songs was light work for him compared to the vocal demands of his serious concert engagements. While these programs added to his earnings, at one point they nearly jeopardized his operatic career. In his memoirs, Merle Armitage reported that Thomas was still appearing in vaudeville in the early 1930s, prompting the management of the San Francisco opera to raise the question as to whether a vaudeville performer was suitable to take a lead role in the company.[12]

Under the Broadway system, Thomas was in great demand, was well paid, and given plenty of work in new productions by Victor Herbert and Sigmund Romberg that have become light opera classics. But no entertainer within this system could have any misunderstanding about how the system worked and who was in control. Success was always precarious. Stars could fall out of favor; composers could run dry after one or two hits. Only the biggest names in the business, Victor Herbert, Romberg, Friml, or Jerome Kern, were bankable and had some leverage with the theater owners. Producers would at least consider their musical ideas, and financial support could be found for any show that seemed likely to be a hit. But for the dozens of excellent songwriters and composers who operated on the fringes of Broadway, and the hundreds who plied their craft in Tin Pan Alley, the only reward they received for their contributions to a musical was a printed credit.

Everything about the financial side of the popular music business was up for grabs in these years. No effective system operated to allocate intellectual property rights, but many hands reached out for a claim. Irving Berlin was shrewd enough to incorporate his own musical publishing company so he could control the distribution of royalties. Even Victor Herbert had to sue to secure royalty payments by pianists and small orchestras in restaurants or little theaters playing excerpts from his popular operettas. Lesser-known songwriters would be pressured to surrender a share of royalties to the producer, or even the singer who popularized the song. After the American Society of Composers and Performers (ASCAP) was founded in 1914, it was still many years before a system of royalty distribution settled into the formulas allocating payments to composers and publishers that is widely accepted today.

In short, American popular music was a world made for freebooters, and Thomas would certainly have understood the leverage his stardom gave him within this environment. As early as 1923, composers were writing songs especially for him, a practice that continued to the end of his career and even after his retirement. In his prime, Thomas was fairly deluged with compositions by hopeful composers. He was always generous in crediting composers when he introduced their songs, a great many of which, from "Home on the Range" and "Marcheta" to "The Lord's Prayer" and "He's Got the Whole World in His Hands," became great successes for both composer and performer. He introduced songs written by his tailor, his summer accompanist, and his regular accompanist, Carroll Hollister. Who else, after all, could put across songs like the "Green Eyed Dragon" and "Sailormen," two of Thomas's most popular recordings and most frequently requested concert favorites? But he fully understood the value that his promotion of the song brought to the enterprise, and knew how to take his share.

In 1957 Thomas recorded a 45 rpm record titled "The Golfer's Lament," composed by Albert Hay Malotte, a long-time friend who had composed several songs for him, including one of the most important songs associated with Thomas, "The Lord's Prayer." There is correspondence in the Thomas Papers that shows him trying to distribute both sheet music and recordings without paying fees to the publisher or record producer — something he had learned in his early days on Broadway. These commercial opportunities were not usually available to artists in the operatic world. Imagine Caruso demanding a cut of Leoncavallo's royalties for "Vesti la giubba"! Yet such arrangements were a fact of life in the world of popular American entertainment, and Thomas knew every angle in the business.

The money to be made from hit musicals or operettas, even from a hit song, was beyond the dreams of the opera world.[13] In the mid–Teens and Twenties, Broadway was just beginning to exploit the potential of popular stage music. Records and radio came along at just the right time to broaden the market and the riches that could be made from this very American art form.

The Broadway system required the skilled cooperation and synergy of composers, directors, set designers, and performers who could learn shows quickly, rewrite scenes to make them work better, and perform night after night (with matinees at least once a week), all under the eye of producers, investors, and theater owners like the Shuberts. Just a few blocks down on Broadway at 39th was the Metropolitan Opera, where the term "hit" might be applied to one production per season, or one every five seasons, with perhaps only half a dozen performances of that production. On Broadway, shows went for broke, and hits could produce a bonanza. The goal of everyone involved with Broadway was to make their fortune with a hit show. It is important to understand this was the value system that formed the foundation of John Charles Thomas's professional career.

Amid the glitter of Broadway, however, there was a strong undercurrent of discontent among the ordinary performers who did not see the big paychecks of the stars. In 1919, Equity actors struck the Broadway producers for better wages. Marie Dressler and Ed Wynn were the principal leaders of the strike, but John Charles Thomas, along with actors like Ethyl Barrymore and others, were on the strike committee. Thomas persuaded Eddie Cantor, then one of the biggest stars on the Great White Way, to come out on strike, and performed with other stars at variety shows to benefit the striking actors, particularly the chorus girls who were paid very little for performances, and nothing at all for their many weeks of rehearsals.

Even the stars were insecure in their hold on the public's favor. In the lucrative but perilous world of the musical stage, a concert career was one more arrow in a young singer's quiver in the event that audiences or Broadway producers lost interest. Recording was equally competitive. Victor dominated the field, but Columbia and other labels were always a threat, and could sign promising new talent or produce a hit record that would sweep the nation. When Al Jolson's "Mammy" became a million seller in 1928, Brunswick kept its manufacturing plant working 24 hours a day to keep up with the demand. Sales on that scale created profits that could be plowed back into new hits.

Success brought substantial wealth to Thomas, wealth at a time when he was both young and when income was generally untaxed. He enjoyed the good life, spending, in the early years,

An early Broadway portrait. (Courtesy of the Archives of the Peabody Institute of The Johns Hopkins University)

twice what he earned. In the Fall of 1916 he bought a home at 64 Washington Mews off Washington Square, and had 64WM for the license plate of the big automobiles he liked to drive, starting with a Buick Phaeton that he purchased in 1916.[14]

He dressed like a fashion plate, and thought nothing of picking out half a dozen silk handkerchiefs at Sulka's for $50, or paying $35 for a shirt. In 1918, a working man could buy a good suit of clothes for $5 — and get a belt or a pocket watch thrown in. Henry Ford created a sensation when he offered to pay his workers the high salary of $5 a day for ten hours of work. Both Armitage and Darby (relying on the testimony of Thomas) report that the young star spent money as fast as he got it. In June 1915 his spending got ahead of itself, and he required a $500 advance from Sam Shubert when he signed to star in *Step This Way*. The loan was treated as an advance on his salary, and no interest was charged. In early October, 1917, the Shuberts advanced Thomas another $2,000, again interest free, to be deducted from his earnings.[15]

Thomas loved the life of a star. He hobnobbed with the greatest musical talent in the city. Sunday dinners at Luchow's, a landmark German
restaurant at 110 E. 14th street in the heart of what was then the musical
theater and literary district, were a regular occasion. Thomas would join
Victor Herbert, Sigmund Romberg, and Otto Harbach for dinner, the
restaurant's small orchestra would play the composers' songs, and Thomas
would sing.[16] The press reported seeing him in the audience at new plays
on nights that he reported himself indisposed for his own performances.
He would certainly have seen the great concert artists who regularly
appeared in New York, like John McCormack, Enrico Caruso, Tita Ruffo,
and the other stars of the Metropolitan. If we can believe his press agents,
Thomas knew these stars, and probably others.

In 1919, Thomas offered a scholarship for a year of study with Adelin
Fermin, who had just moved to the Eastman School of Music in Rochester,
New York, along with a role in a Broadway musical to the best young singer
who applied. It is an important mark of his character that at the height of
his popularity on Broadway he launched an independent concert career,
and planned a sabbatical in Europe to gain experience in opera. This shows
considerable seriousness and maturity. He certainly was not a man following the line of least resistance.

Though he was not among the super rich, Thomas became sufficiently
prosperous to feel the pinch from the income tax which had been introduced in 1914, with a maximum rate before the First World War of just 2
percent. Today, generations have become inured to high taxes imposed by
all levels of American government, and wage earners particularly, who
only see what is left of their income after the tax is taken out, may never
grasp the full scope of income they might have spent but for taxes. In the
case of a performer, who negotiates a contract for a certain fee and receives
his full pay, the tax that is taken from him is much more tangible. For a
man of Thomas's generation, who enjoyed a large income from his own
work from an early age, and continued to enjoy such an income throughout the Depression, the impact of high taxes during the New Deal and the
Second World War could only create a bitter political resentment — and
it did.[17]

Despite the money, Thomas wanted more than Broadway could offer.
His work was comparatively easy, the singing was not demanding, a whole
show might have no more than four or five songs for the lead singers. If
he found the work a trifle boring, the life of a matinee idol offered other
diversions. Even the press commented about the ladies who lined up to
meet this handsome, wavy haired singer, and Thomas took full advantage
of his opportunities.

One rainy afternoon in Boston in 1917, a young theatrical agent whose New York firm of Charles Wagner and R.E. Johnston had just signed the still unknown Amelita Galli-Curci for a national tour, and represented many other leading singers, wandered into the theater where Thomas was offering a matinee performance of *The Highwayman*. Merle Armitage sat through the opening songs of the lead soprano, and then saw Thomas, a "tall, gangly fellow with a sort of grotesque charm," dressed as an eighteenth century gallant in leather hipboots, enter and pour out a lavishly rich rendition of some melodic trifle, quite overwhelming his leading lady vocally and astonishing the audience. After the performance, Armitage went backstage to introduce himself to Thomas. In short order, he told him that he was wasting his talent on such performances, that despite the good pay, sooner or later his waist would thicken, his hair thin, and his days in operetta would be numbered. What Armitage offered Thomas was the services of Wagner & Johnston, a premier New York artist management firm, to promote a series of concerts. Initially, these might not pay as much as musical theater, but with proper management, concerts could sustain a singer throughout a long career.

Thomas, by now an experienced trouper who knew how to manage his business affairs, was frankly uninterested, and told Armitage as much. The Shuberts, he said, would offer him a contract in the next few weeks that would guarantee him employment for a year and make him a rich man — a very rich man. He was speaking of his contract for *Maytime*. Armitage was persistent, however, and, over several dinners and subsequent meetings, finally persuaded Thomas to offer a concert.

Thomas's concert debut took place in the Aeolian Theatre in London, Ontario, on December 2, 1918, and to the astonishment of his new managers, Thomas cleared a profit of $4.88.[18] Armitage tells us that it was unheard of for an inexperienced concert singer to make a profit on his first outing. Yet the sum was hardly enough to tempt a singer away from the rewards of the Broadway stage. It would be several more years before Armitage and his associates were able to persuade Thomas to leave musicals for a serious concert career, but Armitage was determined to keep an eye on this promising singer. Armitage wrote:

> Early in 1918, I went to the Globe Theater and heard J.C.T. in *Maytime*. I was very much impressed with the tone of his voice and I figured that he would eventually become top soloist for [an all–American orchestra Armitage hoped to form during World War I]. I went backstage to the Globe, congratulated him and we became close friends. He invited me to the Astor Bar for a drink and as we chatted I suggested that he would do better in the concert field than musical comedy. As we met two or three times a week, he became more receptive to the idea.[19]

The war came to an end before Armitage could organize his orchestra, and Thomas decided against taking up a concert career at that time. But Armitage maintained contact with Thomas over the next few years, and would approach him with another offer in the future.

During his ten years on Broadway, Thomas had perfected many of the fundamental techniques of his vocal style: first, the articulation and enunciation which was so characteristic of his singing; second, his comfortable assurance on stage — and some of his hamminess as well. Thomas would write an article on the advantages of a background on the musical stage as a preparation for opera and concert work, arguing that the musical stage gave singers a sense of humor that helped them relax and not take themselves so seriously. He learned some things, too, that he could not have learned in opera — that personality was as important as vocal technique in giving a performance loaded with audience appeal, and how to deliver a show-stopper number.

Thomas retained much of the "Broadway style" in his performances throughout his career. Compare his rendition of the "Largo al factotum" aria from the *Barber of Seville* with any other singer's. It has something of the "passion" which Fermin had spoken of as vital in a singer. Thomas looked for vocal material that offered scope for bravura singing, with ringing high notes and a big finish. Thomas's combination of buoyant personality with great singing put his audience in his hands from the beginning. During his years on Broadway, he also acquired a keen sense of the entertainment business, and learned how a star should manage his career. By 1922, he had definitely acquired a star personality, which only comes from many successful performances and the confidence that audiences and producers want you.

3

Europe and the Concert Stage

Thomas's last Broadway appearance was in *Love Letter,* which opened September 4, 1921, played for 31 performances, and then toured for several more weeks. In the Spring of 1922 he sailed to Europe, where he may have made his London concert debut on June 26, returning to the Royal Albert Hall for another engagement October 1 on a program with Luisa Tetrazzini prior to his return to the United States. He may also have appeared in *The Love Letter* in London in the 1922 season, though this is not confirmed.

The primary purpose of the trip was to perfect his French accent and fluency with studies in Paris. He had talked of traveling to Europe since 1916, but the war, submarines, and professional engagements had kept him in New York. One brief newspaper article makes reference to Thomas traveling to France in 1920, but given the desolation in France so soon after the end of the First World War, it seems an unlikely time to travel. On the other hand, we know that he was eager to speak French when he dined regularly with Merle Armitage during the run of *Maytime* in 1918, so it is possible that he would have traveled to France as soon after the War as conditions allowed.

Thomas would return to the United States for concerts during the autumn and winter of each season from 1923 to 1925, though he seems to have spent most of 1926, 1927, and 1928 abroad, visiting Dublin, Edinburgh, Florence and Rome, as well as many other cities on the Continent. His decision to go to France may also have been prompted by the formal end of his marriage. The divorce from Ruby was finalized in Reno in February 1923.[1]

On his return to the United States in the late summer of 1923, Thomas made his only feature length film, a silent movie, *Under the Red Robe,* taking the role of Gil de Berault, paladin for Cardinal Richelieu in a romance set in the reign of Louis XIII. Among the featured players in the film was a young William Powell, as the king's brother, the Duke of Orleans, leader of a conspiracy to seize the throne.

Under the Red Robe was taken from Stanley Weyman's 1893 adventure story. The outdoor scenes of the film were shot on location in Vermont, with the indoor scenes shot in Cosmopolitan Studio's 128th street studio in Manhattan. The film was directed by Alan Crossland (1894–1936), who began directing films in 1916 with a silent called *The Fear Market* when he was just 22. Crossland is best remembered for the first talking picture, *The Jazz Singer* in 1927, starring Al Jolson. *Under the Red Robe* was released in November 1923 and distributed by Goldwyn Pictures.

Cosmopolitan Studios was owned by William Randolph Hearst, and functioned chiefly as a production vehicle for films starring his long-time companion, Marion Davies. Hearst had a particular weakness for historical costume dramas, and this film, like everything associated with Hearst, spared no expense in meeting the highest production standards. The sets, for example, were designed by Joseph Urban (1872–1933), a Viennese-born designer who, through his friendship with Florence Ziegfeld, began designing for Broadway in 1914, including *Love Letter* in which Thomas had appeared, and later *Show Boat*. Urban designed sets for the Metropolitan Opera from 1917 to his death in 1933. Urban was close to both Hearst and Marion Davies, and designed the Hearst Building between 57th Street and 8th Avenue for "the Chief." In the gaudy years of Jimmy Walker, Urban designed lavish interiors for a Central Park Casino that was later demolished under Mayor LaGuardia. His most important commission still standing is the New School for Social Research in New York, particularly its Theater, which flaunts a dramatic combination of Viennese and Deco styling. He also designed Marjorie Merriweather Post's fantasy palace, Mar a Lago in Palm Beach.

Victor Herbert was commissioned to write an overture for the film, but William Frederick Peters is credited with the musical score.

Under the Red Robe is set in a time of chaos when a weak, self-indulgent king sat on the throne of France. Out of this chaos, the title cards inform us:

> a Man arose, a man who read the souls of men —
> Richelieu, a priest and a soldier with a heart of
> fire and a brain of ice.

The times were full of intrigue,

> but through this wilderness of conflict, the little
> stream of human happiness flows on. The slender

threads of human love weave themselves into the
strong fabric of human life — for there are men and
women who know love and honor, patriotism and sacrifice.......

As Gil de Berault, Thomas is arrested early in the film for dueling, then reprieved from a mandatory death sentence by the Cardinal. In return, however, he must capture the leader of a Huguenot rebellion in service to the King's conniving brother (William Powell). Thomas falls in love with the rebel's sister and frees her brother before returning to face the Cardinal's wrath with proof of the conspiracy by the King's brother.

There were a few good moments in the film: a chase on horseback that culminates in a swordfight by two riders circling in the midst of a stream; Thomas's stunt double leaping on horseback from a rising moat bridge to escape capture. The costumes and interiors are lavish, the crowds of extras are impressive. The most affecting scene is near the climax when de Berault returns to the Cardinal's Palace to find him deserted by all of his petitioners and followers save for a single drummer boy — the "remnant of his guard."

One of the hazards of being a cinematic pioneer, however, was that directors were still learning what worked and what did not work onscreen. With its lack of character development, indifferent camera work, and confusing plot line, the audience must have been unclear about where their sympathies should lie. The film has too many leading characters: three protagonists and one undeveloped villain. We are asked to see Cardinal Richelieu in a sympathetic light, but his Protestant adversary, Henri de Cocheforet, is a gallant and noble character whose loyal servant has had his tongue cut out earlier by the Cardinal's men, and bears the brand of the fleur-de-lis on his head to mark him as a heretic. What is a predominantly Protestant American audience to feel about the weak yet despotic King of France and his menacing chief minister? There are even two fascist salutes in the course of the film. Mussolini had only come to power in Italy the previous year, so the upraised arm would not yet have the menacing implications it later acquired, but it could not have been a reassuring gesture for an American audience.

Thomas is energetic in his role, but does not seize the viewer's attention. Among the cast, only Powell went on to make a major career in film, although two other actors, Otto Kruger, as the Huguenot leader Henri de Cocheforet, and Gustav von Seyfertitz, playing his servant Clom, had lengthy careers in a variety of supporting roles. The cast included two tragic characters, Alma Rubens, Thomas's love interest in the film, and Mary MacLaren, who took the role of the young Queen. Rubens, a woman of dark, striking beauty, appeared in another twenty films between 1923 and 1929, but then

Gil de Berault in *Under the Red Robe* was Thomas's one venture into film — a lavish silent feature produced by W.R. Hearst's Cosmopolitan Studios. (Courtesy of Andrew Pop)

fell into a drug habit and died in poverty in 1931. MacLaren was the last surviving member of the cast, dying in Hollywood in November 1985, two months short of her ninetieth birthday. Her film career had included a hundred roles between 1923 and her last appearance in 1949. Sadly, her last decades were spent living in dire poverty as a bag lady.[2]

Victor Herbert conducted the overture at the film's premiere in New York, and Thomas sang, his last appearance under the composer's baton; but the film was a flop, and, despite many offers, Thomas would never appear in another feature film. Yet this setback had no impact at all on his life in Europe.

In Paris, he studied French with two sisters named Yersin, the only instructors accredited by the Academie Française to convert the North American accent into Parisian French. He and Dorothy lived on the Rue Pergolesi, in a fashionable neighborhood perhaps a half mile east of the Arc de Triomphe, and a short distance from the Bois de Boulogne. The Rue Pergolesi is a rather nondescript street with substantial four- to five-story buildings holding large apartments, with the corner butcher shops and patisseries typical of every Parisian neighborhood. In the 1920s, there may have been a few large private homes on the street, but few of these remain today. Thomas walked to his language lessons, going by the home of the Yersins on his way to the Academie Française. On rainy days, one can well imagine him hailing a cab with his loud American whistle.

If New York was the home of Jimmy Walker, Babe Ruth, and jazz in the twenties, Paris was home to Picasso, Gertrude Stein, Ernest Hemingway, and the 1924 Olympics. Scores of Americans discovered its charms, and Paris returned their affection. Thomas was in Paris when Lindbergh landed to the cheers of tumultuous crowds at La Bourget in May 1927.

While in France, Thomas studied repertoire with the great tenor Jean de Reszke for a few months sometime before the tenor's death in 1925. De Reszke is one of the great legends and mysteries of the operatic world. Celebrated as the greatest tenor of his day, before the ascendancy of Caruso, his voice has always remained a mystery because he made no recordings. Only faint hints of the voice can be heard in live recordings made by Lionel Mapleson at the Metropolitan Opera in 1901–02. He began his career as a baritone, however, which suggests that he would have been an ideal coach for a high baritone like Thomas.

De Reszke personally knew three pillars of the French operatic tradition, Jules Massenet, Charles Gounod, and Ambroise Thomas, whose compositions were staples of John Charles Thomas's operatic repertoire. Gounod had conducted de Reszke in a celebrated revival of *Romeo and Juliet* with Adelina Patti in Paris. Massenet had personally selected and coached both de Reszke's sister and his brother, the bass Eduard de Reszke, for roles in his operas.

De Reszke was a paragon of the bel canto tradition of singing, celebrated for his refined, elegant vocal style and careful emphasis on characterization. He was really an artist from a different age, having mastered successively the Italian, French and German operatic repertoire. Thomas was always emphatic that he had only had two voice *teachers* in his life, Blackman and Fermin at the Peabody, so the exact nature of his training with de Reszke is unclear. Although his teaching principles and methods were controversial among some students, de Reszke was widely regarded as a kind and sympathetic teacher.[3] He attached great importance to developing the diaphragm, using the soft palate or hard palate in the mouth for different tones, and would have students sing arias or passages over and over, eighteen times or more during their lessons.

There are two difficulties with Thomas's claim to have studied with de Reszke. First, de Reszke left Paris after the death of his son in the First World War, and moved to Nice. There is no record of Thomas residing in Nice for any length of time. Secondly, the best source for the story is Dorothy Thomas, who would ordinarily be a very credible witness. She says that her husband even went into debt to pay for de Reszke's lessons. However, de Reszke died of pneumonia after a brief illness in April 1925, just when Dorothy and her new husband were arriving in France.

The suggestion that Thomas studied "repertoire" is also somewhat problematic. Nothing in the memoirs of de Reszke's students suggests that the man limited himself to "repertoire." He was a great singer, and a singing teacher. Is it likely that such a man would say nothing about a student's vocal production or singing style? As a young soprano from Brazil, Bidu Sayao was a pupil of de Reszke, but had no recollection of knowing Thomas in those years. Students waited for the master in the hall of his home, and would likely have met and known their fellow students there. The most likely time for Thomas to have studied with de Reszke seems to be between his arrival in Paris in 1922 and his debut at La Monnaie in 1925, before Dorothy joined him in Europe.

If Thomas worked with de Reszke, it is no great leap to imagine him attending some of the final concerts of the legendary bel canto baritone Mattia Batistini (1856–1927), who made his last appearance in London in May, 1925, or meeting Maurice Renaud (1861–1933), the greatest living representative of the French bel canto baritone tradition at the time, past his prime to be sure, but certainly someone any aspiring operatic baritone would want to know.[4]

By all reports, Thomas was a bon vivant. He would golf at St. Cloud in the morning (his score in these years was usually in the high '70s), study and vocalize during the day, attend concerts and shows in the evening, and afterward enjoy the company of friends at late night dinners and parties. He remained, as always, a smart dresser. Two young American students who met him on the golf course in Paris in 1924 were envious of the Dunhill cigarette lighter he carried. These lighters were the latest in swank accessories, and Thomas's model was all the more impressive not only for the watch built into the case, but for its inscription from his Broadway colleagues Fred and Adele Astaire.

Paris was the site of still another of those dubious press agent stories in the Thomas legend. While breakfasting one day, Thomas's attention was drawn to a notice of a vocal audition for the La Monnaie Opera in Brussels. Prompted or taunted by a friend, he boarded a train and entered the competition. Walking on as an unknown, he sang "Vision Fugitive" from *Herodiade*, the "Brindisi" from Ambroise Thomas's *Hamlet*, and the "Prologue" from *Pagliacci*. He won the audition and a place in the company roster, making his debut at La Monnaie on August 1, 1925, as King Herod in Massenet's *Herodiade*.

What is suspect about this story is that the "friend" with whom Thomas was breakfasting, the friend who had a friend who worked in the box office at La Monnaie, who had another friend who knew the manager of the company, was Adelin Fermin, who would certainly have had the contacts and credibility to arrange an audition for a singer of Thomas's reputation. Thomas, after all, was not an unknown. Now approaching his mid-thirties, he was an experienced performer with a well-established career as a concert, recording, and radio artist. One can only conclude that the whole escapade was done as a lark, to see the expression of the judges when this very experienced singer appeared at an open audition and stole the show.

Thomas's contract at La Monnaie ran for four seasons, and allowed him to sing a total of 15 roles. He returned subsequently as a guest artist, making his farewell appearances in *Les Pecheurs de Perles* during the 1931 season.[5]

On his return from Europe in 1922, Thomas met Dorothy Kaehler at a weekend party in Boston, and was smitten by the charm and manners of this 22-year-old college student, particularly her curtsy. As Thomas's interest grew, his friend Charlie Parker took it upon himself to do some research and discovered that this young girl had a very colorful family history. Her grandmother, Nattie Craven, had been the mistress of a prominent California politician, Senator Charles Fair of San Francisco. When Senator Fair died without leaving Nattie any part of his estate, she sued. The judge in the case was the father of a boy who was madly in love with Nattie's daughter Margaret, a stunningly beautiful actress. Another judge might have recused himself from the case. This one chose to consult with Nattie's attorneys on how they might best proceed in their case. The San Francisco press went so far as to suggest that the judge had his eye on young Margaret himself. But Margaret married neither the judge nor his son. Instead, in 1897, she married Henry Koehler Jr., President of the American Brewing Co. of St. Louis. Dorothy was born to that marriage on June 13, 1902. In 1914, her father died, and within six months her mother married George Angue "Boss" Dobyne. The couple divided their time between Beverly Farms, Massachusetts, outside Boston, and Palm Beach. Dobyne's son Robert also lived with the family.[6]

Like Thomas, Dorothy had a close attachment to her mother, but an awkward relationship with her stepfather. The ten or eleven year age difference between her and her suitor may have been one factor in her shy response to his advances, another was that he arrived in her life just as she was about to return to her classes at the University of California at Berkeley. Thomas was not easily deterred, however, and his interest in the young girl may even have spurred him to take up Merle Armitage's renewed offer to launch a serious concert career.

Armitage recalled the events this way:

> One day in January of the early '20s, Johnston, Wagner, and I had a conference. My recent trip through the west, and particularly in California, convinced me that this vast territory was ripe for some new management in the concert field, and we were all convinced that I should open an office in Los Angeles. If we had John Charles Thomas, we all agreed, he would be a magnificent opener for the many engagements we planned in the west. It was decided that we would make one, last, now-or-never approach to John Charles. As I had first encountered Thomas in Boston in 1916, and had kept in contact with him, I was elected to make the move.
>
> John Charles invited me to breakfast at the Algonquin Hotel. We talked over the whole scheme, and I told him that if he would come under the concert management of R.E. Johnston, then I would take him on his first western tour. Painting as bright a picture as I could, I was countered by John Charles's statement that he had made $90,000 the previous year with the Shuberts. "What do you have to offer," he asked? The most we could offer was a concert tour with a minimum guarantee of $35,000, but that would be only the beginning, I assured him. It would mean giving up light opera entirely. John just could not decide. Finally he said, "I flipped a coin with my father once, when we could not decide whether I should study music, or medicine. It turned out just great. Will you take a chance with me and flip a coin now?" My head was reeling, but I managed to say, 'I'll take heads.' Heads it was!"[7]

In a sketch for a movie on Thomas's life, which Armitage circulated at the Hollywood studios in the early '50s, he has Thomas put down the pen after signing their contract and say, "I hope this works out." The phrase has the ring of authenticity.

> ... Preceding this tour, R. E. Johnston presented John Charles Thomas in a New York concert. The prestige of R.E. Johnston, and the appeal of this virile, hand-

some new baritone, brought a capacity audience. Thomas was in excellent form, and the audience, realizing they were present at an historical event, really cheered John Charles to the point that he was forced to sing over seven encores. They just would not let him go. The veteran Johnston, sitting beside me, expressed his satisfaction, 'we have a great success on our hands,' he rejoiced. Next day, the critics, for once, were unanimous.

The West Coast tour ran from Seattle to San Diego. Armitage recalled the energy and enthusiasm of the singer in 1922:

> He loved every day, every problem, every opportunity. To be with him was to live abundantly to enjoy every hour. The commonplace things became charged with new interest, and his ability to see humor in frustrating episodes marked him as delightfully sane. He was a wonderful and colorful companion but never shirked the tools of his profession. He made time for reading, vocalizing, studying, golfing, and ran me ragged with his ineluctable vigor....
>
> During that trip, exhaustion crept into my bones like a sea mist, but John Charles stood out — a lighthouse in the fog, fresher with every performance and as untiring as a soaring eagle. I was worn down and completely outclassed.[8]

The tour was a great success, and in Los Angeles, where his two scheduled concerts were sold out, a third was scheduled for the following week.

Thomas wrote many letters to Dorothy during his tour, and accepted the invitation of Mrs. James Taber Fitzgerald to be her guest for three weeks after the tour ended. Her home was convenient both to golf and sailing off Pebble Beach, and to Berkeley. Thomas returned to Europe in the Spring of 1923, but continued his courtship on his return to the States. The couple was married in Palm Beach on March 5, 1925, two days after Thomas's debut as Amonasro in a Washington D.C. production of *Aida* on the eve of President Coolidge's inauguration. They spent their honeymoon in Havana — not Cuba, but a town in the Florida panhandle — since Thomas still had concert engagements to meet that season. At the conclusion of those engagements, however, the couple sailed to France aboard the *Ile de France*.

John Charles— Johnny, as only Dorothy and Charlie Parker seem to have called him —clearly offered Dorothy a kind of protection and companionship that she needed. As children, both were attached to their mothers and had unhappy relationships with fathers or stepfathers. Circumstances left both feeling somewhat alone in the world, dependent on their own resources. Every acquaintance who recalled Dorothy Thomas always expressed admiration for her, invariably with some such description as, "what a lady." Of their marriage, Ken Darby wrote:

> Dorothy was his complement. She was both woman to his man and mother to his boy. It was he who rang the bells, but it was she who climbed the bell tower and fastened the rope, and she was there to apply a cold towel to the head that

ached when he rang them too long and too loudly. Dependable, forgiving, understanding with a good humor that made her the perfect pivot for his gyrating weather vane career.[9]

When the couple settled in to their accommodations in Brussels, one of Thomas's first visits was to a local bank, where he showed a letter of credit from his New York bank to another American working in Brussels, Newman Smith. Smith, who had never heard of John Charles Thomas, was struck by the very large figure the correspondent bank proposed that he make available to Thomas. When he investigated the sources of his client's wealth, he learned that Thomas had used his Broadway earnings to buy IBM stock and Strauss bonds. After making *Under the Red Robe*, Thomas had become intrigued with the future of film, and bought Eastman Kodak stock. He invested in Brunswick stock after he was signed as a recording artist by that company, and RCA stock after his early engagements on the radio. He also bought Warner Brothers stock, probably after the company bought out Brunswick and hired Thomas to record the Vitaphone films.

Needless to say, these were all very hot stocks in the 1920s. Smith was duly impressed and became a good friend of Thomas, joining him for Thanksgiving dinner on the Chesapeake in the mid–'30s, when Thomas offered his guests black Belgian grapes in memory of their years on the continent.[10]

The motto "Let's Be Ourselves," which hung over the mantle of Thomas's New York apartment in later years, nicely expressed his character. Although he loved Paris and Brussels, he never lost his American informality. A widely repeated story of an experience at La Monnaie tells of the time Thomas nearly forgot a rehearsal for *Parsifal*, and rushed from the golf course to the opera house in an open shirt and plus fours. The stage manager refused to admit him, saying that opera singers did not dress in sporting clothes. Thomas replied that this one did, and eventually located some associates to help him win admission.

There were other difficulties at the opera as well. At one performance the prompter's stage whisper was so loud that Thomas decided the only way to silence him was to cross the stage and put his foot on the prompter's score to prevent him keeping up with the opera. Thus positioned, he continued to perform without interruption. This scene was immortalized in oil, one of eight portraits Thomas commissioned from the artist Victor Abeloos of his operatic roles at La Monnaie.[11]

Thomas also found it hard to put up with some features of Continental life that only Americans would notice. He was appalled by the plumbing in his dressing room, and offered to pay for modern pipes and fixtures. A long struggle with the metropolitan bureaucracy of Brussels ensued, but the new plumbing was eventually installed.[12]

These stories demonstrate the refreshing informality and directness Thomas brought to the world of opera, characteristics that won him many fans in Brussels. In December 1927, while Thomas was in Washington for an operatic engagement, Dorothy underwent an operation after an attack of appendicitis in New York. While her mother boarded a train from Florida to go to her bedside, Thomas went to the Belgian embassy in Washington to wire Brussels that he would be unable to meet his scheduled appearances at La Monnaie the following April. He offered to pay for the cost of a replacement, but the opera house cabled a reply that there could be no replacement for John Charles Thomas, and offered to reschedule his appearances. In any event, Thomas was able to open the season in *Pagliacci* March 11 as scheduled.

Thomas formed several enduring friendships among his colleagues at La Monnaie, particularly with the basso Lucien Van Obbergh and his wife Denise. Van Obbergh was born in 1887, and first appeared with La Monnaie in 1918, remaining on the boards in some 150 roles, until his final appearance in 1956. Thomas found opportunities for Van Obbergh to perform with the Philadelphia Opera in 1931, but the basso declined. Thomas may well have had a part in helping other Belgian colleagues such as Vina Bovy, Clara Clairbert and René Maison secure contracts with the Metropolitan, San Francisco, or Chicago Operas in the United States.[13]

Thomas's operatic career at La Monnaie was nothing short of remarkable. During his debut season in 1925 he sang 13 performances, in *Herodiade*, *Aida*, and *Parsifal*. The following year, audiences heard him in no less than 71 performances, as Harold in *Gwendoline*, again in *Parsifal* and *Herodiade*, in *Les Malheurs d'Orphee*, *Pecheurs de Perles*, *Thais*, *Rigoletto*, and as Tonio in *Pagliacci*. In 1927 he made 35 appearances, adding Don Giovanni to his repertoire, as well as the Count de Luna in *Trovatore*, John the Baptist in *Salomé*, and Hamlet in his final year as a contract performer for the Opera. He made eight appearances in 1930, and just four in June of 1931, all as Zurga in *Pecheurs de Perles*.

The number of performances is remarkable enough. Inevitably, many of them came after just a single day of rest. On six occasions, he appeared on successive nights in different roles. Nor were these small roles in short operas such as Tonio in *Pagliacci*. Take the months of October and November 1926, for example. On Sunday October 24, Thomas appeared at a matinee performance of *Thais*, and the following evening as Herod in *Herodiade*. On Monday November 1 he was Athanael again in *Thais*, Zurga the following evening and Orpheus the next night. Two weeks later, he

With his Belgian colleague Lucien Van Obbergh. (Courtesy of Jacques Fievez)

did back to back performances of *Pearlfishers* and *Thais*, after having offered Tonio earlier in the week. And *Pearlfishers* was scheduled on Thanksgiving, his favorite holiday.

Busy as he was in Brussels during these years, his enthusiasm for air travel allowed him to add even more performances to his calendar. After completing his final performance in *Hamlet* at La Monnaie on June 27,1928 (and attending a large farewell party), he boarded a plane at five in the morning for a six hour flight to London to start rehearsals for *Faust* the next day. The Mephistopheles for these performances was Feodor Chaliapin, the legendary Russian bass, then at the height of his career. Recordings dating from twenty years later demonstrate how Thomas could transform the role of Valentin from the wooden figure he often seems into a vigorous soldier. He concluded Valentin's opening aria, "Avant de quitter ces lieux," announcing his departure for the holy wars, with the interpolation of a ringing A♭. Performances of this caliber are the stuff of great operatic evenings. Despite glowing reviews that took more notice of Thomas's singing than Chaliapin's, *Faust* was Thomas's only engagement at Covent Garden. It is rumored that the great basso, who did not care to share the stage with rivals, had a clause added to his contract with Covent Garden that he would not appear in performance with John Charles Thomas.

Thomas lived at the Astoria Hotel on the Rue Royale in Brussels during the opera season. Each July he and Dorothy vacationed in France. Vichy, where they met and became fast friends with John McCormack, was a favorite stop. They were sometimes joined in Europe by the Dobynes, and one year by Dorothy and Milson Thomas. In late July, the couple usually sailed for New York, and spent August and September at the Dobyne's home in Beverly Farms, Massachusetts, relaxing and preparing for the American concert season, which began in October.

Thomas's recording sessions and concert schedule provide the best means of reconstructing his itinerary during the twenties. We know that he recorded for Vocalion in October and November, 1922, and made his first concert tour of the West Coast that Fall. He recorded with Vocalion in February of 1923, and had concert engagements throughout the United States through June, then recorded with Vocalion again in July and August. He was in London for a concert at Albert Hall in September, 1923, and returned to the U.S. for concerts from November 1923 to March of 1924. He had a recording session in May, 1924, but did not appear in the United States again until a Carnegie Hall recital on December 30 of that year. He offered two concerts in the United States in February, 1925, and of course his operatic debut in Washington in early March. He seems to have spent

John Charles Thomas and Dorothy in Europe c. 1928, possibly with Dorothy's mother, stepfather, and (between John Thomas and Dorothy) stepbrother, Robert Dobyne. (Courtesy of Jacques Fievez)

most of 1926, 1927 and 1928 in Europe, though he made his three Vitaphone films in New York in April, 1927, and was a regular in Palm Beach from December through February in those years.

A newspaper interview in the Fall of 1927 reported that Thomas planned a tour of South America in the summer of 1928, but there is no record of his engagement at either the Colon in Buenos Aries or in Manaus. When he returned for guest appearances at La Monnaie after the end of his contract in 1928, his first performance was usually as Tonio in *I Pagliacci*, in which the baritone sings the opening lines of the *Prologue*. Thomas would step in front of the curtain and announce himself with the line "Pardon, c'est moi; mesdames et vous messieurs. Excussez-moi, s' seul je me presente," to applause that shook the rafters.

Living in Paris and Brussels among other bright, witty, talented young Americans, all making their way in new careers, must have been one of the most enjoyable times of Thomas's life. It was certainly one of the most important periods in his life, and one of the least known. It is unfortunate that he did not relate more of his experiences from these years on the Continent, but he was never a man to dwell in memories. Other Americans in Paris during those years took advantage of the opportunity to collect great art. Baltimoreans like Gertrude Stein and the two Cone sisters amassed great collections on a fraction of Thomas's income. His manager, Merle Armitage, became an avid collector of Paul Klee in these years, but Thomas showed little interest in contemporary art.

What other American musicians did Thomas know or meet in Paris? Virgil Thomson, Cole Porter and Aaron Copland were all there in those years, though somewhat younger than the singer. Thomson was in the Stein circle, and knew Satie and Les Six, important leaders of modern music in France. Thomas would have known Darius Milhaud, one of the Six, from performing

Tonio in *I Pagliacci* was a role Thomas liked to open his season with at La Monnaie. (Courtesy of Andrew Pope)

the lead in the world premier of his opera *Les Malheurs d'Orphee*. Milhaud (1892–1974) would emigrate to the United States after the outbreak of war in 1939, and spend the war years associated with Mills College in Oakland, California.

One figure that it is impossible to imagine Thomas not encountering in Paris is Ernest Hemingway. A sailing companion in later years who shared Dorothy's love of deep-sea fishing, Hemingway was just the kind of crony Thomas would enjoy. Still an unknown but promising writer in his mid-twenties when he first arrived in Paris, Hemingway lived on the Left Bank with his wife in an apartment that rented for $16.80 per month. His first novel, *The Sun Also Rises*, would be published in 1926, just at the time Thomas was comfortably settled into European life. Hemingway and Thomas were both self-made men, and made it their mission to enjoy life to the fullest. They also shared similar conservative political views.

What was different about Thomas's expatriate experience was that he was very comfortably off, more like Cole Porter, or the Divers in Fitzgerald's

Tender Is the Night, than the struggling artists one usually imagines in Paris during the twenties. He went abroad to learn French and acquire a larger operatic repertoire. He was drawn to Brussels because it gave him an opportunity to practice his art. The fact that he was already a successful, established performer meant that the Continent did not awe him. Even the twenty-three-year-old Dorothy caught this spirit. Meeting Chaliapin, by all accounts a most formidable personality, one day on a walk with John Charles, she recorded in her diary that "he was not as tall or intimidating as he seemed on stage, but well over six feet. He looks as if he had lived well and hard. Very *gracieux et plein de gestes distinguees.*"[14]

As American expatriates will, the Thomases enjoyed celebrating national holidays with compatriots. Thanksgiving was a particular Thomas favorite. Roast turkey with creamy mashed potatoes, peas, and dressing that included sauerkraut and bits of ham was his favorite meal. During their first autumn abroad, Dorothy and John Charles invited other friends to join them at a restaurant outside of Brussels for the traditional feast. Over the years, the attendance at this celebration grew until, for their last Thanksgiving in Brussels, Thomas reserved the entire restaurant. In June 1928, Thomas had a large birthday party for Dorothy at the Rouge Clostre restaurant in a forest outside Brussels. He hosted another party at a seaside resort, to which he invited guests from England, and paid their passage to Ostend. At a farewell party in 1928 after his final performance at La Monnaie, singing to a capacity audience on a stage bedecked with flowers, the Thomases hosted a large party at Les Trois Suisses restaurant. This was the man at his best: a warm, friendly, engaging, and generous host.

The 1920s were the decade when Thomas transformed himself from a star of the musical stage to a serious classical concert artist and operatic baritone of the first rank. It was the decade in which he perfected his French language skills, his *bel canto* repertoire, and married the woman who would share his life for the next thirty-six years. After his appearance in *Under the Red Robe,* Thomas made at least three Vitaphone recordings for Warner Brothers as the movies moved gingerly toward the revolution of talking pictures. These films, made between April 19 and 28, 1927, show Thomas in costume performing the "Sweetheart" duet from *Maytime,* and in morning coat delivering a bracing version of Kipling's wonderful Victorian ballad, "Danny Deever," with which he would delight audiences for many years to come, and singing the "Prologue" from *Pagliacci.*

The twenties were the years of Thomas's most prolific recording sessions. He made 37 recordings for the Vocalion and Brunswick labels in the nine years between 1920 and 1929, compared to the two dozen he made for RCA Victor between 1931 and 1944. It is intriguing to speculate that he might have made some recordings in Brussels or Paris, perhaps under another name, but none have ever surfaced.

Thomas's voice underwent a major change as a result of his European training. His earliest recordings as a twenty-five year old in 1915 are almost unrecognizable compared to the more mature voice of the 1930s. In the early Vocalion recordings between 1920 and 1925 the voice is stiff, dark, and rather stilted, almost hooded, as though Thomas was imitating Tita Ruffo, the great dramatic baritone of Caruso's day, whose voice was heavier and, because he was self taught, lacked the refinement of the bel canto style. The Vocalions included a few operatic and oratorio arias, but were primarily songs from Broadway musicals, and traditional songs like "In the Gloaming," or "Nellie Gray."

By 1925, after his debut in Brussels and his training with de Reszke, Thomas's first electric recordings were issued on the Brunswick label. The voice was now closer to the one that would emerge from RCA recordings just six years later — mellow, fluid, confident, without the earlier stiffness. The voice still displays an almost academic bel canto line that has not yet matured into the easy freedom it would find by 1931.

There is something enviable about these years of apprenticeship during the twenties. For all his Broadway success, Thomas was no overnight sensation in the world of classical music. While he enjoyed the good life in Paris, Vichy, Brussels, Palm Beach, and New York, Thomas had the opportunity to sing fine operatic roles with first class opera companies, and still earned a good income from his American concerts, recordings and radio appearances. Discipline and patience were two principles he preached to aspiring vocal students later in his career, and they were principles he practiced. Year by year, he perfected his voice and his art. Thomas was always intensely competitive, and lost no opportunity to build his concert career; but more than most of his contemporaries, he balanced his career with outside pursuits — sailing, deep sea fishing, golfing, motoring, and gourmet dining — all of which gave him enormous enjoyment in life.

One city embodied the enjoyment of life in full measure during the Roaring Twenties, and that was where Thomas moored during most of the months he spent in America — Palm Beach. Like Tivoli or Capri in ancient Rome, Palm Beach was a city built for pleasure, and attracted a peculiar mixture of old money, new money, gangsters, politicians, writers and theater people. While the country at large observed prohibition, liquor flowed freely in Palm Beach, only a few pleasant hours journey away by boat from ample supplies in the Bahamas. Gambling was also available at a well-known local

Dressed as the explorer LaSalle for the inauguration of American Airways service between Chicago and New Orleans, 1931.

casino run by F. R. Bradley that was largely undisturbed by local police because it catered only to the out-of-towners.

Palm Beach could trace its history to the Royal Poinciana Hotel built by Henry Flagler in 1894 in West Palm Beach. The Royal Poinciana attracted northerners looking for warm sunshine to help them recuperate from illness, or simply escape northern winters. The hotel was originally built with 540 rooms, but eventually grew to 1,150, and could accommodate 1,600 diners in its vast dining room. The real development of Palm Beach proper, however, did not begin until the arrival of Addison Mizner and Paris Singer, youngest son of the founder of the Singer Sewing Machine Co. Both men were looking for a spot to recover their health, Singer from high living, Mizner from a damaged ankle injured in a mugging in New York. Singer was looking for a place to build a resort, and Mizner persuaded him to break away from the northern architectural styles and wood construction that looked so bland in Florida, and adopt a more Spanish or Mediterranean style.

Mizner never pretended to be a trained architect or to specialize in any authentic period design. He had traveled widely in Mexico and Latin America, and appreciated how towers, cupolas and vaulted domes could break the flatness of the Florida landscape. His buildings were designed for seasonal occupation, and indulged in open cantilevered staircases, balconies, courtyards and a wide mixture of styles that he blended together under stucco and tile. For ten years, between 1917 and 1927, Singer and Mizner formed a fruitful collaboration until the architect's eccentricity, particularly a fondness for walking around with monkeys and parrots, even into the hallowed rooms of exclusive clubs, finally caused a break. Mizner went on to build a new resort a few miles away in Boca Raton, and both men died in the early '30s after the land boom they launched in the early '20s had turned to a land bust, and the Depression had begun to touch even the fortunes of the very wealthy. After the death of Paris Singer in the 1930s, when the Everglades Club faced bankruptcy, it was rescued by a small group of investors. "Boss" Dobyne was one of them.

The first building constructed by Singer and Mizner became the Everglades Club, though to win construction permits in 1917–18 they had to describe it as a recovery facility for wounded soldiers returning from France. Once the war was over, it was quickly converted to the island's first resort club. The Everglades was a large four-story building, almost a series of buildings, with an additional three stories in the tower. The principal room in the club was the large, two and a half story formal dining room hung with heavy wrought iron chandeliers designed and manufactured by Mizner's own firm, which specialized in the production of roofing tiles and

The Everglades Club, Palm Beach.

other architectural fittings that were compatible with his buildings. The Everglades also had a large open-air dining room, the famous Orange Garden, with large potted trees. There was a room for the "Convalescents Club" to meet, a name kept in honor of the ruse Singer used to build the Everglades, but more likely referring to the hangovers its members nursed there.

Membership in the Everglades was controlled by Singer through annual renewals for each season. Members who violated the rules, or simply did not seem to fit in with Singer's idea of the right society were not renewed. Considering the exclusive nature the club eventually acquired, membership costs were fairly nominal in the early years. A single membership was $75, a family membership $100. Of course the Palm Beach season extended only from Christmas to Washington's birthday at the end of February, so it was deemed prudent to keep membership rates nominal in the years when the resort was just being launched.

Thomas would have come to Palm Beach for the first time in 1924 or 1925 when he was courting Dorothy. That was at the height of the land boom in Palm Beach as speculators rushed to buy lots that they could sell at great profit in weeks or months. A hurricane in 1926, and a second, much more severe storm in 1928 flattened the land market, along with a number of homes. The following year, the Depression further damaged the local economy. Even the rich began to feel pinched. Thomas and the Dobynes, however, floated serenely through these natural and financial catastrophes. Boss Dobyne added a tiled swimming pool to Casa Beata, their mansion facing the Atlantic Ocean on El Brillo Road, and invited

Palm Beach in the Roaring Twenties. Anita Koos (right) joins Dorothy and John Charles at a bathing beauty party in January, 1929.

guests to a bathing beauty contest where all the contestants were winners. A photo from the party shows John Charles, Dorothy, and Anita Loos, the author of the recent best-seller *Gentlemen Prefer Blondes*, at poolside. John Charles is dressed preposterously in tails and swimming trunks, while Dorothy and Anita, one as petite as the other, smile for the camera in their costumes. That photo sums up life in the balmy sunshine of the Roaring Twenties.

The society pages of the local papers regularly carried stories of parties at the Dobynes' villa. A Christmas Eve party in 1930 saw their patio converted into a Basque country inn, "El Torro Furiosa," according to an illustrated poster specially drawn for the occasion. Dinner was served at long tables arranged around a hollow square in which some fifty guests danced to music provided by a local orchestra under colored lights strung in the tropical foliage overhead. This was the Gatsby world of flappers, endless parties, heavy drinking and good times that Anita Loos described in her memors of Palm Beach in the twenties, and Thomas was in the thick of it. Palm Beach was full of nouveau riche mixing with writers and actors from the New York theatrical world, and even a smattering of old line industrialists, such as Henry Clay Frick and Otto Kahn, and a few old society names like Consuela Vanderbilt, mingled with newer fortunes like Atwater Kent, who would become a sponsor of Thomas's radio broadcasts, Marjorie Merriweather Post, and Joe Kennedy. William Randolph Hearst and Marion Davies vacationed down the road at the Breakers. What the resort lacked were the touches of real life and seasonal traditions that were a part of ordinary American life in other parts of the country. Thomas and his circle of friends had a small part in remedying that.

Thomas's spreading fame as a concert and recording star attracted aspiring young local singers requesting auditions and advice about how to launch their careers. In December, 1929, Mrs. Dobyne came up with the idea of meeting this demand, helping local musicians survive the Depression, and enriching the musical life in the resort by founding a band of gypsy singers, the Romanies. Her son-in-law enthusiastically agreed. They became President and Vice-President of the group, which was organized with officers, a board, and by-laws. Both supporters and members were quickly enlisted. Thomas devoted two full days to auditioning fifty singers, selecting twenty for the chorus. Members were required to wear their gypsy costumes to all rehearsals as well as performances.

On Christmas Eve, 1929, the Romanies, including retired Metropolitan contralto Louise Homer, made their first public appearance in Palm Beach, riding around the resort dressed in their colorful outfits, serenading the townspeople in a wagon pulled by two mules.[15] They were surprised to find the staff at some of the larger homes throwing coins at them in the belief that they were real gypsies. The company ended up at the Everglades Club where Thomas emerged from a dinner party to sing the "Prologue" from *Pagliacci*. In time the chorus would grow, adding a small orchestra, with instruments purchased by Mr. Frank Vernon Skiff of Jewel Tea Co.

Younger children, aged 8 to 15, the Tads, came later. The Romanies performed not only at local charitable events, weddings, and parties, but also at one large production each year, and it was supported handsomely. Resort regulars returned from European travels with authentic gypsy costumes, fabric and gear. Annual budgets were in the range of $10,000, probably as much as or more than the Metropolitan spent on a single production. Thomas arranged to hire a conductor to work with the group, as well as a vocal coach, B. Gagliano, from the Metropolitan Opera. A local contractor named Castiglione taught the chorus Italian pronunciation.

In 1930 the Romanies performed *I Pagliacci*, with two professionals in the leading roles. Edward Jardin sang Canio, and a South American baritone, Ernesto Dodds, with the Colon Opera House in Buenos Aries, sang Tonio. A colorful Italian village was set up at the Bath and Tennis Club, and a second performance was offered at the baseball field in West Palm Beach. At the end of the performance, the Romanies escorted Thomas to the train station where he boarded a car for a concert engagement and left the station to the chorus singing "Auf Wiedersehen" from Sigmund Romberg's *Blue Paradise*.

> Let me hold you close to my heart,
> Brush your tears away dear
> While a fond *Auf Wiedersehen*
> You shall hear me say dear.
> Something fills my heart with fear,
> Though I know not why dear,
> Telling me *Auf Wiedersehen*
> this time means goodbye dear.

In succeeding years theme programs were offered, like the "Venetian Nite" in March 1931, "On the Road to Vienna" in 1932, "In Old Madrid" in 1933, and "Carnival in Venice" in 1935. By 1936 the Romanies performed an original Persian operetta, *Baghdad*. Productions and sets grew more and more elaborate. At a performance of *Pinafore* at the Bath and Tennis Club, Thomas made his entrance as Sir Joseph Porter rowing across the swimming pool to board the Pinafore.

By 1938, special guest performers were appearing at the February galas. Richard Crooks appeared in 1938, while Helen Jepson came the following year, and Marjorie Lawrence in 1940. Thomas performed again in *Pinafore* that year, and repeated it the following year, just after the start of the Second World War. He also performed *Falstaff* with the Romanies.

Thomas, who loved choral singing, and was known as "Romany Tom" in the group, performed with them whenever he could. Ernest Charles, composer of "Clouds" and "When I Have Sung My Songs," among a number of other compositions Thomas often featured, was also active with the Romanies. In March of 1941, the Romanies and Thomas performed the Coronation Scene from *Boris Goudonov*. The role of Boris is written for a bass voice, of course, but the scene is primarily a showcase for chorus and orchestra, with some nice high notes for Boris that would have suited Thomas very well. One can imagine the setting, with the Romanies in their colorful gypsy costumes, looking very like a Russian coronation chorus. Tickets were priced at $10 apiece, almost double the cost of good seats at Carnegie Hall, and boxes were offered at $100 for groups of six.

The following year, however, the party ended. With the coming of the Second World War, there were simply too few male voices to comprise a chorus. Efforts were made to revive the group after the war, but by that time Mrs. Dobyne was in poor health, having suffered a stroke and developed diabetes. Thomas was living in California, and local support in Palm Beach dropped off. The organization was disbanded in 1954. By that time, Thomas had founded sister Romanies in Santa Barbara and Apple Valley.

In typical fashion, Thomas lived life to the hilt in the Florida sunshine, enjoying all the parties, clubs, golf, sailing and other types of fun the resort offered. Typically, too, he found opportunities to combine work with pleasure, appearing on a weekly broadcast from a South Florida radio station. He was already a veteran radio performer, having first broadcast from a station in New Jersey under the sponsorship of Brunswick. That show became a favorite of fishing crews in the Atlantic. At a time when even announcers, much less opera performers, dressed formally in radio studios, Thomas came directly from his yacht to the Florida studio, and stood barefoot before the microphone, ready to return to the sea after the broadcast. That informality had to end when the station management began inviting a paying audience into the studio to hear the baritone.

As his American concert career grew and he relocated permanently to the United States, Thomas and the Dobynes looked for another residence that would be closer to his parents. In 1934, the Dobynes sold their Massachusetts property and settled in Easton, Maryland, on the Chesapeake Bay, where they could enjoy yachting and golf. Thomas would sail his 110-foot yacht, the *Masquereder*, from Easton to Palm Beach, and live aboard it with Dorothy while visiting the Dobynes. The yacht was christened the *Masquereder*, Thomas liked to say, because it allowed he and Dorothy to masquerade as millionaires, even though they were not. This arrangement of living near or with their parents, (Thomas bought a home for his mother in Palm Beach about a mile down the road from the Dobyne's mansion) was a convenient way of dealing with Thomas's extended absences on concert tours. The Thomases would not buy a home

In Palm Beach with a prize catch. (Courtesy of the Archives of the Peabody Institute of The Johns Hopkins University)

of their own until their purchase of a house in Los Angeles in 1942. Thomas also kept a suite at the Berkshire Hotel, at Madison and 52nd Street in Manhattan, which he opened after Thanksgiving each year for the opera and concert season, but he preferred to use it as an office and usually stayed on the *Masquereder* when he was in town for any length of time.[16]

John Charles Thomas and Dorothy aboard the *Masquereder* near Easton, Maryland. (Courtesy of the Archives of the Peabody Institute of The Johns Hopkins University)

Easton was not an island like Palm Beach, but it was a small, isolated town of just 7,000 residents. Life there was quiet and pleasant. In the 1950s, Thomas joked with an interviewer that he had lived in Easton since he was a teenager, but he was still treated as a newcomer. He must have meant that he had visited Easton during summers after his parents moved to Towson. In his youth, scores of cruise boats left Baltimore's Light Street docks on weekends to carry Baltimoreans to a variety of Eastern Shore weekend resort destinations like Easton or St. Michaels.

The Dobyne property at Easton comprised a few hundred acres at Ingleside, some four miles east of town on the wide mouth of the Miles River just opposite St. Michaels. The Dobynes lived in the large, white clapboard home fronting the river; John Charles and Dorothy lived in a smaller house nearby. Life was lived on the water. Thomas and his father-in-law would go to the golf course by motorboat. When he was not golfing, Thomas's life in Easton was anchored at the Miles River Yacht Club. Travel to Baltimore would have been by boat, since no bridge yet spanned the Chesapeake Bay. To reach New York, Thomas would either have entrained at Baltimore, or traveled farther up the Chesapeake on his yacht to catch the train at Havre de Grace. For longer stays, his crew sailed the *Masquereder* to a Manhattan mooring, and he lived onboard. The comparative isolation of Easton offered John Charles and Dorothy an opportunity for quiet relaxation, and ample time for the baritone to practice his music.[17]

Newly settled into his life in Palm Beach and Easton after returning to the United States, Thomas watched his concert and radio career grow even as the Depression settled grimly over the lives of most people in the United States. He was engaged by the Philadelphia, Chicago, and San Francisco operas, but found the barriers to joining the nation's premier opera company, the New York Metropolitan Opera, still formidable.

Two other factors enabled Thomas to make his transition to the concert and operatic world. His personality had always had an element of the impetuous and unsettled. His marriage to Dorothy began to change that. While he became more peripatetic than ever, traveling regularly between the East and West coasts, from Florida to Massachusetts and then Maryland, between Europe and America, he became a more contented person, particularly after he made a home in Easton. A second element of stability came in the form of Carroll Hollister, who served as Thomas's accompanist at the height of his career, from the fall of 1933 to May 1, 1945. At six feet, 150 pounds, with blue-gray eyes, Hollister was a rather thin, patrician figure, eleven years younger than Thomas. He had been born in Danbury, Connecticut, in 1901, the son of a Congregational minister, and attended Amherst College for one year before transferring to the Institute of Musical Art in New York. He made his debut as accompanist to Elena Gerhardt in 1925, and was accompanist to violinist Mischa Elman from 1929 to 1933. He was a superb accompanist, who, like Thomas, always performed from memory, without music.[18]

A quiet man, Carroll Hollister was a collaborator in the fullest sense of the term, keeping Thomas up to the highest artistic standards. It became his job to pore over new music and the many songs offered Thomas by hopeful composers to select material that best suited the Thomas voice and style. During the summers, he worked with Thomas daily, rehearsing material for next season's concerts. During the concert season, from October to April, he and Thomas traveled around the country in the glamorous, if unenviable, life of wandering minstrels. When one looks at the marked transformation between the very experienced concert singer which Thomas had become by 1932 and the superstar he would become within a few short years; between the good recordings he was making for Brunswick by 1930 and the warm, rich voice that poured from the RCA recordings and surviving radio broadcasts from later in that decade, it is very tempting to point to Hollister as the single most important difference in Thomas's emergence as a major vocal star. When Hollister left Thomas in 1945, the singer's repertoire and performances deteriorated precipitously. While they were together, Thomas was always generous in acknowledging Hollister's support, whether on the concert stage or in a radio broadcast, and introduced a few of his compositions at his concerts and on radio programs. He was generous too in the salary he gave Hollister, which was not always the case with other successful performers.

An aircheck survives of a 1934 radio appearance by Thomas which must have been one of Hollister's first appearances with the baritone. Thomas sings "What Is This Thing Called Love." The piano accompaniment is vaguely remote, almost like the two artists are performing the same music, but in different settings. Within a few years, however, Hollister's accompaniment is inseparably a part of the performance. Just how integral it is can perhaps best be seen in the many "character" and humorous songs which were a signature of Thomas concerts. Listen to the opening bars of "Sailormen," "Green Eyed Dragon," "Blow Me Eyes," or "Long Ago in Alcala" and you recognize at once that it is the piano accompaniment that sets the whole tone of the piece — and sustains the lighthearted spirit to the end.

As Thomas's popularity grew, and his concert career expanded once he settled permanently in the United States, he went through a number of changes in his management. He had begun his concert career under the

Carroll Hollister and John Charles Thomas at the beginning of their association, in 1933. (Courtesy of the Archives of the Peabody Institute of The Johns Hopkins University)

management of R.E. Johnston and Merle Armitage. When Johnston died, Armitage decided that he no longer wanted to spend so much time on the road, and left the agency business. During the 1930–31 season, Thomas was under the management of NBC Artist Services, but switched to Charles Wagner in 1933. By the end of the decade, both NBC and CBS were offering high fees to sign Thomas, fees which Wagner was unwilling to meet, so Thomas returned to NBC. [19]

Thomas was quick to adapt to new media, and was booked regularly on radio after returning from Europe. Indeed, he was a pioneer in performing on radio when many artists and their recording companies feared that the new medium would hurt record sales. When station WEAF set up a new radio studio at 195 Broadway in early 1923, Thomas was present. On New Year's Day, 1924, Victor Records decided to offer the public two of their most popular Red Seal artists, John McCormack and Lucrezia Bori, on a special holiday broadcast, and found that they sold 200,000 records of the artists in the following week, and that McCormack's upcoming concert at Carnegie Hall was sold out overnight! Because the artist's royalty on each Red Seal record could be as much as $1 in those years, artists were soon lined up to perform for the radio audience. Thomas's recording company, Brunswick Records, soon launched a musical quiz program, *The Brunswick Hour Musical Memory Contest*, with a monthly prize of $5,000 for the listener who could identify both music and performers who had appeared over the past four weeks. Listeners were urged to buy Brunswick discs to prepare for the quiz, and elaborate measures were taken to conceal the artists as they arrived at the station. Thomas

With John McCormack, whom Thomas replaced as host of the Vince radio program in March, 1934. The two men had known each other in Europe in the 1920s. (Courtesy of the Archives of the Peabody Institute of The Johns Hopkins University)

appeared on the program, though his voice must have been instantly recognizable. He sang on General Motors' *Family Party* on NBC in 1928, appeared regularly on the Atwater Kent show during 1929, then for Maxwell House in the following year.[20] On March 21, 1934, he succeeded John McCormack in a two-year stint as star of the Vince program, which aired at 9:30 Wednesday evenings in the East, the night following Lawrence Tibbett's 8:30 P.M. show for Packard. Curiously enough, Thomas and Tibbett, the most famous baritones in American, did not meet until 1935. Thomas was a regular guest on Ford's Sunday evening show from January 1937 until 1940, and also made appearances on the RCA Golden Key program and the Chesterfield show in 1937. He appeared on the Coca-Cola program between December, 1940, and May, 1941. In addition, there were frequent guest appearances on special holiday programs such as Mother's Day, which helped his record sales and built up demand for him as a concert artist.

It was on a Mother's Day program sponsored by the Golden Rule Insurance Company in May of 1934 that one of Thomas's most celebrated broadcast battles with regulators and the networks began. At the end of the program, he leaned into the microphone and quietly said, "Good night, mother." Ken Darby relates the uproar that followed:

> NBC execs came into the studio and made it clear that personal messages would not be broadcast (a violation of FCC rules). John eyeballed the executives and placed a hand on his (*sic*) shoulder. "I am represented by the company that hires you. I am the property of NBC and RCA. When I sing on any of your affiliated radio stations, or on the network itself, please convey to your superiors that it will be my custom to close whatever portion of the program I have been engaged to do with 'good night, mother.' It is important for you to understand this because any contractual document between me and NBC will contain that stipulation. Good night, gentlemen."[21]

The dispute got into the press, and Thomas repeated his threat to quit the radio altogether if he were not allowed to send this message. NBC and the FCC eventually relented, but the incident could only have fed Thomas's resentment of corporate and official bureaucracies.

The comfortable tenor of Thomas's new life was interrupted by unhappy family news in June, 1935, that would raise profound psychological questions for Thomas and the lifestyle he had embraced. Returning to Palm Beach from a concert tour that month, Thomas received a wire from his mother that Milson, who had looked wan but alert the previous Christmas, was failing. Thomas flew to Towson, where his seventy-year-old father died at his vicarage on June 21, 1935. A funeral service was held June 24, after which Milson was interred in Druid Ridge cemetery.

John Charles with his mother, Dora Thomas. Thomas was a devoted son who regularly signed off his radio performances with "Good night, mother." (Courtesy of the Archives of the Peabody Institute of The Johns Hopkins University)

It had been an eventful year. John Charles Thomas had joined the Metropolitan Opera company, he had relocated with his in-laws from Massachusetts to Easton, he had bought his first Packard, and his first boats. He had arrived. Then his father died.

Thomas reflected later to a friend that he wished his father had lived

John Charles Thomas with his prized Packard, c. 1934. (Courtesy of the Archives of the Peabody Institute of The Johns Hopkins University)

to see all his work and effort reach fulfillment. Somewhere deep inside, he was still looking for the approval of the strict parent who had opposed his pursuit of a singing career and his acting in frivolous Broadway shows; the father who presided over his marriage to Ruby, very likely with premonitions of its failure; who had seen him marry a wealthy heiress eleven or more years his junior, and seen the awkward family life she was leaving to marry his son. John Charles Thomas seems never to have won the approval of his father, and was deeply conscious of it. Unresolved issues lingered from his pious family upbringing. In conversations with his mother after his father's death, John Charles confided that he was uneasy about the wealth and "goods" he had acquired from his singing. His father had always emphasized the importance of deeds rather than "things," and he was not sure that it was right to surround himself with so many possessions. His mother reassured him that so long as he did the "deeds," he was entitled to keep the "things."[22]

Thomas seemed comfortable with that advice. Within a year, he sold

The *Masquereder* anchored near Easton, Maryland. (Courtesy of the Archives of the Peabody Institute of The Johns Hopkins University)

the *Masquereder* for a larger yacht, the *Moon*, which he re-christened *Masquereder*. At 110 feet, his second yacht was a longer, sea-going ship with accommodations for six passengers and a crew of seven, with larger staterooms and more deck space. The crew was American save for a Hungarian cook and a Bahamian seaman particularly skilled at finding promising locations for deep-sea fishing.

Having become well established on the concert stage, at major opera houses, on radio, and as a recording artist under contract with RCA after 1931, Thomas as late as 1934 still faced one great — winning a place in the nation's premier opera company, the Metropolitan Opera of New York.

4

Astride the Divide: Classical and Popular Artist

When John Charles Thomas set out in 1922 to move from the Broadway stage to the world of concert artist and Grand Opera, he was setting himself a formidable challenge. Just how formidable is shown by the fact that no Broadway performer has made the same transition since. Try to imagine Robert Goulet or Brian Stokes Mitchell establishing a second career as an opera singer. Difficult as it would be today, it was much harder in the 1920s when there was a strong bias against American artists at the Metropolitan.

In 1922, the only American who was a regular member of the company without European training and experience was Rosa Ponselle (1897–1981). While she is now regarded as having one of the finest voices of her century, she had only been considered at the Metropolitan in 1918 because the threat of submarine attacks on passenger ships prevented European singers from crossing the Atlantic during the First World War — and because Enrico Caruso pushed her cause. The manager of the Metropolitan Opera, Guilio Gatti-Cassaza, told them both that if she failed, the door would be closed to American singers for many years. The next American to join the company was the baritone Lawrence Tibbett, who had the good fortune to step into a major role as understudy when another baritone became indisposed. Without that famous break, no one knows how long he would have been kept in supporting roles at $100 per week.

Gatti's bias against Americans was almost malicious. In 1926 he hired Marion Talley, a nineteen year old from Kansas City. She had starred in a local production of *Mignon* at age 15, and her hometown raised money for her to study in Italy and then live in New York, in hopes of launching a career at the Metropolitan. Gatti praised her almost excessively, and she performed more than fifty times at the Met. Talley had a warm, lovely

75

voice, as her recordings attest, but two marriages and a failed venture in Hollywood dulled the brightness of the voice and her career. She retired from singing at age thirty. Talley's fate confirmed all Gatti's misgivings about American singers, and he lost no opportunity to point out that Americans simply did not have the stamina required of great operatic voices.

Another factor that deterred American singers from consideration by the Metropolitan was that they did not fit the image of an opera singer in the 1920s. That image was one of formidable aloofness. Their haughty faces stared out from the pages of musical trade journals in sober formality, like real-life versions of the characters Margaret Dumont played in Marx Brothers comedies. Within a decade, the aura of grandeur and exclusion surrounding opera and classical music would change, both on concert stages and in the pages of the trade journals. A whole generation of American singers, including Tibbett, Richard Crooks, Nelson Eddy, and, not least, John Charles Thomas, would be responsible for that shift. Thomas, in particular, would introduce light-hearted pieces at the end of his concerts, intended to allow audiences to relax and enjoy the charm of simpler music than the serious fare of opera, lieder, and art songs that comprised the first part of his concerts. By the late 1930s, the Metropolitan would have in its roster not only Ponselle, Tibbett, Crooks and Thomas, but Richard Bonelli, Leonard Warren, Helen Jepson, and Helen Traubel. Yet the process of transformation, and the artistic price, would leave its mark on both Thomas and American popular and classical music.

The absence of American artists on the Metropolitan's roster was a sore point in the early thirties. In May 1932, Clarence Whitehill, a French-trained American baritone and twenty-two-year veteran with the company, publicly resigned in protest over Gatti's anti–Americanism, citing the company's persistent pattern of hiring Italian artists at the highest salaries and offering them the choicest roles. He specifically mentioned the Met's failure to engage John Charles Thomas among his reasons for resigning. Gatti expressed his regret at Whitehill's remarks, suggesting that they might have been prompted by the company's inability to continue his contract as a regular member in the coming season. Gatti also pointed to the fact that in the 1933 season, the Metropolitan would offer the fourteenth production of an American opera during his tenure.

A number of American singers, such as Gladys Swarthout and Frederick Jagel, came forward to defend Gatti by pointing to American singers such as Ponselle, Tibbett, Grace Moore, Alma Gluck, Anna Case, Mario Chamlee, Marion Telva, and Paul Althouse who were or had been members of the company. Anyone knowledgeable about the world of opera would recognize at once that only Ponselle and Tibbett were true stars from this list. Alma Gluck had sung only three seasons at the Met, between 1909 and 1912. Grace Moore is a difficult case. In her day, she was certainly considered a star, having debuted at the Metropolitan in 1928 and made some early sound films in Hollywood. New York critics never found her voice strong or sure enough for opera, and she took very few roles at the Metropolitan, returning to lucrative operettas like *The Dubarry* on Broadway, and going back to Hollywood in 1934 and 1935 for her most successful films. Her operatic reputation has not endured. Curiously, Richard Crooks, who had made his Metropolitan debut in February, 1933, was not listed among Gatti's American recruits, and does not seem to have entered the growing controversy.

When Gatti announced his own resignation as manager of the Metropolitan in the fall of 1934, Herbert Witherspoon, a basso then teaching at New York's Juilliard School and serving as Director of the Chicago Opera Company, was named as his successor. Thomas had enjoyed great success in Chicago, and had a good relationship with Witherspoon. The two had plans for a much larger role for Thomas in the Metropolitan's repertoire. A friend recalled the dejection, so rare in Thomas, when he took a phone call reporting Witherspoon's sudden death from a heart attack soon after being named as Gatti's replacement. Edward Johnson was quickly appointed the new General Manager and held the post until 1950. Thomas was never offered the roles he had hoped to sing under Witherspoon.

As steep a cliff as Thomas was scaling to enter the realm of opera, he had significant advantages that would ease his way. First, there was his voice, which by 1934 had become a remarkable instrument; then his name and personality, which had become well known throughout the country. He also had money. One of the most important decisions Thomas made after his return from Europe was to liquidate his investments in the stock market. Over a period of months in 1928–29, Thomas, on the advice of his manager, Marcks Levine, converted the balance of his substantial holdings to cash, which he spread out in deposits among a number of large banks around the country. After the Depression hit, he kept his funds in cash, as well as real estate, such as the home he purchased for his mother in Palm Beach. He held onto his IBM and RCA shares, which remained sound investments. While the Crash and subsequent Depression would have many consequences for Thomas's career, financial ruin was not one of them.

Money allowed Thomas to live comfortably and continue to build his concert career while practically volunteering his time to the Metropolitan.[1] This marked an important difference between Thomas and his operatic colleagues. Some, like Lawrence Tibbett and Richard Crooks, had substantial concert and recording engagements. Most of the stars did some concert and radio work, and certainly could have done more had it suited their personalities. But their careers and reputations were all tied to the Metropolitan in a way that Thomas's was not. Indeed, few opera stars since have enjoyed quite the same independent stature that Thomas had. This fact allowed him to keep the opera in a certain perspective. He respected the Metropolitan as the nation's premier opera house, and wanted to succeed in both the popular and operatic realms. But he also knew that the great majority of his audience were not interested in opera, and built his career on pleasing them.

Thomas had one other advantage over his colleagues at the Met. As remarkable as it may seem today, in return for its agreement to broadcast the Metropolitan matinees on Saturday afternoon during a time when the opera was without a sponsor, NBC was given a franchise on all radio appearances by Metropolitan artists. That clause was omitted from Thomas's contract since his pre-existing radio contracts were already well established, and, as it happened, many of these were on NBC. Nevertheless, he remained a free agent while artists like Lawrence Tibbett and Rosa Ponselle chafed under their obligation to the network.[2]

By 1930, Thomas was under contract with three major opera companies in the United States— Philadelphia, Chicago, and San Francisco. His roles in the early seasons were primarily *Pagliacci*, *The Masked Ball*, and *Faust*. Always the showman, Thomas would do cartwheels onto the stage for his *Pagliacci* entrance. In Chicago, he took a high G and A♭ in the "Prologue," but refused to take a solo curtain call despite a storm of applause from the audience. A recording of Thomas singing the "Prologue" in a live performance attributed to Philadelphia has much more vitality than his youthful 1922 Vocalion recording. Despite poor sound quality, it leaves no question as to why audiences demanded more. If there was a secret to Thomas's performance style, it was his ability to find the decisive moment in a song or aria when he could take hold of the lyrical line and move it to a swelling climax while maintaining bel canto vocal breath control.

Thomas sang two roles in German, *Tannhäuser*, whose "Evening Star" aria was always a standard in his concert repertoire, and, more surprisingly, Jokanen in Richard Strauss's *Salomé* in September, 1930, in San Francisco, as well as Los Angeles the following month. When he sang the role with Maria Jeritza, he created a sensation by peering out of the well between the legs of his temptress.

Thomas performed small roles like Valentin in Gounod's *Faust*, and debuted as Scarpia in *Tosca* in Philadelphia in January, 1932. Although no

This sketch of Thomas and Hollister illustrates their image at the peak of their careers: not as performers of hearty novelty songs, but serious classical artists offering programs with something to please everyone. (Courtesy of the Archives of the Peabody Institute of The Johns Hopkins University)

recording seems to have survived, a Thomas Scarpia, along with his Athanael in *Thais*, would certainly be near the top of recordings one would like to hear.

Thomas first performed *Thais* in the United States during that same 1932 season in Philadelphia, with superb collaboration from the beautiful Helen Jepson, whom Mary Garden had coached in the role. She and Thomas would later repeat the opera at the Metropolitan, where, to Jepson's deep disappointment, manager Edward Johnson required her to "cover up" her revealing costume just prior to the performance, thus undermining much of the opera's dramatic effect. Thomas also sang Athanael with Marjorie Lawrence, who, while primarily known as a Wagnerian at the Metropolitan, had trained in France, and had all the lyrical qualities required for the role, with a slightly weightier voice than Jepson's.

Throughout his career, Thomas had a number of opportunities to sing new works. At La Monnaie, he had performed the role of Orphée with great success in the world premiere of Darius Milhaud's modern, harmonic opera, *Les Malheurs d'Orphee*. On December 30, 1924, he made his Carnegie Hall debut as Duda the Jester in Rimsky-Korsakov's *Sadko* under the baton of Kurt Schindler, with Marguerite D'Alvarez and his friend, tenor Mario Chamlee, as principals.

On May 20, 1933, Thomas created the role of Wrestling Bradford in the world premiere concert version of Howard Hanson's opera *Merry Mount* at Ann Arbor, with Rose Bampton and Frederick Jagel, along with the soon to be famous Nelson Eddy in a small role. The opera was set in Puritan New England, and Thomas even took wrestling lessons from a professional wrestler to prepare for the role. Hanson was for many years a prominent composer at the Eastman School in Rochester, New York, and one wonders if Adelin Fermin, who moved to Rochester from the Peabody, might not have been instrumental in getting Thomas the role. Lawrence Tibbett was chosen to perform the role at its Metropolitan premier the following February, within a week of Thomas's Metropolitan debut. On November 23, 1935, Thomas performed the title role in *Gale*, in Chicago. The composer, Ethel Lezinska, the conductor of the Women's Symphony in Chicago, put up $4,000 to finance the production, including a thousand dollars for Thomas's fee. No sets were ever constructed, however, and the performance was little more than a public rehearsal, at which Thomas reportedly sang no more than half the words in his role.[3]

His behavior was deplorable. That it was rare in Thomas's case cannot excuse it. Yet it does show two important traits in his character. First, he was not without a strong streak of professional laziness, which only grew during his career. Then, too, he had learned very early to appraise the commercial and artistic merits of a production. In this case, one suspects that he was simply not going to burden himself by learning a role and an opera that would never be heard again.

On most occasions, however, he prepared very seriously for a new role, learning bull-fighting techniques, for example, when he hoped to be offered the role of Escamillo in *Carmen* at the Metropolitan. His approach to the toreador was different from the conventional pose of indifference to Carmen's attentions. Thomas's Escamilo wooed Carmen, singing his lines with a soft, seductive air. At the Met, this role went to Ezio Pinza.

As Scarpia in *Tosca*. (Courtesy of the Archives of the Peabody Institute of The Johns Hopkins University)

Thomas seems to have performed the role only once, on November 29, 1941, in Chicago. It must have been a remarkable performance, with Bruna Castagna as Carmen, Eva Turner as Michaela, and Jan Kiepura as Don José.

Curiously enough, although Figaro in *The Barber of Seville* would become one of his signature roles at the Metropolitan from 1938 on, Thomas never performed that role during his early years on the American opera stage. Even the elder Germont in *Traviata*, one of his most popular roles at the Met, was performed only three times in San Francisco and Los Angeles in 1930, and once the following year in Portland with the touring Chicago Civic Opera, with Claudia Muzio and Tito Schipa, before his debut in the role at the Metropolitan in 1934. The reviews in Portland suggest that he stole the show, first with a fine duet with Muzio, "Dite al giovine," then receiving a thunderous ovation with his rendition of "Di Provenza al mar." The performance in San Francisco with Clara Clairbert and Gigli in September 1930 did not go so well. Thomas was left floundering when he stepped on stage to hear Violetta singing in French. Their duet became one of those experiences that conductors and performers dread, with the soprano singing to an intermittently mute partner and an anxious orchestra. Thomas was unable to recover until the *Di Provenza* aria later in the scene. Clearly, this was one of those performances where a shortage of funds had prevented orchestral rehearsals. Thomas was probably caught between trying to improvise French lyrics for a role he had not sung in Brussels, and making the Italian phrasing blend with the soprano's French. When the episode was recalled in later years, he expressed no irritation. Although he could have a hot temper, on some occasions he simply shrugged off a misadventure. This was his attitude toward conductors who let their orchestras drown his voice. If the orchestra overwhelmed him, he let it go. He would not strain his voice to make himself heard above them. Yet surviving recordings of live performances show no indication that this was a problem. From a live recording of the trio from *Faust*, with Frederick Jagel and Ezio Pinza, it is clear that Thomas had no difficulty holding his own with voices as large as any in opera.

It is now common to recall the Depression with a kind of nostalgia for the art produced under the WPA, everything from the murals of Thomas Hart Benson to Orson Welles' productions of Shakespeare in Harlem. For anyone trying to make a living in the arts, however, they were very bleak times indeed. The Depression had a profound and overwhelmingly negative impact on the entertainment world, as it did on every other aspect of American economic life. True, classical music was heavily patronized by the wealthy, but year by year, fewer Americans felt wealthy after 1929, and classical music was one expense that many were willing to reduce. In 1932, the Philadelphia Opera announced the suspension of its season due to economic conditions.

The Metropolitan saw the departure of a number of its stars in 1930, some, like Amelita Galli-Curci, Margarethe Matzenauer, and Frances Alda, were ready to retire in the normal course of their careers. Others, like Beniamino Gigli, refused to take a pay cut and sailed home to Italy when the Met imposed a $1,000 cap per performance on their stars. Rosa Ponselle, probably the greatest singer in the Italian wing, not only took the pay cut, but saw her appearances cut to just eight weeks in the 1934-35 season. In 1936, she sang two Santuzzas in *Cavaleria Rusticana* at $500 each, and made only five other appearances at $1,000 each. The following year she retired from the Metropolitan. While the pay scale has never been offered as a reason for her early departure, it could hardly have been an inducement to stay. Ponselle's standard fee for concerts was $3,000. Flagstad, who also earned $1000 per performance at the Met, received an extraordinary $7600 at one concert in Los Angeles in 1939.

Perhaps even more threatening to the Metropolitan than the loss of major singers was the rumor in 1933 that A.C. Blumenthal, who had succeeded Florence Ziegfeld as producer of *Show Boat*, planned to open a new opera company under the management of Paul Longone, with Thomas, Maria Jeritza, Claudio Muzio, Dusolina Gianini, Pasquale Amato, Gigli, Chaliapin and Tita Ruffo in its company. Thomas and Jeritza were reported to be signed to appear in *Tosca*.

To launch a major opera company in the depths of the Depression might seem either a reckless venture or an empty threat, but the idea must have shaken the Board of the Metropolitan. Depression or no, entertainment was still making money in both New York and Hollywood. There would be no trouble finding musicians or a hall in which to stage performances. Shuttling stagehands and lighting technicians between Broadway shows and the new opera house would have been very cost efficient. Managers with Broadway experience would have offered flashier productions than the old lady of 39th street could mount. At the very least, a competitor might divide the market of operagoers when every ticket sale was vital to the Met's survival. Longone went on to manage the Chicago Civic Opera, but the mere threat of such a rival might have been sufficient to induce the Met to sign Thomas to a contract for the 1933-34 season. On February 3, 1934, he made his debut as the elder Germont in *La Traviata*. His dressing room was papered with congratulatory telegrams, which were preserved and are filed today in his Papers.

Thomas's debut was something of a sensation. The performance itself, a benefit for the Vassar scholarship fund, offered the best casting the Met could furnish, with Rosa Ponselle as Violetta and Tito Schipa as young Alfredo.[4] But Thomas seems to have been the singer the audience came to hear. Don Gilbert, later the Western regional manager for NBC, was present and recalled the performance:

> Dorothy's ... tension disappeared the moment John Charles made his entrance. The audience released it all in a spontaneous hullabaloo of cheering and applause. Then came the voice — instantly triumphant and it remained so throughout the entire performance. During the curtain calls following Act II, Rosa Ponselle stepped out of the spotlight so that Thomas could have the full benefit of the furor he had created. He gently kissed her hand; bowed again and again. Then, as the cheering continued, he strode downstage with what appeared to be the obvious intention of making a speech! The applause diminished as the audience anticipated the demolition of a Met tradition. Instead, John Charles bowed, walked upstage, turned and bowed again in silence, then made his exit. The applause was deafening.[5]

By the time Thomas was singing at the Met during the long dreary days of the Depression, conditions were fairly shabby. Even during the Golden Age of the Metropolitan in the teens and twenties the operatic

gold was entirely vocal. Acting and production values were often low. The
lighting, scrims and stage designs that can add so much visual drama to
Grand Opera today were undreamt of in the twenties and thirties. Singers
commonly wore leggings rather than bare a leg on stage. Scenery might
consist of a dropcloth, and the waves of the Rhine river were fixed or mov-
able plywood forms.[6] There was no money for more than one rehearsal with
the orchestra and some quick cues about where the spotlights would fall
for the principals. Thomas complained that the dressing rooms were filthy,
the stage mechanisms were antiquated, and unpleasant odors permeated
every space behind the curtain. Costumes were the responsibility of the
principals, and used for all productions in every city. The idea of a consistent costume design for a production was unknown. New productions
were extremely rare. Year after year, the same war-horses would be trot-
ted out, the same performers, the same productions of familiar *Pagliaccis,
Traviatas, Aidas, Rigolettos* and *Trovatores*. Scenery for an opera scheduled to be repeated within a week was stored in the alley, exposed to the
elements, because there was no storage space within the building.

Ten years later, after Thomas had left the Metropolitan, Virgil Thomson would describe the peculiarities of the nation's premier opera company succinctly in a *New York Herald Tribune* column entitled "What's
Wrong with the Met":

> The conducting staff is first class. The singing company is an excellent troupe....
> The orchestra is second-class but fair. The chorus is a disgrace. It sings in no
> recognizable language and habitually off pitch. That is when it sings at all; one
> third of it comes in at about the fourth measure usually. The stage direction is
> timid, and for new productions, pretty sketchy. There is a vast store of none
> too fresh costumes and of water-soaked scenery. Lighting is effected by equip-
> ment of antediluvian model and largely without rehearsal. All this is obvious
> to anybody who goes there often. And yet, in spite of it all, some beautiful per-
> formances turn up. There is no reason to suppose that the beautiful perform-
> ances are planned any more than there is to think the less fortunate ones are.
> An accident of balanced casting ... will do wonders.... [But] even the best bal-
> anced cast rarely stays together for more than one or two performances. [7]

In his first season, Thomas made only three appearances, twice in *Traviata,* and once in *Pagliacci.* He did not appear on the Metropolitan boards at
all in the 1935-36 season, and just half a dozen times each in the following
two seasons. His most active season was that of 1938-1939, when he performed a total of 17 times. On February 10 and 11, 1939, he appeared on successive evenings in *The Barber of Seville* and *Thais.* He would repeat that feat
on February 20 and 21, 1942, in performances of *Pagliacci* and *Aida,* though
both of these are smaller roles than Figaro or Athanael. He made only two
appearances with the company in the 1938-39 and 1939-40 seasons.[8]

It would be hard to see how Thomas could have been satisfied with his casting at the Met. While there were wonderful productions like *Thais* and *Traviata*, with Ponselle, Sayao, Schipa, and Crooks, *Barber* with Pons, and a *Faust* with Albanese and Pinza, many of the performances were with second tier performers, like a *Pagliacci* with the American tenor Arthur Carron, or out of town performances in Brooklyn, Newark, or on tour in Philadelphia, Baltimore, or Dallas. The Depression may again be at fault, with the Metropolitan trying to stretch its budget and employ as many of its company as it could, but it was simply not a fulfilling artistic relationship for a singer of Thomas's mettle.

Thomas c. 1935. (Courtesy of the Archives of the Peabody Institute of The Johns Hopkins University)

Notwithstanding the down-at-heel aspects of the old house, vocally, this was one of the great ages of American opera. With the presence of Melchior and Flagstad, Lotte Lehmann, Friedrich Schorr, and later Helen Traubel, the German wing of the Metropolitan was arguably at its best in the '30s. The Italian wing was strong, but aging. Giovanni Martinelli, who celebrated his 20th year with the company in 1933, would be around to mark his 30th anniversary at the Metropolitan a decade later. Some seasons brought exciting new productions of American operas, such as *The King's Henchman* by Deems Taylor, *Merry Mount* by Howard Hanson, *The Emperor Jones*, or *Peter Ibbetson*, all produced as vehicles for Lawrence Tibbett. In 1932, a *Boccanegra* was mounted for Tibbett, Jepson, Martinelli, and a young Leonard Warren. In 1938 and the following year, for a glimpse of what opera might be, the Met offered *Otello*, again with Martinelli, Tibbett and Jepson. These highlights aside, there were areas of astonishing neglect for a great opera house. The French wing, despite the embarrassment of riches represented by Georges Thill, Thomas, Richard Crooks, Helen

Jepson, Bidu Sayao, and Lilly Pons, even Jussi Bjoerling briefly, was all but moribund. The rare fresh productions were likely to be something brought out for Pons, like the much-reduced *Daughter of the Regiment* in 1940. Mozart rarely appeared on the boards, and when it did, it was chiefly as a vehicle for Ezio Pinza. The prevailing taste of the era ran to Wagner, a very ponderous, stultifying Wagner, and this profoundly limited the opportunity for productions of Bel Canto operas for which Thomas's voice would have been best suited.

    The two operas that became signature roles for Thomas at the Metropolitan were *La Traviata* and the *Barber of Seville.* Thomas's rendition of "Largo al factotum" as Figaro's opening aria in the *Barber* was invariably a hit, sung with all the gusto demonstrated on his recording, whistle included. The role of Figaro suited Thomas's comedic talents perfectly. We usually think of *Traviata* as a vehicle for a soprano and tenor, yet it offers two fine opportunities for a bel canto baritone to show his mettle, as well as one of Verdi's finest ensemble scenes in the gaming room. The role of the elder Germont in *Traviata*, the stiff parent appealing to the courtesan to loose her grip on his wayward son, also suited Thomas's limited acting skills. He had fun with the part by dressing himself to look like Uncle Sam.

Figaro in *The Barber of Seville*, one of Thomas's most successful roles. (Courtesy of the Archives of the Peabody Institute of The Johns Hopkins University)

    Paul Jackson has described Thomas's singing in both roles. Of the December 11, 1937, *Traviata*, he writes:

Traviata may be one of the ultimate star vehicles for sopranos, but the star of this performance is undoubtedly

John Charles Thomas' sonorous Germont.... Thomas ... offers a generalized, dignified presence whose conversational manner gives the scene a welcome spontaneity. "Bela voi siete," he cries with surprise, as though he has only just recognized Violetta's beauty. By the time he reaches the duet proper he has grown impatient with [the conductor's] lethargy.... By the end of the scene, Thomas is conducting with the voice, and Panizza and Bovy are forced to tag along with his ground swell of tone as he sprints through to the end. "Di Provenza" is the vocal highlight of the afternoon.... [T]he breadth of line and resplendent top voice are nigh irresistible; as if to prove he can be subtle if he chooses, he trots out a delicious diminuendo on the final tonic of the aria.... For him, singing is as easy as falling off a log.

He finds more room for criticism in Thomas's Figaro from January 22, 1938, and April 10, 1943, respectively:

Thomas tosses off ["Largo al factotum"] as casually as though he were licking a lollipop. Less praiseworthy are his badly smudged fioriture in the "Dunque io son'" duet — eventually he just gives up on most of them and, since he got away with it, repeats the offense in the opera's concluding "Di si felice inesto."

John Charles Thomas doesn't even bother with [Rossini's turns].... He, too,

As Giorgio Germont in *Traviata*, the role of his Metropolitan Opera debut in February, 1934. This photo is probably with Helen Jepson as Violetta. Note his resemblance to Uncle Sam in costume. (Courtesy of the Archives of the Peabody Institute of The Johns Hopkins University)

is somewhat out of vocal form, for he avoids some of the expected high-note interpolations and muffs the final high G of the aria. His playing to the audience turns the clown into a buffoon (the gasp for breath in the middle of his spelling out of R-O-S-I--N-A as Tuminia holds the long note, is just one of his repellent tricks). In spite of it all, he is still a vocal spendthrift, full of spirit, sometimes vocally nimble, and when Figaro gives his address to Almaviva, able to dominate the Rossini orchestral crescendo.[9]

But concerts, radio programs, and recording royalties paid the bills, not opera. Thomas's special appearances were attended by enormous audiences, 20,000 at the opening of a three-day music festival at Madison Square Garden in September, 1933; 30,000 at the Hollywood Bowl; 100,000 at Soldier Field in Chicago in August, 1934; and 165,000 at Chicago's Grant Park in 1938.

He also found time to perform in operetta, which he always enjoyed. In 1938, Armitage signed Thomas to a two week run in *Blossom Time* for mid–June at the Curran Theater in San Francisco. This was to be the beginning of the Los Angeles Light Opera Company, with which Thomas would remain associated for two decades. The production came about through the efforts of producer Edwin Lester, who had been offering revivals of aging operettas like *Desert Song, The Red Mill,* and *Rose Marie* in Los Angeles since 1935. Unlike New York, where the musical was evolving toward more contemporary compositions, Los Angeles preferred "light opera in the grand opera manner." But it also wanted to see stars, not second rate vaudevillians.

Lester had first seen and admired Thomas on Broadway in 1916. When he approached Merle Armitage with the *Blossom Time* offer, he was told that Thomas would agree, but only if it were a two week engagement at $7500 per week. However, he was willing to sing as many performances as the producer liked at that fee. It turned out to be the perfect arrangement for Lester. He persuaded his friend Homer Curran to take the show at his theater in San Francisco after the opening week at the Philharmonic Hall in Los Angeles, and thus was born a great tradition of light opera on the West Coast. After sixteen years away from operetta, Thomas found great satisfaction now, and for the rest of his career, in taking an occasional role in musical theater.

He was scheduled for eight performances per week, with matinees on Wednesday and Saturday. Armitage did not immediately publicize Thomas as the star. Instead, he let the press report that the Operetta would headline a major star, and offered advance sales of tickets for this mystery performer at a discount. The best seats thus went to the adventurous few, but initial sales were less than $10,000. Within the first week after the announcement that Thomas would sing the lead, ticket revenues were $15,000, and the final sales amounted to $50,000. The story perfectly illustrates both Thomas's business acumen and the sense of fun with which he and his associates approached their work. The following year, Thomas returned for an appearance in the *Gypsy Baron*, which received even more enthusiastic reviews not only for his singing, but for his cartwheels and whip snapping skills.

Concert tours were a well-established form of entertainment in the thirties and forties that has largely disappeared today. To be sure, major artists still perform concerts around the country, and around the world. But there is nothing like the extent of classical musical programming today that existed at the height of Thomas's career. Year after year, Thomas, like other artists of the period, would schedule concerts in the major metropolitan centers—perhaps five or more in New York or Los Angeles. In these major urban centers, concerts were largely in the hands of impresarios such as Sol Hurok in the East, and L.E. "Bee" Behrmann on the West Coast. In smaller cities, concerts were usually sponsored by community music guilds who used big name performers to draw in a large audience in hopes of getting some to return for subsequent concerts by lesser known artists. An artist like Thomas, who could demand fees of $2500–$3000 per appearance, plus a percentage of the house, would agree to appear in a smaller town for $1,000 or $1500 if it was conveniently located en route to his next engagement in a major city.[10]

Thomas performed as many as 90 concerts in a season. In 1931, he had no less than 97 concert engagements in 76 cities in 27 states, including appearances with the Chicago and Philadelphia operas, and the St. Louis and Los Angeles Symphonies. It is hard to imagine the demands of such a schedule. Only an artist with robust health, which Thomas had, and an even temper, which he did not, could attempt such a schedule year after year. To be sure, Thomas and Carroll Hollister had first class tickets and stayed in the finest hotels. They were entertained by the gentry in the hinterlands and the leading members of sophisticated society on the metropolitan stops on the tour. Even so, the regimen of a concert tour, with as many as three or four performances a week, was as grueling as it was unrelenting.[11]

The simplest details, such as laundry and meals, required careful attention if complications were to be avoided. Every evening the accompanist faced a new instrument in a new hall. The singer must take care to keep his voice rested and untroubled by colds. Thomas preferred at least two days rest between concerts, and instructed his management to avoid scheduling successive performances. The morning after the concert, he

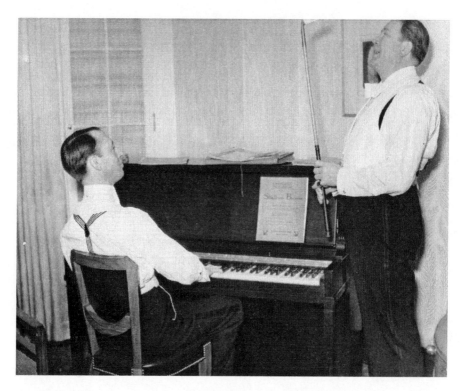

With longtime accompanist Carroll Hollister before a concert. (Courtesy of the Archives of the Peabody Institute of The Johns Hopkins University)

packed, made his farewells to collected dignitaries, and was off to the train or airport for the next engagement. With all this, in a concert career that lasted over thirty years, Thomas claimed that he only canceled one performance.[12]

Even with the most solicitous managers, problems were bound to arise. At a concert in San Francisco one evening, Thomas exploded when he discovered a printer's error in the Program. Merle Armitage tried to reason with him that nothing could be done at this point, but Thomas's anger was so great that his shouting backstage could be heard by the audience. When he finally went on stage, he had to compose himself for a time before he could begin his performance. After the concert, his good temper was restored, and he sent a note of apology to Armitage, regretting that his manager had not joined him for their customary post-concert steak dinner.

Of all the fine singers of his or any generation, Thomas was one of the few who made the concert stage the principal focus of his career. It not only required hard work, willingness to travel, to cheerfully meet with the leading members of whatever group had sponsored the concert series in a given city or town after the program, and complete freedom from stage fright, but a love of and need for the applause of a live audience. This is what Thomas liked best about the concert season: stepping out upon a new stage, or before a familiar big city audience, and offering them a new program that they would enjoy and respond to with enthusiastic ovations.

Most of these concerts were highly enjoyable for artist and audience. Thomas was involved in one particularly unpleasant episode, however, that made headlines around the country in January, 1934, just prior to his Metropolitan debut. He had been booked for a concert in Dallas just after New Year's. Shortly before his scheduled appearance, the concert organizer informed him that, unfortunately, they had not sold sufficient tickets to meet his fee, and asked him to go on for less. Thomas refused.

With the exception of the Dallas press, news reports did not criticize Thomas, but the story did leave the impression that Thomas was more concerned about money than the disappointment of his audience. It was certainly not auspicious publicity on the eve of his Metropolitan debut. What the press did not report was that this was the third time the concert organizer had pulled this surprise on her artists. Thomas's view was that it had to stop, and he would take whatever criticism came. It is a classic vignette of the man and the times.

A typical Thomas concert schedule during these years illustrates just how hectic life could be during his six months on the road. The 1939-1940 season began with a concert in San Francisco on September 30, an appearance in Detroit for the Ford radio program followed on October 8, Dallas on October 10, Fort Worth October 12, Washington, D.C. October 15, Savannah and Atlanta October 17 and 19, New York October 22. It continued at this pace around the country by train and plane until June 2 and 4, 1940, with two concerts in San Francisco.

Most concert singers would prepare one program each season, which they carried from town to town across the country. Thomas's repertoire was remarkable, literally hundreds of arias, art songs, hymns, and popular tunes. He would prepare at least four basic programs in a season, each of which could be expanded or altered with substitutions, with sufficient notice given to the printers. What distinguished the Thomas concert from those of contemporaries was the deliberate inclusion of works by American composers, and the lighter "character" songs that were his signature pieces and which every audience looked forward to hearing in the final section of the program. The inclusion of American compositions—by contemporary composers—was a deliberate decision of Thomas fairly early in his concert career, but one that was never accepted by critics used to the more conventional repertoire of opera arias and art songs.

His concert repertoire evolved over the years, and it is interesting to compare programs from the twenties to those of the late thirties. Rather surprisingly, Thomas offered considerably more lieder in the early years, and in general performed fairly traditional fare. His humorous "character" pieces were a staple of his earlier concerts, but they got better over the years, and perhaps there were more of them.

Thomas always tried to put his audiences at ease. In part, he achieved this simply by showing them that he was at ease himself, and by saying a few words—often more than a few—as an introduction to his pieces. If he forgot the words—a rare occasion, but it happened when he introduced "Nocturne," the first song ever composed especially for him by Pearl Curran, at a Town Hall concert in New York in 1923—he acknowledged his mistake and began again. Just as rarely, he might miss a high note. When

John Charles Thomas regularly performed to overflow audiences at his concerts. This appearance was in Calgary, Alberta, Canada. (Courtesy of the Archives of the Peabody Institute of The Johns Hopkins University)

this happened at one New York concert, he said, "Now wait a moment, folks, I know I can get that," and did on his second try.

At other times it was not Thomas who made the mistake. At a concert in Canada, where programs traditionally began with "God Save the King," particularly in wartime, Carroll Hollister's fingers wandered into the Episcopal doxology "Praise God from Whom all Blessings Flow." He began again, and fell into the same error. Thomas saved the situation by explaining to the audience that he and Hollister were both preachers' sons, and old habits died hard. Then there was the concert on a warm evening in Baltimore when Thomas returned to the stage after the intermission without his hairpiece. Few gestures could be better calculated to make an audience feel at ease — but it was not a calculated gesture, it was simply Thomas following his motto, "Let's be ourselves."

One other feature of Thomas's concert presentation should be mentioned. He and Carroll Hollister both performed, as photographs attest, entirely from memory. There was never sheet music, which some singers rather ostentatiously use today, nor even the ubiquitous small book of lyrics that most performers clutch in their hands in the event of a memory lapse.

A Thomas concert program would usually begin with an Italian art song that served to limber up the voice. "Tu lo sai" was a very frequent opening number. This would be followed by a series of opera arias and art songs, culminating in a dramatic number to finish the first part of the concert, such as "Per me giunto" or an aria from *Thais*. But there were variations on this. In Ottumwa, Iowa, in 1938, Thomas offered a series of lieder. In another concert, he offered several songs in Yiddish. Between songs, he would talk informally to the audience about the music, or perhaps read a poem, always with the purpose of making the audience feel comfortable.

While Thomas took a break after his first cycle of songs, Carroll Hollister would perform two or three piano selections. Thomas would return with a short series of art songs, then leave the stage for intermission. After intermission, Thomas returned with American and English songs. Thomas enjoyed having a little play on his names in his programs, so it was common to hear a piece by Ambroise Thomas in the first half, or American composer Ernest Charles in the second half. He often included Negro spirituals, being particularly fond of the arrangements of Henry Burleigh. Women composers, such as Carrie Jacob Bond, Louise Reichardt, a young blind girl, Beatrice Fenner, or Clara Edwards, were also well represented. Selections from operetta or musical shows figured often enough on his radio programs, but were never heard as part of a Thomas concert program. Finally, he would leave the audience with a humorous favorite, such as "The Stuttering Lovers," "The Old Skinflint," or crypto-spirituals such as "The Land o' Degradashun" or "David and Goliath," before being recalled for encores.[13]

A concert program from an April 14, 1936, concert at the State Teachers College in West Chester, Pennsylvania, survives with notations by an audience member. It shows notations for numbers Thomas and Hollister both added to the printed program. Thomas added "Mattinata" by Cavollo to his first segment, and three encores, "O Dry Those Tears" by Del Riego, "Sailormen" by Jacques Wolf, and "Home on the Range." Hollister added Debussy's "Clair de Lune" to his segment.

Critics were generous in praising the beauty of Thomas's tone, his diction, his peerless mastery of the French style, and his effective communication of the music. Virgil Thomson reviewed Thomas's Carnegie Hall concert of November 26, 1940, when the singer was at the height of his powers, and wrote in the *Herald Tribune* the next morning:

> John Charles Thomas pleases all. Not necessarily everybody all the time. But at some point or other in each program, everybody. Last night he gave us old Italian songs of finest vintage, poured to perfection. He gave us works from French and German masters who bridged the nineteenth and twentieth centuries. There was a famous operatic aria, "Eri tu," from Verdi's *Ballo in Maschera*. There was a group of highly dramatized American folk songs that included even a Negro spiritual. All were executed with consummate art, and all were enthusiastically received by some part of the large audience. Most were applauded heartily by the whole house.
>
> Mr. Thomas has a different style of delivery for each kind of thing he does, and each style is appropriate to its kind. What permeates all the styles is his remarkable and instinctive musicality....
>
> I call his musicality instinctive, because only those with melody in the soul ever sing so easily or pronounce so clearly. He does not pronounce the words to a vocal line; he makes a vocal line out of the words sung. Naturally they come out clear in any language. And naturally the music comes out as melody.
>
> ... If Mr. Thomas were not such a fine musician, it would be difficult to forgive him for making every number a wow. If he were not such a natural musician, his lighter numbers would be ham. Gifted so rarely and schooled so soundly, everything he touches becomes, in a different way and for a different public, beauty.[14]

Yet there was often an undercurrent of discontent in other reviews. One critic suggested that the baritone's tempos were more his own than the composers, that he was not quite at home with German lieder, and grumbled that "Vision Fugitive" from *Herodiade* was not particularly good opera, nor even the best Massenet. Most were quick to dismiss the lighter pieces that closed a typical Thomas concert as not worthy of the artist or individuals of better taste in the audience.

In retrospect, one smiles at the fastidiousness of critics in such an age of abundance. Those writers were not only able to hear Thomas in concert, but Pinza, Ponselle, Tibbett, Crooks, Flagstad, and other great singers of the era. They could even tune them in from week to week on regularly scheduled radio programs. More troubling, the critics seemed never to want to hear what Thomas was working so hard to achieve with what seemed like so little effort, an integration of the classical repertoire with the better art songs of contemporary American composers. Listening today, we hear a singer who presents all this material with his own signature vocal style, his mannerisms, accent and enunciation, all of which add to the charm of an artist making the music his own. Listen to Thomas growl out his warning to Aida in the Nile scene, or his guttural Italian before the climax of the "Prologue" from *Pagliacci*, the broadly elaborated vowels of his singing in English, and you ask — who would have him any different?

Thomas paid little heed to his critics, and felt that what hurt him most in their eyes was his decision after a Town Hall concert on March 24, 1940, to devote two thirds of his future concert programs to works in English. The critics were not really hostile to Thomas, how could they be? He sang these lighter contemporary works with such charm and enthusiasm that they were irresistible.[15] They were simply saying that in trying to please a mass audience, to sell as many tickets as possible in the biggest concert halls, Thomas inevitably had to neglect the elements of his repertoire that appealed to a more discriminating audience.

To understand why critics then and now are impatient with Thomas's performances, we must consider some of the elements of classical singing, Thomas's voice in particular, and his recorded repertoire. The most obvious difference between a classically trained voice and popular singers is the fullness of vocal production. Classical singers project a large, full-toned voice, not always a large voice, but a tone that is full, centered and on pitch. Less obvious, the vocal production and tone is uniform and even throughout the scale. This was the point of those painstaking exercises Thomas learned from Adelin Fermin. The best way to illustrate these features in Thomas's voice is to take a simple, well-known song, say "Swing Low Sweet Chariot." Everything about his singing of this traditional spiritual seems easy and straightforward. It is certainly not a difficult piece. Yet the perfect, easy placement of the voice is obvious, as is the steadiness of the line. There is no breaking of phrases to grab a breath. He can modulate the tone to sing the verse more softly, and the same evenness of tone and production is maintained. That is the fundamental characteristic of good classical singing.

As you listen to the range of Thomas's repertoire, from children's songs and simple pieces like "Home on the Range," to his "character" songs, art songs, and opera arias, the same elements are present. The children's songs can be very touching, and the simplicity of a piece like the "Lord's Prayer" is deceptive in that it requires considerable art to *keep* it simple. The effect of such music falls apart when sung too dramatically, as it often is in amateur performances.

There is considerable technique entailed in Thomas's rendition of pieces like "Tally-Ho," where he mimics both galloping huntsmen and a panting fox, "The Green Eyed Dragon," "Blow Me Eyes," or "Long Ago in Alcala," technique that must be self-effacing in order for the songs to retain their charm. The same is true of the finest American popular songs; Jerome Kern's "All the Things You Are," for example, or even "Smoke Gets in Your Eyes," rely on the interpretive art of the performer to bring out the poignancy of the lyrics within the bare simplicity of the musical line. To perform them badly is easy; to make the familiar memorable is art.

Yet for all the art in such songs, repeated listening eventually exposes their cloying sentimentality and artistic bareness. That does not happen, critics would argue, with more sophisticated music. Rather, one grows to appreciate all the more the art and technique, the phrasing, emotional coloring, the vocal agility and sureness required to perform them well. The difficulty, the frustration with Thomas is that he left so little of that level of work to evaluate. Of the eight operatic arias that he recorded commercially, only two, "Salomé c'en est fait" and "Nemico della Patria," fully reveal his voice. The rest, like the four classical art songs he recorded, simply leave us wanting more. That was what the critics were saying. They did not want to settle for a Hershey bar from a singer who could easily offer fine Belgian chocolates.

The classical repertoire provides one measure of a singer's art, but the native idiom provides another. To hear John McCormack sing the text of Yeats' "Cloths of Heaven," or Flagstad, Melchior, and Bjoerling perform Scandinavian material, is to touch some native bedrock where art and nature bond. In his repertoire of American songs, Thomas left a more enduring legacy. His singing reflected a nationalism that may have been more pronounced among American artists of the thirties than earlier decades. You did not have to paint WPA murals or ride the rails with Woody Guthrie to feel this nationalism. Paul Robeson gave expression to it through spirituals or the "Ballad of John Henry," Tibbett in patriotic songs, and Thomas through regional novelty songs such as "Lindy Lou" or cowboy songs or sea shanties or songs in Negro dialect. All were expressions of national pride in an American musical style. Even "Open Road," from the Viennese operetta *Gypsy Baron* by Strauss, was invested with an American spirit when sung by Thomas.

A wonderful example of Thomas's attempt to marry European art and American song occurred in a concert in Baltimore on April 27, 1939. It was the annual concert by the Glee Club of the B&O railroad, beginning, of course, with "I've Been Working on the Railroad." Thomas offered operatic and classical songs in his first section, two German lieder, "Per me giunto" from *Don Carlos*, and three French art songs, then returned at the end of the program with "Sing a Song of Sixpence," the "Toreador Song" sung with the Glee Club, and finished with "The Lost Chord." Very few classical singers would find themselves as much at home in such a concert as Thomas did.

Thomas considered contemporary American composers to be as fine as European composers, and he was willing to be their champion on the concert stage. It was a timely gesture. Both the Depression and the impending world crisis had fostered greater nationalism, and over the next few years, in the early years of the war particularly, there would be a deliberate effort to offer classical music in English. In 1943, Rodgers and Hammerstein's *Oklahoma* became a musical declaration of independence from the mold of middle European operetta that had long been the dominant musical form on Broadway.

Who were the leading American composers between 1934 and 1945? Jerome Kern, George Gershwin, Vincent Youmans, Frank Loesser and Cole Porter may be among the best known today, but there were many women, such as Blanche Seaver, Pearl Curran, and Beatrice Fenner, and a host of writers who are relatively little known today — Sydney King Russell, William Worthington, Campbell-Tipton — but whose art perfectly suited Thomas's style.

Thomas had great success with two or three American songs that will forever be linked with his name. "Home on the Range" was a sixty-year-old saddle song when Thomas transformed it into a national standard.[16] In 1934, Albert Hay Malotte wrote to Thomas offering his setting of "The Lord's Prayer." Thomas and Hollister immediately appreciated its potential, and found an early opportunity to introduce it. At an informal Sunday concert for the Dutch Treat Club, whose members were drawn from the New York theatrical and entertainment world, Thomas was asked for an encore after his recital. When he asked what the audience would like to hear, one man shouted, "I don't care if you want to sing the Lord's Prayer." When Thomas did, there was not a dry eye in the audience. Soon after that, he performed it in a choral setting with the Romanies in Palm Beach. "He's Got the Whole World in His Hands" and "The Green Eyed Dragon" were also introduced by Thomas, and few have ever matched the magic of Thomas's ferocious Dragon.

Ferde Grofé is best remembered today for his Grand Canyon Suite, but he also collaborated with Paul Whiteman on the song "My Wonderful One," which Thomas sang on the radio. (Courtesy of the Archives of the Peabody Institute of The Johns Hopkins University)

But Thomas performed more serious music with American themes as well. When asked to appear at ceremonies celebrating the completion of the Golden Gate Bridge in San Francisco in May, 1937, he sang "The Prayer of Fr. Serra," by Charles Hart, accompanied by chorus and orchestra. A splendid recording survives from a radio broadcast on the RCA Magic Key program the following month. Combining a celebration of historical heritage with optimism about the future, it presents Fr. Serra as a visionary, looking forward to the modern state of California.

> Look Ye I have beheld a vision
> I have seen the parched land become a pool
> And the thirsty land springs of water.
> I have seen the desert blossom like a rose
> And the wilderness bear corn and all the fruits
> And a highway shall be there
> And feet of many nations shall go up and down on it.

The one example in the patriotic genre that served Thomas best was George Kleinsinger's "I Hear America Singing." Kleinsinger had begun developing this piece as a Walt Whitman cantata as early as 1932. It took shape in a CCC camp (Civilian Conservation Corps), where the composer had found refuge from hobo life, and was expanded in 1935 when Kleinsinger directed a performance of some of his material at a politically oriented summer camp. In 1937, the International Ladies Garment Workers Union offered the composer a $100 commission to revise his work for a special performance for Mrs. Eleanor Roosevelt at Madison Square Garden in June, 1940, with Thomas as soloist. NBC broadcast it nationally on the eve of the Democratic Convention that summer, and it soon became a popular concert favorite for orchestras around the country. Thomas was strongly identified with the work for many years, but it served other baritones as well, from William Warfield to Robert Merrill.

"I Hear America Singing" was, and is, a fine example of American composition from the era. Proudly nationalistic and optimistic, drawing on America's literary and political heritage while looking hopefully toward the future, it fully expressed American buoyancy, even after years of Depression, and was thus a perfect vehicle for Thomas's robust singing. He recorded the work in March, 1941, and RCA released it on four sides of two 12-inch disks. Only Thomas's wide popularity could explain RCA taking such a gamble, for even today such musically or poetically literate recordings are rarely produced for marketing to a mass audience.

Still another example of the American music that Thomas performed were a number of songs in Negro dialect. These had long been something of a staple novelty among classical singers. Richard Crooks recorded a series of Stephen Foster songs, for example, among which "Camptown Races" had the most pronounced Negro dialect. Nelson Eddy's "Shortnin' Bread" was one of his most popular recordings, and Lawrence Tibbett, Rosa Ponselle, and other singers all included such dialect songs in their concerts, broadcasts, and recordings. Even John McCormack recorded a gently beautiful "Mighty Lak a Rose" with the lightest Negro dialect garnished with an Irish brogue. But Thomas probably made such material more integral to his repertoire than most singers, everything from "Land o' Degradashun" and "Swing Low Sweet Chariot" to "Ev'ry Time I Feel de Spirit." While he could call on his father's revival camp meetings to get some of the feel of the Negro spirit in these songs, they were still distinctly "white." The orchestration of "Ev'ry Time I Feel de Spirit" has hints of Aaron Copeland. And that was the point. All of these songs are colored by American nationalism of the New Deal era, celebrating regional and racial elements in the American character. At the time, it was all accepted as very appropriate.

It was in pursuit of more such material that Thomas approached the

Famous friends: with Jerome Kern (left) and Oscar Hammerstein, two of Thomas's favorite writer/lyricists. (Courtesy of the Archives of the Peabody Institute of The Johns Hopkins University)

well known balladeer and collector of American folk music, John Jacob Niles, after a Carnegie Hall concert at which Niles had performed "The Roving Gambler." Thomas asked Niles if he could write a set of songs on the gambler theme for him. Niles recalled that Thomas was annoyed that Paul Robeson regularly repeated the same material he had sung on his Vince Radio broadcasts earlier in the week, and wanted to have a set of songs that Robeson could not match. Niles delivered four songs to accompany "The Roving Gambler": "Gambler Don't You Lose Your Place at God's Right Hand," "The Gambler on the Big Sandy River," and "The Gambler's Wife," which had already been composed for Gladys Swarthout and was frequently used in her concerts. Just as he was ready to deliver the commissioned pieces, Thomas asked Niles to compose another that would "show off my high notes." Niles produced "The Gambler's Lament," which Thomas altered, to the composer's irritation, with the addition of a major chord at the end to indicate the Gambler's hope for final redemption.

The story is a good one. "The Roving Gambler" was certainly a popular song in Thomas's concert and radio repertoire. As a folk purist, Niles was entitled to object to the alterations made by Thomas and Hollister to "show off his high notes," but that is exactly what a concert performer would do to maximize the audience appeal of a song.[17]

Two men who had no reluctance whatever in giving Thomas solid commercial hits were Jerome Kern and Oscar Hammerstein. There was no other composer whose songs Thomas recorded as often or as successfully as Kern. Where would baritones be without "Old Man River"? It was one of Thomas's first recordings for RCA in May of 1932. His recordings of "The Last Time I Saw Paris" in March of 1941, "All the Things You Are" and "The Song Is You" in January 1942 may well be the definitive versions of these standards. In early 1945, Kern and Hammerstein dropped by Thomas's home to pitch "A Funny Old House" to him. They had written it for their 1934 Broadway Show, *Three Sisters*, and Thomas sang it on a Westinghouse broadcast a few weeks later, but it never became a standard. He would have had better luck with "Why Do I Love You," which he sang in a sweet duet on the radio with a very young Dinah Shore.

The songs of Kern and Hammerstein were frequently featured on Thomas's radio broadcasts. He once asked Kern what his biggest selling song was. Kern said it wasn't even close, "Smoke Gets in Your Eyes" (lyrics by Otto Harbach) far outsold all the others. Thomas sang it with the King's Men Quartet three months after the composer's death, on a special Westinghouse broadcast devoted to Kern's music in February, 1946. Radio audiences heard Thomas sing "Long Ago and Far Away," that masterpiece from the pens of Kern and Ira Gershwin, but RCA missed the chance to record it.

Thomas probably knew Oscar Hammerstein at the beginning of his career, when he had written the lyrics for Sigmund Romberg's *The Desert Song*. Thomas often performed "One Alone" and the "Riff Song" from that operetta on radio. What other singer can convincingly perform both "Kansas City" and "Oh What a Beautiful Morning"? Thomas recorded both. The only other Rodgers and Hammerstein song he performed was "You'll Never Walk Alone" from *Carousel*.

Thomas never found great collaborators, such as the pairing of McCormack and Kreisler in recordings of Rachmaninoff songs, nor did specialist groups seek him out to record something comparable to McCormack and Kipnis's recordings for the Hugo Wolf Society, or Richard Crooks' recording of Schubert's *Schöne Mullerin* cycle. Apart from a selection of American art songs and unreleased lieder recordings, there is no indication that he made any effort himself to record a more selective repertoire.

Thomas brought something from his father's revivals and his Broadway experience to his concerts that made him a great performer. It was that instinct to please the crowd with a show- stopping number, as well as the sheer infectiousness of his personality, that made him such a popular concert singer. But something found in other artists was missing. The intimacy of a McCormack record — or performance — came from the artist's ability to invite the audience to share his art. That is rarely conveyed in a Thomas record or performance. When it is, in "Sylvia," "I Heard a Forest Praying," the unpublished "E'en as a Lovely Flower," one has a hint of what he might have left us.

The reputation of even the most popular singers depends on their recordings to preserve their reputation. Unfortunately, the times and the marketplace did not serve Thomas as well as his talent deserved. After recording for the Brunswick label between 1924 and 1929, Thomas transferred to RCA in 1931 when Brunswick was being sold by Warner Brothers to the American Record Company, which eventually became Decca. The switch had a great impact on his career and his legacy. RCA was then the premier classical recording studio in the United States, if not the world. Thomas's association with RCA meant recognition as one of the elite of recording artists, but RCA already had one American operatic baritone in their catalogue, Lawrence Tibbett. They saw Thomas as a crossover artist whose popular songs could reach out to a broader audience, and it was many years before his operatic singing was properly marketed by the company.

Phonograph records had reached their peak sales in 1921, and fell from that point throughout the '20s and '30s, as radio replaced records as the popular entertainment medium. It would be 1947, a full twenty-six years, before record sales exceeded their 1921 levels. Whereas RCA Red Seal records, the premiere label for operatic performers, had sold for $1.50 before the First World War, or as much as $8 for some famous single-sided ensemble performances, by the mid–Twenties, it was difficult to maintain the price at $2 for a two-sided 12-inch record. Other music was not only more popular, but more profitable for recording companies. Al Jolson's "My Mammy" and "Swanee," for example, each sold over a million copies.

By the mid–Twenties, Columbia, Victor, and other record firms had created special divisions for "race" and hillbilly records. The standard fee for artists on these labels was $25 per side, with a nominal royalty of $5.00 per 10,000 sold. Those recordings, far more collectible today than most Red Seals, invariably outsold classical and operatic performances, which never accounted for more than 40 percent of the record market. Yet the classical business remained important for Victor, which had by far the greatest number of major artists under contract, because it represented a level of prestige.

The concept of the Red Seal, or prestige labeling, will be difficult to understand for today's readers in a time when labels or music producers have become undifferentiated, and where neither the public nor studios seem to distinguish between a country music hit and a classical recording. At the beginning of the century, however, class was very important, and Victor's Red Seal signified culture and quality, against the black labels of popular but lower-class music.

Thomas and other singers of the era helped erase this class division — to a point. One summer in the 1930s, José Iturbe, a refugee from the Spanish Civil War who would later become a familiar character in MGM films alongside such popular singers as Frank Sinatra, declined to appear on the same stage with Benny Goodman and his band in Philadelphia, claiming that this would be incompatible with his stature as a symphonic conductor. Other American conductors quickly volunteered to take Iturbe's place, but he insisted on being paid his full fee for the performance he had refused to conduct.

The Depression, however, would compel the record studios to reevaluate the role of classical and operatic recordings in their business. After 1929, Victor was forced to reduce both the number of new recordings and the royalties paid to artists. It lost singers like Beniamino Gigli, and for a time Giovanni Martinelli dropped off its list of recording artists. Recording whole operas was unheard of. When it was attempted, as with Gigli's recording of *I Pagliacci*, the supporting cast were non-entities. Recordings of Mozart were offered, and Donizetti's *Don Pasquale*, with Schipa, but these were not successful. Columbia produced opera sets with unnamed artists. In Europe, EMI launched a brave effort to record *Die Walküre*, with Lauritz Melchior and Lotte Lehmann under the baton of Bruno Walter, in 1938, only to give up as political conditions in Germany and Austria deteriorated. At the other end of the spectrum, one found such pitiful offerings as the young, lovely voiced Helen Jepson racing through as many as three songs on each side of a record, and Thomas himself squeezing "Love Can Be Dreamed" and "Mine Alone" onto one side of a twelve-inch Red Seal. Recording technology, which was moving to magnetic tape in Germany, simply stagnated in the United States.

The recording business was thrown into more confusion by an ongoing struggle between the American Federation of Musicians, ASCAP, record manufacturers, and the film and broadcast industry. While the musicians union and ASCAP fought to get broadcasters to pay royalties for the records played on the air, and movie studios asserted their complete rights to soundtracks they had produced, court decisions eventually ruled that no royalties were owed on recordings played over the air unless they were commercial broadcasts. It was a war of all against all for a diminishing market. All the while, low sales in the Depression eroded the margins of both record producers and performers. In an effort to expand its sales, RCA approached the Woolworth chain of dime stores to carry the company's records. If Woolworth's had agreed, this arrangement would have undercut hundreds of small business record shops across the country. But Woolworth balked at carrying 75¢ or even 50¢ records, and pressured RCA to produce a 10¢ record — which they did!

What record companies were looking for in this environment was an artist who could induce the popular audience that bought lighter music to purchase the higher priced classical recordings. John McCormack had filled this role for years. Stowkowski filled something like this crossover role for orchestral music. With popular songs like "Home on the Range" and "The Lord's Prayer," Thomas held some promise of appealing across market sectors for a new generation of record buyers. To put it more crudely, Thomas offered Victor a "twofer." They could probably pay Thomas less than high priced European opera singers whose recording careers came to an end with the Depression, and he was a crossover artist whose popular songs could appeal to a wider audience than most opera singers.

Thomas's niche at Victor became a kind of trap. "Home on the Range," "Trees," and character songs like "The Green Eyed Dragon" undermined his reputation as a serious artist. While he made superb recordings of such rarely performed arias as "C'en est fait ... Salomé demande" from Massenet's *Herodiade*, and "Zaza piccola zingara" from Leoncavallo's *Zaza*, as well as such popular standards as "Largo al factotum" from the *Barber of Seville*, and "Di provenza al mar" from *La Traviata*, as well as a number of "art" songs by American composers, they were few in number and never succeeded in winning him the recognition he should have had in the classical repertoire.

His first recording for RCA in May, 1931, came out as #1525 in the catalog — "Home on the Range" and "Trees." His next recordings, in October, 1931, were in a similar vein — mock Negro dialect songs "Lindy Lou," "Gwine to Hebbin," and "Old Man River," with the lovely "Sylvia," a baritone favorite composed by Oley Speaks, on the reverse side of "Old Man River." In February, 1932, Thomas recorded his first operatic arias for RCA, with the "Evening Star" aria, "O du mein holder Abendstern," from *Tannhäuser,* and "Di Provenza al mar" from *La Traviata.* The difference between the earliest RCA recordings and those Thomas had put out on the Brunswick and Vocalion labels even as little as two years before is dramatic. From the beginning, the RCA recordings are warm, vibrant, and nicely forward in the microphone, where the Brunswick and Vocalion material sounded stiff and distant. This first "Di Provenza" still retains, if not the stiffness, some of the formality of the earlier recordings. Its 1939 replacement is much more relaxed and confident in the familiar Thomas manner, and is particularly notable for its sweeping phrases produced in one breath.

Thomas would have five more recording sessions in 1933 and 1934, producing such familiar favorites as "The Green Eyed Dragon," "Sailormen," and the "Lord's Prayer," all commercial successes, and then silence. He recorded *nothing* with RCA between October 1934 and May 1938. There were four recording sessions between May 26 and June 2, 1938, another on November 30, 1938, which produced just six songs on three records; two of these were French (half of his recordings in this language with RCA). Two songs from the 1938 sessions would not be released until they were paired with recordings of his August 1939 sessions, which are arguably Thomas's finest. Four lieder recordings from the May–June 1938 sessions have never been released.

In one week between August 17 and 24, 1939, at RCA's Hollywood studios with Frank Tours conducting, Thomas made the majority of his operatic recordings—his last operatic recordings as it turned out, and his last foreign language recordings. If not for these sessions, audiences today would have little conception of the caliber of singing of which Thomas was capable. The voice is at its peak, full bodied, dramatic, warm, and beautifully lyrical. How, one asks, after listening to "Nemico della Patria" from *Andrea Chenier*, or Iago's "Credo," can any character who sings so beautifully be a villain? And how could Victor fail to make more recordings by such a singer?[18] There were three sessions in 1941, but two of those were for "I Hear America Singing." There was only one recording session each in 1942, 1944, and 1945.

What accounted for the failure to record Thomas between 1934 and 1938, and why wait until January 1942 to find a pairing for two songs recorded in August 1939 by a singer at the height of his popularity? The best explanation is the dire business environment of the Depression. Even during the New Deal, when the economy was supposedly on the mend, if people had money, few were ready to spend it on something as nonessential as a phonograph record. A twelve-inch Red Seal cost $2, the equivalent of four or five lunches to those who could afford to eat at a lunch counter. By contrast, Benny Goodman's records cost 50¢, and Fats Waller's "Ain't Misbehavin'" just 35¢. Besides, radio, which broadcast live and recorded performances to suit every taste, was free.

The release of recordings from the 1939 sessions in January 1942 might

have been an effort to rush recordings onto the market in the face of immi-
nent wartime restrictions on new recordings, or to offer some new recordings during the impending musicians' strike.[19] Companies like RCA were
allowed to release a limited number of recordings each year using rationed
shellac, but these were to be pressings from existing recordings, not new
ones. RCA released five Thomas records in 1941, ten songs, then quickly
issued five more in January 1942 to beat the wartime ban.[20]

Just as the Depression was lifting and 23 new records were released
to shops between May, 1938, and January, 1942, the war limited production and distribution of his records—seriously affecting Thomas's earnings. The wider impact of the war on opera and concert performers will
be discussed in the following chapter.

All of the fault for Thomas's rather modest recording legacy, however,
may not be due to RCA's shortsightedness or economic conditions. Ken
Darby noted that Thomas "was not too keen about recording: the art had
not proceeded far enough to satisfy him." This is difficult to understand.
For all its technical limitations, recording in the late '30s and early '40s
was still quite good. Some of the microphones developed then are still
sought out by vocal artists. The engineering talent was first rate, and the
rich creamy tube sound that so suited Thomas's voice was the norm in
recording studios. The industry had even developed the technology for
long-playing records, though these sixteen-inch recordings were restricted
to use on radio broadcasts since no one felt the commercial market would
accept a new recording format. Between 1943 and 1946, Thomas would
have a sixty-two piece orchestra at his disposal. Costs were such that he
could easily have afforded to pay for several private recording sessions to
preserve his art, but he did not.

It was on broadcasts over the airwaves, however, rather than recordings, that the widest public heard Thomas, and those broadcasts had much
more the flavor of a live performance than his records. He was sponsored
by Vince tooth powder from 1934 to 1936, and made appearances on the
Ford Radio Hour broadcast from Detroit on Sunday evenings between September 1936 and October 1940, the *Coca Cola* program between Decem-
ber1940 and May 1941, and the *RCA Magic Key* in 1936 and 1937.

Thomas sang a number of pieces on these broadcasts that were never
recorded by RCA, including a splendid "Vien Leonora" from *La Favorita*
for *Ford* in March, 1940, and "Per me giunto" from *Don Carlos*; as well as
a fine "Toreador Song" from *Carmen*, along with a seductive "Beau soir"
by Debussy, both from an April, 1939, *RCA Magic Key* broadcast; an unexpectedly warm "Songs My Mother Taught Me" by Dvorák on the *Golden
Rule Insurance Company's Mother's Day Program* of May, 1941; and some

delightful "character" songs, such as "Mah Little Banjo" and "The Old Black Mare."[21]

These two aspects of Thomas's repertoire — art songs and "character" songs — are so much a part of his art that they require some comment. One can count at least seventeen art songs among Thomas's recordings, primarily by American composers. Listeners will have their own favorites, but most would probably include "Sylvia," "Your Presence," "Come to Me in My Dreams," "Where My Caravan Has Rested," and "Fulfillment" as among his best recordings in this genre. "Boats of Mine," Anne Stratton Miller's setting of the Robert Louis Stevenson poem, which Thomas did not record but sang on the radio, should also be listed.[22] What mark these as particularly fine examples of his singing is that they all have a graceful, relaxed tempo that allows full expression to Thomas's long, sweeping bel canto line. Both "Home on the Range" and the "Lord's Prayer," which were long identified with Thomas's popular repertoire, share this characteristic tempo and display his vocal beauty at its best.

Recordings of these art songs could not have been expected to sell in great numbers. Their inclusion in Thomas's recording sessions, therefore, must have represented some remaining commitment to art in what by the late 1930s had become a very commercial career. Of all his recordings, the art songs seem to be the best examples of Thomas's deeper musical taste.

The theme of a song was also an important factor in the effectiveness of Thomas's interpretation. Apart from a piece like "In questa tomba," which is not really representative of the repertoire, Thomas was not a compelling lieder singer. Lieder often requires the singer to weave a mood of introspection, melancholy and longing that was simply not in Thomas's character. His lieder show a very fine quality of voice, long line, and dramatic emphasis. But only the latter is a requirement of fine lieder singing, and the missing elements of reflective angst is much more telling. In the American art songs Thomas recorded, the mood may be reflective, but there is an element of hopefulness, satisfaction, or fond recollection that is congenial to his own personality, and makes his interpretation very effective. One would think that Tchaikowsky's popular "None but the Lonely Heart" would be well suited to Thomas's voice, but a recording from a radio broadcast shows that it became lifeless in his hands. Sombre melancholy was just not in his personality. The cycle of Kashmiri Love Songs by Amy Woodforde-Finden is more effective, but still not quite in the class of Tibbett's popular recording of the second Kashmiri Love Song.

If one compares Thomas's lieder recordings to those of the German baritone Heinrich Schlussnuss, there is no question that Thomas has the finer voice and far better vocal line. Schlussnuss seems to gulp for breath after every four words in Mendelsohn's "On Wings of Song," where Thomas carries it along in long sweeping phrases. But Schlussnuss has a native speaker's feel for the language and perhaps the mood of the piece.[23]

Thomas's personality worked to his advantage in the many "character" songs he recorded. Of these, "The Green Eyed Dragon" and "The Barber of Turin" are bravura pieces that it is hard to imagine any other singer making his own. But there is another group, like "The Farmer's Pride," "Tally Ho," or "Old Black Mare" (from a radio broadcast), with fewer vocal pyrotechnics, that engage the listener with anticipation of the surprise one knows is coming at the end. In addition to the customary qualities of vocal line and beauty of tone, what makes these songs effective is Thomas's ability to convey the prankish mood of boyish high spirits— more than convey it, to sing it. With Thomas, the song or aria had to be congenial to his own character, or to be purely lyrical as in the classical Italian art songs, to be fully successful.

The absence of such synergy between role and character may explain why Thomas never made a Hollywood film during the heyday of the American musical. Given his wide popularity and readiness to try new media, particularly ones that paid well, it is surprising that he never appeared in films when musicals were at the height of their popularity in the early thirties. The fact is, he was not interested in any of the projects that were offered him, and the few he was interested in were not marketable. Moreover, by the thirties, Thomas had long since lost his matinee idol looks, and the operettas that suited Nelson Eddy would not have worked the same way with him.

A half dozen scripts for film projects were offered to Thomas, beginning with *Sing, Fool, Sing* in 1936. None of these projects suggest a lost Hollywood classic. At one point, David O. Selznik expressed an interest in producing a Technicolor film with Thomas as the star. *The Glory Road* by Adele Rogers St. John and Mark Kelly would have had Thomas playing a man grown bitter about the failure of peace at the end of the First World War. He buys a farm to get away from the world, then finds his faith in mankind restored through music.

Kingdom Come was developed in 1940 for Warner Brothers, and was actually scheduled to start shooting on May 20, 1940. The plot involved a singer who becomes associated with a Mission serving the unemployed that is threatened with closure. The film delivered a message critical of the "crutch " of public or private charity, and was to use some of Thomas's most popular songs, such as "The Green Eyed Dragon," "He's Got the Whole World in His Hands," and "I Love Life," as well as works by Percy Grainger, Albert Hay Mallotte, and Jaques Wolff. Given Hollywood's aversion to "message" films, it is surprising the film got as far into planning and production as it did. With the fall of France to the Germans the very month *Kingdom* was scheduled to go into production, however, it became unthinkable to distribute a film pointing out unpleasant divisions in American society, and the project was shelved.

The Great Answer was an RKO and Ginger Rogers property that circulated among studios in 1944, based on the story of Dunkirk from a book by Margaret Runbeck. *Then You'll Remember Me* was to be a life of the nineteenth century Irish composer and baritone Michael Balfe, which included a role for Jenny Lind. When one thinks of the dozens of biographies of composers that Hollywood turned out in these years, one can only wonder if Balfe was not just a little too obscure for the studios.

One of the most intriguing projects would have had Thomas starring in a comedy set in Victorian London, titled *Dr. Arthur Saville's Crime.* Thomas would have played Lord Saville, a nervous, suggestible nobleman who is told by a fortune-telling prankster that he is about to murder someone. After several bungled attempts to fulfill this destiny, and having broken off his engagement in order to spare his fiancée the pain of the trial and dishonor he assumes will follow his crime, Saville finds himself walking forlornly on London Bridge that night. He spies the Cockney fortuneteller peering over the bridge, and realizes what fate intends for him. A few minutes later, a London bobby passes and asks his lordship if anything is the matter. Saville's satisfied answer as he gazes down on the ripples of current washing over his tormentor's hat is "not now." The film required no singing, but would have suited Thomas's own puckish personality very well.

At least one of Thomas's Westinghouse radio broadcasts was filmed, and is available from a popular video library under the title "Behind Your Radio Dial." Thomas sings "In the Gloaming" and "Come Thou Almighty Lord," and just as in his earlier Vitaphone films, his deportment is relaxed but motionless. Showing little expression, he simply pours out the sound. For much of the time that he sings, he stands before the microphone with his arms folded across his back. It is a posture he would not have been able to assume in any live performance, but suggests that this was the way he sang in rehearsal, utterly relaxed but giving himself a little more support by keeping his arms across his lower back.

By the late forties and early fifties when Met colleagues like Ezio Pinza and Lauritz Melchior were finding success in films, one movie was made that would have seemed an ideal vehicle for Thomas. It was the 1949 film *Everybody Does It*, starring Paul Douglas as the owner of a wrecking and construction business whose wife, Celeste Holme, aspires to an operatic career. Although the wife has very little talent, a sympathetic soprano discovers that Douglas has a great baritone voice. Douglas bears some resemblance to Thomas, which suggests that this might have been the project an employee of Thomas remembers movie executives trying to persuade the singer to take. His fee was prohibitive, however, so they turned to the then unknown Douglas.[24] One might even think the Disney studios could have found a role that suited Thomas's comedic gifts in one of their animations— as they did, for example, for Salvatore Baccoloni — but nothing seems to have been offered to Thomas.

With or without a movie career, Thomas had clearly reached the pinnacle of his concert career by 1939. He and Carroll Hollister were ready to plan a major tour of Europe that year, and prepared a series of concerts at the Town Hall in New York in anticipation.[25] Each concert would showcase arias and songs in French, Italian, English, or German respectively. Though Europe was suffering through the same economic slump facing America, and dollar transfers could well have been a problem, the tour would have been a major highlight in Thomas's career, carrying his name and voice to an international audience it could not reach any other way.

The five-nation concerts were offered on Sunday afternoons at the Town Hall in New York, to great critical success. Looking at the program today is like glancing over some menu from the Edwardian age, where course after course offered an excess of rich food to suit every taste. Consider the French program on October 22, 1939, which began with:

Chanson Religieuse (a 13th century troubadour song by Guiraut Riquier)
L'Amour de Moy (15th century)
Chanson à Manger by Charles Lemaire (d. 1704)
Bois Epais (from *Amadis* by J.B. Lully)
Air from *Les Deux Avares* André Modeste Gretry
La Procession César Franck
Le Mariage des Roses César Franck
Chevaux de Bois (The Merry-Go-Round) Claude Debussy
Beau Soir Claude Debussy
Ballade des Femmes de Paris Claude Debussy

Promesse de mon Avenir from Massenet's *Le Roi de Lahore* was substituted in the printed program just before the Intermission according to one reviewer.

Intermission

D'une Prison (Verlaine) Reynaldo Hahn
La Danse Macabre Camille Saint-Saens
L'invitation au voyage (Baudelaire) Henri Duparc
Mignonne Gabriel Pierné
Larmes Gabriel Fauré
L'Angelus (Breton folk song) arranged by Bourgault-Ducoudray

Me suis mise en danse (Bas Quercy) arranged by Arnold Bax
Kaddisch Maurice Ravel
Chant du Forgeron Darius Milhaud
Sainte Maurice Maurice Ravel
La Belle Jeunesse Francis Poulenc

The concert was very well received, with the audience demanding many encores, beginning with "Au Pays" by Auguste Holmes.

For the British Concert, December 3, Thomas and Hollister were joined by a violin, viola, cello, and flute ensemble from the NBC Symphony Orchestra. The Italian Concert on February 11, 1940, again started with 17th and 18th century works, then operatic arias, and concluded with modern songs by Resphigi, Donaudy, Sadero and Bimboni, again with regional offerings from Tuscany, Naples, and Sicily. The German program, February 25, began with a selection of five Schubert songs, then five Brahms lieder, the Mahler "Songs of a Wayfarer" cycle, and concluded with five pieces from Hugo Wolf. The American Concert on March 24 began with Revolutionary War–era songs, folk songs, and a poignant Negro spiritual, "Take My Mother Home," by Hall Johnson, drawn from Christ's words from the Cross to the apostle John.[26] That was followed by works by Edward MacDowell, Charles Ives, and Virgil Thomson, and concluded with songs by other contemporary composers.

Despite the success of the series, the outbreak of war in Europe in September, 1939, meant that there could be no tour for the duration. When the Germans quickly conquered Belgium, Holland, and France in May, 1940, the Europe Thomas loved in the twenties had vanished. Thomas's recording of Jerome Kern and Oscar Hammerstein's "The Last Time I Saw Paris" in March, 1941, captures the bittersweet mood of the time perfectly. Two months later, on May 9, 1941, another link with his early years was also broken when Adelin Fermin died in Rochester, New York, at age 74.

5

The Man Who Loved Life

> I love Life, so I want to live
> To drink of life's fullness
> Take all it can give.
> — Mana-Zucca

No song in John Charles Thomas's repertoire better summarized his zest for life than Mana-Zucca's "I Love Life." The same energy found its way into his wardrobe. A *New York World Telegram* reporter described Thomas as "a huge man, jovial in loud tones, [who] wears rakish wide brimmed hats and suits in keeping. Exactly the sort of man you would expect to have calling your odds on the seventh race or the next fight." He went on to explain that in the radio studio, Thomas sang with his coat off, and soon had his collar loosened.[1]

At the beginning of his career, Thomas had dressed like a fashion plate, perhaps as compensation for his humble family background. During the war years he was a sporty dresser who liked loud colors. Describing Thomas's appearance at their first meeting in August, 1942, Ken Darby recalled that he wore magenta slacks, a salmon colored jacket, a maroon shirt with a white necktie and maroon beret.[2] Thomas once had special shirts made — cherry red with a yellow stripe — for himself and the members of Darby's quartet, the King's Men. His home and automobile were equally tailored to his personality. After the luncheon meeting, Thomas showed Darby his customized station wagon, with its hand tooled leather upholstery, radio, heater, a bar in the back and a loudspeaker which Thomas used to berate other drivers' poor road skills.

How should one describe the personality of John Charles Thomas? The publicity packets distributed by his management described a man who disliked puns and punsters, had a violent dislike of insincerity, and did not believe in fortune telling (though his concerts were sometimes scheduled at numerologically coincident times, such as one at 3 P.M. on March 3). He liked movies, and preferred small dinners to large cocktail parties. For their evening entertainment, he and Dorothy played cards with friends. Thomas was a light sleeper and an early riser, hence the christening of one of Dorothy's boats *Tip-Toe*. He rehearsed his singing all morning every day, even on vacation. He was a 32nd degree Mason. His favorite poets were Ruskin and Shakespeare, although his favorite poem was "Poor Robert of Sicily" by Browning. Thomas's favorite composers were Brahms, Verdi, and Beethoven, his favorite opera *Aida*, his favorite operatic role Hamlet, his favorite hymn "Adeste fidelis." As a young man President William McKinley had been his hero, and his politics strayed little from those boyhood ideals. In 1940, the man in public life that he most admired was Charles Lindbergh.

Close friends portrayed a more complicated personality. They found him open, generous and trusting, but at the same time moody, secretive, and suspicious. Harry Budd of San Francisco recalled that Thomas could be cruel and kind; a hard bargainer—for concert fees, for example—but also generous; gregarious, but a man who liked his quiet hours.[3] He could not brook criticism of his singing. He had a pride and ambition to excel, for example, in golf, where he would resent losing a $3 bet. He was an indefatigable sportsman. Frank Chapman, who in 1937 had first introduced Thomas to "Lord Randall," a song which became a great concert favorite, recalled that Thomas could fish all day, play 18 holes of golf, then after an hour or two of rest, give a concert in fresh voice the same evening.

A favorite story is told of Thomas after a long day of sailing and drinking during a regatta in Easton. Late in the evening he staggered along the dock to a group of boys and demanded with some bluster, "I'm John Charles Thomas. Row me out to my boat." The young fellows complied, and as they were rowing back to the dock, heard a voice boom out across the water in the dark, "My name is John Charles Thomas, and this is my boat," followed by the boat owner's insistence that it was *his* boat, and then, as the boys neared the shore, the opening phrases of "Home on the Range." Presumably, Thomas eventually found his own boat, and was able to sleep it off the next morning.

Sometimes his drinking could be more reckless. Helen Jepson recalled with delight the occasion she and Thomas drove back to New York with Fermin after a performance in Philadelphia. Thomas was drinking and speeding, and threw his bottle out the window when he heard a police siren. He argued with the policeman, was given his ticket, and drove on to New York. Jepson thought he probably did not pay the ticket.

Thomas was an inveterate prankster. On Broadway, he was known to begin singing while the soprano was still holding her last note in a song. At a performance of *Blossom Time*, and perhaps more than one, he broke up an ovation for the soprano by cartwheeling onto the stage. In the opera house, he would get his hat plumes caught in a soprano's hair, or complain *soto voce* of his soprano's weight while bearing her across the stage in the last scene of *Rigoletto*—and pinching her bottom through the sack. When John McCormack could no longer reach the final high notes of his best known song, Thomas would annoy the great tenor by asking why he no longer sang "I Hear You Calling Me" at his concerts. McCormack finally exploded, "You know damn well why I don't sing it." A favorite joke he liked to play on golfers the first time they teed off with him was to place a foam rubber golf ball on their tee and watch their dismay as the ball floated a few yards down the fairway. He once invited a vaudeville sleight of hand artist to be his guest in Easton, without, of course, informing his family of the man's occupation. Thomas thought the ensuing consternation was all great fun as watches, jewelry, and silverware disappeared. On another occasion, at a party in California during the Second World War, Thomas shaved his head, put on a silk robe and added two long fake teeth to impersonate a Japanese.

Thomas was often invited to perform at the White House during the Roosevelt years, for the President claimed publicly that "Home on the Range" was his favorite song. In private, after years of hearing the song played at political appearances, the President expressed his dislike of the piece. Thomas had been a featured guest at the Press Club Dinner on May 9, 1936, an annual event where speakers could make off-the-record jokes about politicians. He sang at a Carnegie Hall gala celebration of the President's birthday in January, 1943. The two men must have had a strange relationship. Both were hearty jokers who enjoyed "needling" friends, yet they were at opposite political poles. Thomas once introduced his father-in-law to the President by saying, "Mr. President, this is my father-in-law, George Dobyne, a staunch Republican who hates your guts." Roosevelt replied with a laugh, a handshake, and possibly an inner grimace.

The years of Thomas's prime, from 1934 to 1943, saw him settled in to a comfortable routine. He rehearsed new material in Easton during the summers, accompanied by Carroll Hollister or a local music teacher and composer from nearby Cambridge, Maryland, Margaret Carreau. The singing would sometimes cause farm laborers to pause to listen to him in the fields—to the annoyance of the landowner, "Boss" Dobyne.

Thomas was very serious about all aspects of his performance. At one point he "kidnapped" Gino Meroli, a native Italian speaker, by luring him

Although Thomas later opposed President Roosevelt, he was often invited to sing at the White House in the early years of the New Deal. Pictured here with FDR and fellow singer Morton Downey. (Courtesy of the Archives of the Peabody Institute of The Johns Hopkins University)

to a train at Grand Central Station in New York then locking him in a first class compartment with a ticket to Easton, where he stayed to help Thomas perfect his Italian pronunciation. But while he worked at his craft, vocalizing and singing every day of the year, summers were for fishing and yachting. Thomas simply had a great capacity for self-enjoyment, which comes out vividly in his music. By late summer, he would learn what his schedule would be at the Met for the following season, after which his management would confirm his concert appearances. Easton was usually the site of his first concert of the season in mid to late September, often as a benefit for the children's wing of the local hospital. His appearance at the local Avalon Theatre, a small house with a charming Art Deco interior that seated perhaps 400, was the highlight of the Easton social season.

When not on the road concertizing between October and March, he would break away from his scheduled appearances during the winter to energize himself in the warm sunshine of Palm Beach. Thomas's principal forms of relaxation were golf and yachting. Of the two, golf was the more enduring. He took up the game in 1913 as a diversion from the tedium of rehearsals and performances while performing in de Koven's Gilbert & Sullivan company. He carried his enthusiasm for the game to Paris and Belgium, and to his subsequent residence in Palm Beach, Easton, Los Angeles, and Apple Valley. In those early years he played with wooden clubs, and was delighted when he broke 80 for the first time, in March, 1925, the same week of his opera debut and his second marriage. Dorothy also golfed, and was better than her husband. In the early '30s, Thomas played with Bobby Jones in Atlanta, and scored 81 in the game. In 1958, nearing seventy, he was still able to score 76. An adherent of the "use it or lose it" school of singing, he often sang as he walked the fairways, just to keep his voice in shape.

Yachting was just becoming a popular sport for the affluent when Thomas took it up in the 1930s. In an interview for an article in *Motor Boating* in April, 1936, Thomas recalled exploring caves along the shores of the Chesapeake Bay with his father, and longing to have just a small boat to row on the water. In 1925, he and Dorothy took a house in Beverly Farms, Massachusetts, on the North Shore, and chartered a 48-foot boat for two weeks. That hooked them on sailing. When they returned from Brussels in 1933, Thomas began haunting shipyards, yacht brokerage offices and poring over advertisements in the boating magazines hunting for a yacht. He finally settled on an 85-foot houseboat with rooms for six and a crew of five, which he bought in March, 1934, at City Island in Palm Beach.[4]

Thomas christened his new yacht the *Masquereder*, because he said it allowed Dorothy and him to pretend they were rich even if they were not. Two months later, they sailed down Florida's Inland Passage to Key West and invited Ernest Hemingway to join them for deep-sea fishing. Dorothy recalled the events of one day as Thomas and Hemingway were swimming off the boat, and the crew was enjoying its daily issue of grog.

> Suddenly, we found ourselves swimming through and dodging around scraps of lettuce, apple cores, strings of celery, cabbage leaves, fruit rinds and coffee grounds! Johnny yelled, 'Dive everybody!' and we did, swimming under water around the stern and coming up on the starboard side.
> Ernest and Johnny were a sight, garnished with leftover spaghetti and parsley. All of us were so scroungy we had to hose each other down.
> The ship's cook had taken that moment to dump garbage from the bow galley and the onshore current carried it straight into our faces.[5]

Deep-sea fishing was more Dorothy's pastime than Thomas's, but he loved being out on the water, and would vocalize freely as they sailed off Palm Beach or in the Chesapeake. The ship was kept in Easton through Thanksgiving or even later, and the Thomases and guests often had Thanksgiving dinner aboard her as they cruised the Bay. Mother Thomas made silk pennants for the ship, and the crew had special uniforms. Adelin Fermin came aboard the *Masquereder* that first winter of 1934-35 to help Thomas rehearse for his concert season and perhaps for some of his operatic performances. Thomas had Christmas and New Year's dinner with his parents on board the *Masquereder*, a late date to be on the Chesapeake, then returned to his scheduled concert engagements. When he was in New York, he often lived and slept on board, using his mid-town apartment as an office.

Yachting did not completely satisfy Thomas's love for life on the water. In Palm Beach, he owned a cabin cruiser, the *Pecheur*. In 1935, he bought a Class E runabout that he christened *Myne* and then another hydrophonic class boat with a 225-cubic-inch engine called *Myne II*, built by Walter Bunkee of Dover, New Jersey. He won first prize in the 1935 Miles River regatta at Easton, and another first place trophy in the 1935 Chester River race, and entered many other races in Florida and New York. A third speedboat, called the *Tip-Toe*, rounded out the Thomas fleet. He won admission to the "Hell Divers" Club when he was thrown from one of his boats at high speed.[6]

In 1942, heavy U-boat activity off the East Coast, the expense of maintaining a yacht with wartime rationing of fuel, and a pending move to Los Angeles led Thomas to sell the *Masquereder*. He first offered it to the Navy, which said it was too large for their needs, whereupon he sold it to a Cuban national. En route to its new home, the Navy changed its mind and

Left: Dorothy Thomas was responsible for making her husband a deep-sea fishing enthusiast. *Bottom:* On the Miles River in *Tip-Toe,* his racing boat. (Courtesy of the Archives of the Peabody Institute of The Johns Hopkins University)

confiscated the ship, only reimbursing the owner after a prolonged appeals process. The yacht was used during the war as a navy hospital ship in the Caribbean.

Because it was somewhat unusual for a man to take an interest in cooking in the thirties, many publicity releases during his career highlighted Thomas's love of cooking, and even offered his recipes for tomato sauce and fried chicken. His advice to cooks was to think about what they wanted to eat, then make it. There is a photo of him and Conchita Supervia looking hungrily at a prospective turtle soup, but for a man who spent much of his life on the Chesapeake, there is no record of his interest in blue crab or the other delicacies

With soprano Conchita Supervia, contemplating a forthcoming turtle soup. (Courtesy of the Archives of the Peabody Institute of The Johns Hopkins University)

of the Bay. In fact, he seems to have had very mundane tastes. He made his spaghetti sauce in five-gallon batches. His favorite meal was roast turkey with creamy mashed potatoes; his favorite breakfast—fried chicken and waffles, with fried potatoes, or fried tomatoes smothered in gravy. On his tour of Australia in 1947, he insisted on a clause in his contract that all accommodations would include kitchen facilities, and was photographed preparing a steak, his customary post-concert supper. He loved kitchen gadgets, and was among the first to buy a popcorn popper. His Los Angeles home boasted a very large wine cellar as well as a walk-in freezer, which he used to give his salad lettuce extra crispness before serving.

During the Second World War Thomas took up farming. He raised chickens, turkeys, ducks and pheasants in Los Angeles, and sold eggs to the Victor Young orchestra members at 60¢ a dozen — less than the wartime market price. In Easton, his vocal students bought him a sow that got him started in raising pigs, which occasioned some of the most delightful photographs of farmer Thomas beaming happily at an enormous sow, nearly five feet long, as she lies on the ground suckling her pigs.

Even if his denim workclothes look a little too well pressed in these photographs, Thomas clearly enjoyed outdoors activity — and during the war, farming was not only a patriotic duty, but carried useful tax benefits. Raising hogs seemed like a practical way to make the Easton property, which he and Dorothy managed during the Dobynes' last years, income producing. Thomas read everything he could on pigs, and consulted with farmers around the country for advice on breeds and operations.

In 1954, while on a concert tour in Harrisburg, Pennsylvania, he hired a taxicab to drive the 150 miles to Hagerstown, Maryland — in the years before interstate highways— to meet with the Burdick family and discuss his pig operation. He bought several boars and sows from them, and left two complimentary tickets to his concert. He finally selected a cross between Poland Chinas and Chester Whites that he called China Whites, a pure white breed that was unusual at the time. The breed had the maternal characteristics of the Chester Whites, and would be used to cross with other breeds to produce large litters. Pork production was undergoing a transition in this period from an era when hogs were as valuable for their lard as for their meat, to a time when lean meat became more and more prized. Thomas built barns, watering troughs, installed wooden exercise runs for his pigs and automatic feeders for his "pig palace." Still, as he later admitted to Ken Darby, "the pigs never did pay."

All his life, Thomas was an active member of social clubs, particularly yachting and country clubs. The most important of these, however, was his membership in California's celebrated Bohemian Club. He was first invited to attend a gathering of the Bohemian Club in 1932, and was elected to membership in 1934, after paying a $550 initiation fee. He had performed in an opera production, *The Legend of Hani*, as a guest of the Club in 1934, and two years later inaugurated, or in the usage of the Club, "sired" Preachers Sons' night, which became a tradition at the semi-annual encampments.

The enthusiastic hog farmer. (Courtesy of the Archives of the Peabody Institute of The Johns Hopkins University)

Thomas was in his element in the heavily alcoholic atmosphere of informal male companionship at the Bohemian Grove.[7] His membership in the Club grew in importance for him after his retirement, because it kept him in contact with important national leaders of business and government and allowed him to maintain his sense of status within the Grove as his own

Thomas spent heavily to maintain a modern hog operation. (Courtesy of the Archives of the Peabody Institute of The Johns Hopkins University)

celebrity waned. He could also play the role he seems to have increasingly enjoyed as an aging Falstaff, lording it over a band of merry pranksters. The Bohemian Club had suspended its gatherings during the War, so the assemblies of 1946 and 1947 were particularly cheerful gatherings. Thomas built his own "Doghouse" campsite in 1945. This complex consisted of three buildings: a small theater stage, a separate cabin for the bar, and a Lodge with a large kitchen, a living room dominated by a rugged stone fireplace, and bedrooms for at least six guests. Hand hewn beams dominated the interior, while the exterior of the Lodge was sheathed in redwood bark. A motto was carved over the fireplace, much like that in his New York apartment:

> I love this little house because
> It offers after dark
> A pause for rest, a rest for paws
> A place to moor my bark.

Thomas invited Ken Darby and members of his quartet, the King's Men, to several gatherings in the Grove from 1946 on, paying at least some of their membership fees. At the 1953 encampment, he invited them to join him for a late supper at a nearby cabin. Darby recalled the evening in his biography:

> John Charles said: ... There's someone who needs serenading and I'd like you [the quartet] to sing a few. We aren't going back to the Grove for dinner tonight.
>
> He led us down a long path meandering among the cabins of the resort hotel next to the golf course. The conversation was disjointed and irrelevant, John Charles choosing to remain silent.
>
> In the farthest corner, surrounded by redwood saplings and a small forest of ferns, was a white cottage with a veranda. John Charles stepped quietly up onto the porch, opened the screen door and knocked gently.... (W)hen the door opened, the person standing there was beyond any expectation. She was tall, dressed entirely in white — except for a rose scarf tied loosely around her neck — and even her hair was white....
>
> John Charles introduced each of us by name, calling her "Mary".... The room was softly illuminated by two lamps on tables beside a beige couch, and tall tapers burned in candelabras on the dining room table that was set for six! So she wasn't all that surprised! When I turned back, John Charles had his arm around her waist; her eyes were looking straight into his— on the same level — and she was saying "...you look tired, John. Come sit down and I'll pour you a big drink."[8]

After dinner and a serenade, the quartet returned to their cabin while Thomas stayed the night with Mary, whom Darby assumed was a long-time mistress.

Other opera stars were members or guests of the Club, but none had quite the standing of Thomas. Lauritz Melchior was a guest one summer, and sang two songs, "For You Alone" and Grieg's "Ich Liebe dich," to great applause. As he prepared to sing again, Thomas took over the stage to move the show along. Melchior stomped off in good humor, muttering, "I ask you, vot chance does a tenor have in a program run by a baritone?"

Lawrence Tibbett, a native Californian, was also a member of the Bohemian Club, and had always been a close friend of Thomas during their years at the Met. Whatever rivalry existed between them for roles was treated as a friendly competition. Essentially, however, they performed different repertoires, Tibbett taking the heavier dramatic roles, Thomas specializing in the lighter roles of Rossini and Verdi. Thomas cheerfully substituted for Tibbett on several occasions when the latter was indisposed due to his drinking problem. They had fun singing together in the Bohemian Grove, where photos show their famous duet in 1936 in "When We Two Were a Maying." Tibbett got Thomas's goat at the 1939 encampment by holding the final note of the "Credo" from Verdi's *Otello* after Thomas, who was singing it solo, finished. Their friendship was broken by an unfortunate remark by Tibbett about Dorothy, probably spoken when he was in his cups.

The popular tenor James Melton apparently upset the Club's members when he made a hasty departure from the Grove one year. Although Thomas was not present, correspondence shows him taking the side of the offended members.

Most members of the Bohemian Club were wealthy conservatives who chafed at their long years out of power during the New Deal. Charley McCarthy got the spirit of the Grove right when he wisecracked to his partner during the 1946 encampment, "Bergen, this country's in a hell of a shape when you have to go into the woods to find Republicans." Thomas was an outspoken isolationist in 1940–41, and was just as outspoken against the Hitler regime. He was convinced that the Europeans would somehow eventually remove Hitler, or as he put it, "kick his ass out of Germany."[9] In the 1940 election, Thomas supported Wendell Willkie, and appeared at the candidate's formal acceptance speech in Elwood, Indiana, in August. Willkie was a candidate of Henry Luce and the Time-Life organization and certainly no isolationist.

Despite his support for Willkie, Thomas was convinced that FDR would keep America out of war. His resentment of Roosevelt and the left wing New Dealers represented by Henry Wallace grew during the war, and he was furious over what he and other conservatives considered the sellout of Poland and Eastern Europe at Yalta. Although the Westinghouse program devoted a show to celebrating the United Nations, and he several times sang a song titled "One World" on the show, Thomas was privately scornful of the UN and gave it forty years before it became a corrupt bureaucracy like the IRS. In later years his view of the Warren Court was just as critical.[10]

While some of these views may seem far from the mainstream today, in his time, Thomas was a centrist Republican, albeit one most at home with the southern California country club set. We tend to recall the Roosevelt era as a liberal epoch, but this misjudges Roosevelt's political caution and the strength of the Republican Party even during its long years out of power. Roosevelt preferred to be all things to all factions, and frequently frustrated the liberal elements in his administration by his reluctance to get very far in front of public opinion. Although Congress remained in the control of the Democratic Party from 1931 to 1947, the Republican Party made strong gains in the 1938 elections, and came within ten seats of controlling the House after the 1942 elections. Even during the high tide of New Deal liberals between 1933 and 1939, the Liberal wing of the Congressional Democrats was always offset by the conservative southern delegation, led by Vice President Garner, so that Republicans were never without some influence.

Thomas was relatively active in Republican politics, and even considered running for the U.S. Senate in the 1950s. In April, 1952, General Eisenhower came to the spring encampment at the Bohemian Grove and gave an inspirational speech by the lakeside. Afterward, Thomas reported to Darby that "I talked with him, I asked a bunch of questions and he gave me all the right answers. You wait. Ike will be the next man in the White House." Thomas campaigned heavily for Eisenhower that autumn, particularly in California.

Despite Thomas's stature in the entertainment world, and his active role in politics, the presumptuousness of his interrogating a man who had been at the center of international affairs for ten years, and had high level experience in Washington dating back to the twenties, is a bit breathtaking. Of course the Bohemian Club had high-powered businessmen and politicians among its members, including former President Herbert Hoover, but few could match the General's experience in dealing with world leaders and Cold War policy issues.

Thomas was just as self-centered in his personal life as in his social world. Both of Thomas's biographers, Ken Darby and Merle Armitage, raised the question of why this man who could delight audiences with renditions of buoyant children's songs, from "The Green Eyed Dragon" and "Sailormen" to "A Child's Prayer," who entertained orphans on his Christmas show, and who performed at Shriners Children's Hospitals and at annual benefits for Easton Children's Hospital never chose to have children of his own? Dorothy Thomas told Ken Darby after her husband's death that she had always wanted children, and was disappointed not to have them.[11]

Friends had slightly different recollections of Thomas's feelings toward children. A few recalled that he doted on children, while others said he never inquired about their children or showed any affection toward them. Darby recorded that Thomas was very welcoming to his son Peter when his father brought him along on a visit to Apple Valley. On the question of why the singer did not have children, however, both Darby and Armitage reached the same conclusion. Behind Thomas's own assertions that a concert career did not allow time to raise children, it seemed clear to both men that Thomas had always been the center of attention, and wanted to keep it that way.

Ken Darby offers the best portrait of Thomas's personality in the later stages of his career, and the conversations he records are not always flattering to his friend. The two men were clearly members of a John Charles Thomas admiration society, and the picture that emerges is of an aging Falstaff presiding over a court of admirers. Thomas was not always like this. All the elements of this somewhat crusty personality can be seen from earlier years, but there was a lighthearted, engaging Peter Pan quality about the younger man even into the 1940s that fell away in the last decade of his life.

6

The War Years and After

The bombs that fell on Pearl Harbor and ushered America into the Second World War also brought enormous changes to the cultural climate in the United States, not least to its musical culture. The concentration of young people in the military during the war, and the sentimental attention paid to wives and sweethearts on the home front, stimulated a subtle shift toward something like a youth cult in the world of commercial music. Over the next decade, that trend evolved from big band music and crooners to rock and roll, while another part of the popular music audience was drawn to new Broadway musicals very different from the old operettas. From the end of the war, and into the early Fifties, these changes meant a sharply declining audience for concert singers like Thomas, trying to reach a broad, general audience.

The war itself had a more immediate impact on professional musicians. After long years of Depression, jobs for musicians suddenly became abundant. Thousands of musicians were called up or volunteered for the armed services. Radio networks, symphonies, and other entertainment programs needed as many musicians as they could find — and were even willing to pay them union scale.

At the same time, wartime restrictions complicated, and even jeopardized, the production of musical entertainments of all kinds. From early 1943, the use of public or private transportation, such as automobiles or taxis, to attend "entertainment events" was prohibited. As a result, Boston, Baltimore, and Hartford canceled their opera seasons.

Gasoline rationing discouraged the use of buses for tours by bands, and travel regulations and restrictions on the railroads, which now fell under the direction of a war control board, complicated travel for concert artists like Thomas. Civilian plane travel during the war was all but unknown. Hotel accommodation was less predictable as businessmen and military officers moved around the country on official business. There were smaller inconveniences for concert artists as well, like restrictions on tailoring that discouraged the making of vests, pleated trousers, and even trouser cuffs.

Other restrictions were specifically directed at the music business. The shellac used for record production came from India, and had to be rationed. Recording studios were restricted to a quota for record production, and that quota was linked to their pre-war production. Since fewer records could be manufactured, studios tended to market better-selling popular music, thus cutting into the income of classical performers like Thomas. To add to the problems of record studios, James Petrillo, the President of the American Federation of Musicians, called for a walkout by musicians on July 31, 1942, which meant no new recordings could be made. Vocalists like Thomas were exempted from the strike if they used only piano accompaniment.

After years of trying to maintain record prices in the deflationary climate of the Depression, RCA had been forced to cut its classical record prices in half in August, 1940, following rival Columbia's lead. Now the industry was suddenly faced with inflationary pressures from all sides: higher wages for studio musicians, wartime material shortages, even shortages of production workers, while price controls hampered its ability to pass these costs along to consumers. After thirteen months, Decca capitulated to this pressure in September, 1943, and signed the contract proposed by the musicians' union. Columbia fell into line in the Fall of 1944, followed quickly by RCA.

More than the inconvenience of wartime restrictions, taxes presented a serious threat to the continuation of Thomas's career. New Deal economists fundamentally mistrusted free enterprise, private investment, or capital accumulation, and designed tax rates accordingly. In 1938, the tax rate on incomes over $150,000 was 64 percent. Wartime rates passed in 1942 and 1943 raised it to 90 percent.[1] If the Roosevelt Administration had had its way, taxes would have been higher. On April 27, 1942, the President sent a message to Congress in which he called for confiscation of all incomes, after taxes, above $25,000. "I believe that in this time of grave national danger ... no American citizen ought to have a net income, after he has paid his taxes, of more than $25,000 a year. It is indefensible that those who enjoy large income from state and local securities should be immune from taxation while we are at war."

A performer with Thomas's earning power was basically working for free after the first few months of the concert season. The prospect of overcoming bureaucratic hurdles in order to get dependable train transportation and hotel bookings around the country for sixty or seventy concerts each season, only to hand over all your earnings to the government, dimmed the allure of concert tours. Giving up concert tours, however, meant the risk of losing your audience at age 52 or 53, and starting all over after the war — if you still had your voice.[2]

Thomas maintained his concert schedule for the balance of the 1941–42 season, and performed a few concerts in the Fall of 1942. During the spring of 1942, however, he was approached by the Westinghouse Corporation to host a Sunday afternoon radio program. The timing of the offer could not have been more fortuitous. While attending a party at a movie director's home in Santa Monica in 1942 during a War Bond tour, Thomas had admired the property and asked his host if it were for sale. The director said that it was because it was "too close to the Japs."[3] Because of the submarine attacks off the East Coast, and the failing physical and mental condition of the Dobynes, John Charles and Dorothy were ready to sell their Palm Beach property and relocate to Easton. When he consulted his mother, she readily agreed to leaving Palm Beach. With those decisions made, Thomas moved quickly to buy the 37-acre property on a hillside at 3100 Mandeville Canyon Road. Among its other amenities, the house had a walk-in freezer and two commercial film projectors that could be used to show films on a screen that descended from the ceiling. [4]

He wired Charlie Parker to come out from Easton and supervise some changes he wanted on the property. Thomas persuaded Westinghouse to broadcast the radio program from the West Coast rather than New York, and settled in to southern California living by the fall of 1942. After his last performances at the Metropolitan in late February, 1943, Thomas dropped his lease on the New York apartment at the Berkshire, and split his time between Easton and Southern California.

The Westinghouse Program began airing in January, 1943. Thomas's team for the broadcasts would consist of Victor Young, conducting a sixty-two piece orchestra, a sixteen-man chorus directed by Ken Darby, and storyteller John Nesbitt, who offered a 5–8 minute segment of warm nostalgia with a subtle plug for Westinghouse. The show's producer was Clarence "Clare" (pronounced Claree) Olmstead. Two factors are particularly striking about the collaboration of the principals on the Westinghouse show. First, they were all at the peak of their form and complete professionals. Second, it was, with one exception, a remarkably happy company during the three-and-a-half-year run of the program.

Victor Young had been born in Chicago in 1900, but after the death of his mother, he and his sister were abandoned by their father, a tenor

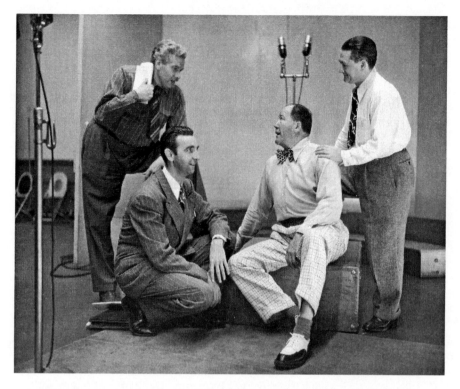

Left to right: Clare Olmstead, producer, Ken Darby, choral director, Thomas, and Victor Young, orchestra conductor for *The Westinghouse Program*. (Courtesy of the Archives of the Peabody Institute of The Johns Hopkins University)

with the Chicago Opera, and the children were sent to Poland to live with their grandparents for fourteen years. Their grandfather, a tailor, was able to enroll the children in the Warsaw Conservatory, where Victor studied violin and his sister piano. One of his teachers was Roman Statlovsky, who had been a pupil of Tchaikovsky. In 1917, Young got caught up in the First World War when he was interned first by the Russians in Kiev, after performing at a recital, and then, after escaping with the help of a Bolshevik officer who admired his playing, by the Germans on his return to Warsaw!

At the war's end, he was determined to return to America, and arrived in New York in 1920. He eked out a living there until he journeyed to Los Angeles to meet his fiancée, who had arranged an audition that led to a position as concertmaster in Sid Grauman's theater orchestra. Young moved to other concertmaster positions in Chicago, and then to New York to play with Ted Fio Rito's orchestra. He was also a talented composer, and had his first hit song in 1928 with "Sweet Sue." He would subsequently write "Lawd You Make the Night Too Long"(1932), "Street of Dreams"(1933), "Ghost of a Chance"(1933), "My Foolish Heart"(1950), "When I Fall in Love"(1952), and "Three Coins in the Fountain" (1954) .

In 1929 Young began working for radio shows, and in 1931 was hired as musical director of radio and recordings by Brunswick, which eventually became Decca Records. Had Thomas not left Brunswick at that moment for RCA, the two would have been collaborators at an earlier stage in their careers.

Young had written un-credited music for Hollywood studios in 1929, and again in 1932, but in December 1935, he signed with Paramount Pictures, moved to Hollywood and quickly showed a genius for versatility in writing scores for films ranging from *The Road to Zanzibar* to *For Whom the Bell Tolls.* He also continued to compose for Broadway reviews, such as *Love Parade.*

Young worked for most of the Hollywood studios during his career — Columbia, Goldwyn, MGM, Republic, RKO, 20th Century–Fox, and Warner Brothers. His association with the Crosby-Hope road pictures led to later work for Hope's *Paleface* with Jane Russell, and Crosby's *A Connecticut Yankee in King Arthur's Court* and *The Country Girl.* By 1939 he was writing incidental music or full scores for an incredible 37 films a year, 33 in 1940, 23 in 1941, and eighteen in 1942. The Westinghouse show offered a breather, so that by 1945, he was responsible for only seven films. By 1952 and 1953, he was getting assignments like *The Quiet Man* and *Shane,* and wrote scores for *Johnny Guitar* and *Three Coins in a Fountain,* as well as *The Country Girl* in 1954.

It is easy to name Young's great scores, but there were dozens and dozens of studio projects that landed on his desk which offered little scope for serious composition: *The Gracie Allen Murder Case* and *Buck Benny Rides Again* were only two from that dreary pile. Precocious and ambitious, Young was valued in Hollywood as a fast worker with a seemingly endless supply of melodies falling out of his sleeve. One orchestra member recalls being invited by Young to a party at the home of director John Ford where Young sat down at a table during the party and wrote out all four parts for a string quartet that he led in his spare time. Like Thomas, he could have done far better work had he not been caught up in the lucrative Hollywood music mill. Whether he put great effort or little effort into his compositions, the studio reaction was always the same: "That's terrific, Vic, now see what you can do with this."

In 1944, a theme Young had composed for the movie thriller *The Uninvited* became a big hit when it was released as "Stella by Starlight." He led the orchestra in this song several times on the Westinghouse program.

Young shared Thomas's taste for drinking and carousing with friends, and elaborate practical jokes. In *Music for the Movies*, Tony Thomas tells of the classic joke Young pulled on Max Steiner:

> Young drove up from Paramount to have lunch with Steiner at Warners ... and found Steiner rehearsing the orchestra in the main title to a new film... . [U]nseen to Steiner, [he] wrote the theme on a piece of paper ... and drove back to Paramount... . [T]he following morning he recorded the piece with his own orchestra. He then called Steiner and invited him up to his house that evening for a poker session. By the time Steiner and a pair of other card-playing musicians arrived, Young had wired his record player to his radio. Some time during the game, he switched on the radio, which triggered the record player — and out came the Steiner music. After about twenty seconds, Steiner's eyes came up from his cards and he started to tremble. "Oh, my God."
> "What's wrong, Max?" innocently asked Young.
> Steiner shook his head. "I don't understand. That music. Is that something new?"
> "Hell, no," said Young, "I listen to this program all the time — they've been playing it for years." ... Soon [Steiner] said, "Vic, I'm not feeling too well, I'd better go."[5]

Young was much loved by the musicians in his orchestra, and is universally remembered for his cheerful good humor, musical brilliance, and businesslike efficiency as a conductor. The players, many borrowed from the Los Angeles Philharmonic, were amused at Young's conducting style. For all his classical musical training, he conducted as though leading a jazz band, starting with his arms in an outstretched position and swinging them back in to his body rather than giving a downbeat.

As musical director for the Westinghouse show, it was Young's responsibility, along with Darby and Olmstead, to select the pieces to be performed each week, and sketch out their orchestrations. There is little indication that Thomas participated in this process. Pencilled substitutions in the program might have been at Thomas's direction, or based on collective decision-making. Young brought his sketches to the Saturday rehearsals, went over them with the arrangers, then left it to the copyists to write out the individual parts for the member orchestra.

Thomas stood at his microphone behind and to the right of Young. Both men kept eye contact to assure that their tempos remained consistent. At the end of a two-hour rehearsal, the orchestra was ready to perform for the broadcast the following morning. No one ever took the music home for further practice.

After the war, Young's career continued to flourish, culminating in his Oscar for *Around the World in Eighty Days* in 1956. His untimely death of heart disease that year cut short a brilliant career.[6]

Ken Darby (1909–1992) was the head of choral music for the Disney studio, and had been musical director for MGM's *Wizard of Oz*. He would accompany Thomas on the "all star numbers," with his King's Men quartet. He would later win Oscars for *The King and I*, and *Porgy and Bess*, and had the distinction of providing the choral backup for several early Elvis Presley films.

By 1943, John Nesbitt (1910–1960) was a well established narrator of "Passing Parade" shorts at the MGM studios. His stories on the Westinghouse program essentially followed the same nostalgic pattern, recalling early automobiles, offering tributes to the household maid who was a common feature in middle class homes before the Second World War, re-telling the story of famous inventors, musicians, or outlaws like Billy the Kid.

The final member of the team was, of course, Carroll Hollister. With the forces of a full orchestra and chorus to support him, Thomas did not use his long-time accompanist on the show, but he was always in attendance for rehearsals. As it happened, Hollister was able to fill his time with other activities.

When Carroll Hollister shipped his household possessions west from New York in April, 1942, one of the crates was accidentally dropped and broke open on their arrival at the Union Pacific depot in Los Angeles. Freight handlers found that it contained communist literature and notified the FBI. Subsequent investigation by the Bureau disclosed that Hollister's shipment contained eight boxes containing some 3000 communist publications. His annual concert tours travelling around the country with Thomas since 1933 were obviously a perfect cover for the unobtrusive accompanist to distribute communist literature to comrades in major metropolitan centers.[7] Hollister's affiliations should not have been a surprise to the FBI. He had been one of the founders of the Musicians' Committee to Aid Spanish Democracy during the Spanish Civil War.

Over the following several months, FBI agents observed meetings at Hollister's home, taking down license plate numbers to identify others in attendance. Informants revealed that Hollister was a "key figure in the communist party in Los Angeles," with a leadership role at the Hollywood Canteen, where he served as vice president under the titular leadership of Bette Davis. The Canteen, modeled on the Stage Door Canteen in New York, provided free entertainment for servicemen by Hollywood stars and popular entertainers. The actor John Garfield was also a vice president, and screenwriter Dalton Trumbo later appeared at meetings of the Board of Directors. Both men were associated with communist activities, and Trumbo subsequently achieved notoriety as one of the ten uncooperative witnesses who took the Fifth Amendment when subpoenaed to testify before the House Un-American Activities Committee in 1947. While the FBI records indicate nothing more subversive on Hollister's part than support for mixed racial dancing at the Canteen, a common tactic of the communists at that time was to win influence in such popular organizations for propaganda purposes as well as to redirect funds intended for such non-political purposes as GI entertainment to support communist activities.[8]

Hollywood was a major hub of communist activity during the war, and perhaps the Party's most lucrative financial base. Many screenwriters were active communists, or sympathizers. While they might not have been able to write films entirely to suit the Party line, they were in a position to insinuate many themes of the class struggle into their work. The Party had no interest in creating propaganda films that no one would see. It was much more useful to insert sly suggestions of ideology in popular films that would be widely seen. And it was just as important to try to block films or scripts that would have carried messages hostile to the communist ideology. Even extras sympathetic to the party were able to contribute subtly to the cause by portraying workers as oppressed victims of society, or the wealthy as dissolute and decadent exploiters. While this may sound silly today, communism in the thirties and forties was a religion, and its tenets were taken very seriously by believers. Party members were put through the most demanding dialectical contortions during that era, but most never missed a turn in the Party line.

A long-time Party member like Hollister would have spent most of the thirties guarding vigilantly against infiltration of the movement by Trotskyites—and trying not to fall under suspicion himself. He would have had to overlook the hundreds of thousands of deaths from famine in Russia that resulted from collectivization, the purging and execution of scores of old Bolsheviks, and then Red Army officers in the late 1930s. Outspoken in their opposition to fascism from the early thirties or before, party members switched, literally in the course of an hour, from denunciations of Hitler's Germany to insistence on American neutrality when the Soviet Union signed a non-aggression pact with Germany eight days prior to their joint invasion of Poland. The Anti-Nazi League was quickly replaced by the American Peace Mobilization (APM), and the American League for Peace and Democracy that discouraged American cooperation with Britain in resisting German aggression.[9] When the Soviet Union invaded Finland in 1939, American party members opposed any effort to portray the Finns sympathetically.

Hollywood Party members were interested in more than simply exercising subtle ideological influence on the American mind through the film industry. Herbert K. "Herb" Sorrell led the Conference of Studio Unions, a communist front, in several violent strikes in 1945 and 1946 in an effort to win control of all union labor on studio lots. He came close to winning, a victory that would have put the communists in an even better position to intimidate the studios into producing films more consistent with communist ideology, or at least not produce films hostile to communism. More important, control of union dues from studio labor would have been a very lucrative source of income for the movement. These were the battles that gradually turned Ronald Reagan from a supporter of the New Deal to a conservative political activist.

For Hollister, the retiring accompanist, these were heady days to serve the Party in Hollywood. He might well have imagined himself emerging from Thomas's shadow to play a significant role in the new America that would emerge from the Second World War. He might have smiled at the illusions of the wealthy Thomas and his reactionary friends. The Roosevelt Administration was already laying the groundwork for mistrust and suspicion of the wealthy. Confiscatory taxes and a centrally planned and controlled economy were in place and widely accepted. Henry Wallace, a man with "progressive" left wing sympathies, was Vice President, and might have been expected to be the Democratic Party candidate for President when Roosevelt left office. Harry Hopkins, another "progressive" whom some have thought a possible Soviet agent, was the President's closest advisor.[10] Earl Browder, the head of the Communist Party USA, was convinced that he was able to exercise personal influence on the President and American policy through an agent with White House access. The Party's agent was deceiving Browder about this, but his own confidence in his special influence could well have percolated down to other Party members.[11]

In the wider world, Party members must have been very confident about the movement's prospects after the end of the war and the triumph of the great leader Joseph Stalin. It was clear that in a post-war Europe, communists, with their record of resistance to Fascism, and the military and political support of Russia, would be in the best position to gain political control of newly liberated states throughout Europe. One could already envision the British Labour Party vanquishing Churchill's Conservatives in post-war elections and introducing a socialist government — which they did. The Party would prove to be a major electoral force in France and Italy for many years. In the context of this larger movement of the *Weltgeist*, Hollister's role on Thomas's radio show must have seemed insignificant indeed.

With the end of the Cold War, the interest of historians in the nature and influence of the communist movement in Hollywood has faded. It is easier to think of blacklisted Party members as martyrs to free speech than as subversive foreign agents. But a question about Hollister's relationship with Thomas remains compelling. How could these two men, with such antagonistic political convictions, remain artistic collaborators for twelve years? Did Thomas know Hollister was leftist or even communist? On Hollister's part, the simple answer may have been that there was a Depression. He could scarcely expect to find a better position than that of accompanist to Thomas, and it offered ample opportunity to make clandestine contacts with political sympathizers around the country. More than that, however, he could well argue that his work with Thomas brought both a greater appreciation of serious music to the masses, and genuine popular entertainment, both of which were goals of socialist culture.

As for Thomas, it is difficult to imagine that he did not know Hollister's political leanings. But he could hardly expect to find as fine an accompanist who shared his conservative views in that era! Even more, however, it is quite possible that Thomas appreciated the humor of the situation. Dragging Hollister along to the Bohemian Club encampments, making him listen to the well-lubricated opinions of conservative businessmen, would be exactly Thomas's idea of an extended practical joke. And so the partnership continued: the revolutionary muttering sullenly about the advent of impending Revolution; the conservative confident that sooner or later good sense would sweep away the New Deal.[12]

While these political tides churned beneath the surface, however, Thomas and Hollister were busy putting on a radio program at 11:30 every Sunday morning. Westinghouse was wholly committed to war production during the war, but saw their Sunday program as a way to keep the company's name before the general public. If John Nesbitt's stories happened to feature electronic apparatus like selenium switches used in lighthouses, or heavy electrical machinery, that was sufficient to satisfy the corporate sponsor. Most often, however, the theme was heavily nostalgic — stories about the old west, about the early Model Ts, colorful characters from the gold rush years in San Francisco — always with a satisfying nod to the future that America would build out of the struggles and challenges it had faced and overcome in the past. Both storytelling and live radio is experiencing a small revival today, and, listening to Nesbitt weave his tales over the airwaves, it is easy to imagine the appeal of this program as it was broadcast into the family living room, with children as well as adults getting caught up in tales of Billy the Kid, lost gold mines, or ships in danger on the seas.

Thomas had, of course, been familiar with the Southern California scene since the '20s, and could not have picked a more exciting time to move to Los Angeles. Despite the strains of war, with heavily camouflaged factories, blackouts, the cancellation of all horse racing, even a ban on broadcasting weather reports for fear of giving information to the enemy, and nighttime curfews for aliens—including Europeans who had fled the Nazis and found refuge in America — Hollywood offered a most inviting environment. Los Angeles was still a land of undeveloped coastal hillsides, with orange and date groves stretching out in all directions under eternally blue skies and clear desert air. In 1940, the census reported a population of 1.5 million for Los Angeles, and 2.7 million for Los Angeles county. By 1950, the population would grow by nearly 50 percent, to 2 million in the city and 4 million in the county. Thomas set about creating a new life for himself, mixing with old friends like Basil Rathbone and getting to know the latest Hollywood celebrities.

For Hollywood, the war brought a new boom, the last hurrah of the studio system before the advent of television. The arrival of gifted composers, writers, and actors fleeing the Nazis enriched the studios artistically and culturally. Emigré intellectuals like Arnold Schoenberg, Thomas Mann, and Aldous Huxley were drawn to Los Angeles, along with lesser-known artists and performers fleeing Europe, very like the crowds of extras found on the set of *Casablanca*. Victor Young took advantage of the influx of this new European talent by commissioning refugee composers to make arrangements of American folk tunes in a classical idiom, such as "Mary Had a Little Lamb" in the style of Shostokovich and Ravel, or a surprisingly good "Yankee Doodle" á la Beethoven by Stahl.

The half hour Westinghouse broadcasts signed on with Thomas booming out the opening phrase of "Home on the Range" and introducing the cast. Thomas would generally start off with a solo, followed by an orchestral piece, followed by a medley from the chorus, then another song by Thomas at the midpoint. John Nesbitt would offer his story, followed by the orchestra again, with Thomas and ensemble in a final number before his sign off with Robert Franz's "Widmung," or "Dedication," sung in English.

The mood in the studio was relaxed, with the good humor of the conductor and star creating a pleasant working environment. The entire company were highly skilled professionals producing high quality shows. One imagines people tuned in across the nation on quiet Sunday afternoons (the 11:30 A.M. West Coast broadcast was scheduled to reach the large East Coast audience at 2:30 P.M.), whole families listening before the big Sunday afternoon meal. Thomas owned the mike, and introduced each number. There were no guests, and neither Young nor Darby ever spoke, though Thomas might offer some one-sided banter, such as when he introduced the orchestra's performance of "I'm Through with Love" with "I hope it's not true, Vic." Nesbitt simply read his story and closed with "another step in time's passing parade."

Surviving rehearsal recordings show that Thomas could be testy at times. Responding to some unseen action on the set, Thomas asks in an aside, "Do you have to do that now?" At another rehearsal, when someone from the cast tried to show him a message while he was performing "Brown Bird Singing," he sang "I'd better not look at that until I'm through... Sweeter songs of love than the brown bird ever knew" without missing a beat, and even keeping the song's rhyme scheme.[13] Thomas joked at one session that the members of the chorus always thought they could tell what he was going to sing by the color of his clothes. For example, brown slacks or coat would suggest "Brown Bird Singing" on the program. "Well today," he said, "I'm wearing a purple shirt and lavender trousers, I wonder what they think I'll sing." A voice from the chorus called out, "There Are Fairies at the Bottom of Our Garden." On Easter Sunday, 1945, Darby recalled that Thomas walked into the studio looking like he had fallen into half a dozen pots of egg dye. His outfit consisted of a ripe pumpkin sport coat over a grass green silk shirt with a corn yellow necktie, with orange slacks, maroon and white shoes, persimmon socks, all topped off with a purple beret. The orchestra immediately struck up "Somewhere Over the Rainbow." Despite a script that was usually followed tightly, there were spontaneous moments too. After hearing the orchestra perform a piece he liked, Thomas would say "Let's get the words to that one, Vic."

The general musical flavor of the Westinghouse show would be described today as Light Classics or "Pops." In the program's early months, there was an emphasis on American music. The show would usually feature one or two light classics, very often works of Grieg, Chopin's *Polonaise*, or Kreisler's *Liebesfreud*, mixed with show tunes, old standards, and many newly popular Latin rhythm numbers like "Peanut Vendor" and "Jamaican Rumba." Thomas would sing selections from his familiar repertory, along with standards from Victor Herbert or Jerome Kern, and almost always a hymn, which was both appropriate for the Sunday time slot and very popular during the war. With fewer operatic or classical pieces, the program was almost the reverse of the standard Thomas concert, where show tunes, Gilbert and Sullivan songs or popular numbers like "Rancho Grande" were never performed. The material offered on the Westinghouse broadcasts was very similar to that which Thomas had used over the years on his earlier radio broadcasts.

Even with this popular programming, the general level of performance was quite good, and on occasion, exceptional. These were, after all, experienced Hollywood studio musicians under one of the ablest orchestra leaders in the country. To hear orchestra and soloist cut into familiar operetta tunes such as "Tramp, Tramp, Tramp" from *Naughty Marietta*, or the "Riff Song" from the *Desert Song*, is to hear a genre done at its best. With pieces like "Shaller Brown," arranged by Percy Grainger, Sir Landon Ronald's "Prelude to the Cycle of Life," Vincent Youmann's "Through the Years," or Cole Porter's "Begin the Beguine," the ensemble outstripped itself. These were the kind of showstopper numbers, reminiscent of his early Broadway days, that Thomas could do better perhaps than any other singer. Not every piece can be a showstopper, but critics who miss this aspect of Thomas's art overlook one of his greatest talents in performance.

The programs frequently included numbers from Thomas's Broadway days, such as "Tommy Lad," "A Mother's Song" from *Her Soldier Boy*, and a medley of "You Are Free" and "I Love the Girls, Girls, Girls" from *Apple Blossoms*. The contrast between the rather stiff recordings on Vocalion in the '20s and his robust and confident rendering of these numbers as a mature artist is dramatic. Thomas also performed contemporary hit songs, from "White Christmas" to Vincent Youmann's "Great Day."

Thomas's appreciation for singing with choral accompaniment stretched back to his boyhood in his father's church, and directing Methodist choirs at summer camps. Performing with a full orchestra and the King's Men was very fulfilling artistically, and when Thomas spoke fondly of the company on the final show, he was expressing gratitude for the real comradeship that had grown up among the performers over three and a half years. As we shall see, Thomas remained close to the King's Men personally and professionally for the rest of his life. Apart from his long-time association with Carroll Hollister, this was the only close artistic collaboration he ever formed with other musicians.

There were a handful of special programs that stood apart from the weekly offerings. A Johnny Appleseed show produced for Easter, 1945, with Thomas taking the role of a fiery revival preacher, suggested memories of his childhood in the Pennsylvania coalfields. For a Christmas show, the troupe offered a dramatization of the popular short story "A Juggler for Our Lady" that was repeated the following year. Two shows were dedicated to the memory of great American composers, Victor Herbert and Jerome Kern, shortly after the latter's death in 1943. Plans for the V-E Day program included a medley of Service songs, and Beethoven's Fifth Symphony — with a penciled note: "must be scored immediately!"

The orchestra was at its best performing popular numbers with the lush Hollywood sound that was at its height during the war years. Cole Porter's "Begin the Beguine" comes to mind. More serious music, particularly the

The Westinghouse set in Studio B of NBC's Los Angeles headquarters. (Courtesy of the Archives of the Peabody Institute of The Johns Hopkins Universit)

operatic selections, sometimes suffered from too little rehearsal. Opera requires a tight discipline between singer and orchestra, with the dramatic emphasis in the right places. There was an occasional raggedness in these selections, in part due to a habit Thomas developed of holding back momentarily before beginning a phrase. He may have been trying for a rubato effect, but it sounds like he was on the verge of missing his beat. Of course the orchestra had to follow their conductor, not the singer. With operatic numbers that were performed more frequently, however, such as "Nemico della patria," the results could surpass the versions recorded by RCA. Young keeps the orchestra perfectly teamed with Thomas, supporting the baritone's dramatic phrasing, and sustaining the overall dynamic of the aria beautifully.

Thomas excelled when responding to a challenge or the inspiration of the moment. Occasionally the orchestra would play something that appealed to Thomas, and a few weeks later he would join the orchestra in singing the piece. One of the finest recorded examples of his singing is a "Tristesse eternal" that he sang in response to a modern, slightly swing-

Thomas in full voice on a Westinghouse broadcast. (Courtesy of the Archives of the Peabody Institute of The Johns Hopkins University)

ing adaptation of this Chopin Etude that was then being popularized as the title song of the film *A Song to Remember*. His introduction hints that *this* was the way the music *ought* to be performed. The performance is almost electrifying, with a compelling rhythm and bravura high notes.

In March, 1945, Thomas offered the audience "Somewhere a Voice Is Calling," a touching remembrance of John McCormack, whose health was failing, and who would not survive the year. The following month, after the death of both Ernie Pyle and Franklin Roosevelt, a moment of great emotion throughout the country, Thomas's performance of "Farewell" was riveting. Three operatic rarities which he never recorded rewarded the patient listener: "Il balen" from *Il Trovatrore,* "Per me giunto" from *Don Carlos,* and "Promesse de mon avenir" from the rarely performed Massenet opera *Le Roi de Lahore.* "Nemico della Patria" from *Andrea Chenier* was one of the most frequently repeated opera arias on the program, and the slight variations in Thomas's rendition demonstrates the concert artist's prerogative of altering his interpretation from one performance to another.

The aria offers fine scope for powerful dramatic singing at its climax. But in one or two performances, Thomas transformed it into a piece of gentle lyrical beauty that catches the listener expecting the standard dramatic interpretation off guard. Was he simply tired that day, or experimenting with something new? Variations on a Jerome Kern standard like "All the Things You Are" were more expected. There, instead of his recorded version with a strong ending on the reprised chorus, Thomas substituted a soft ending, Young and the orchestra repeated the verse, and then Thomas finished *forte*.[14]

As might be expected, there were a number of songs with wartime themes. Caroll Hollister wrote a stirring "Marching Song of Freedom" that Thomas performed three times.[15] "God of Battles" was composed to lyrics written by General Patton. "When My Boy Comes Home" was another of those songs, written for Thomas by Albert Hay Malotte, which had everything required of a popular song, but vanished like so many other wartime songs at war's end.

While Thomas could render such rousing anthems with suitable verve, on other occasions he showed signs of being all too familiar with his material. His voice could be husky, his speech a little slurred (at 11:30 in the morning!) and the singing came very close to parody, most notably in the third performance of "Begin the Beguine" or the "Major General's Song" from *Pirates of Penzance*. When this happened, it was Victor Young's job to retire those numbers from the show's repertoire. When Thomas found himself in vocal difficulty on high notes, Darby would bring the chorus to a crescendo to cover the star. The same technique could be used just as effectively to exploit Thomas's vocal range, as in one performance of the "Serenade" from *The Student Prince*. The only way to tell that Thomas is singing baritone, rather than tenor, is that the chorus comes in to sing the highest notes.[16]

The first reaction of today's listener might be that the whole program tended to be corny—confirming the judgment of critics who had shaken their heads for years at Thomas's concerts. The quartet pieces may be the hardest to listen to today, with medleys of "Buckle Down Winsocki," "Bicycle Built for Two," and "In the Good Old Summertime." But these selections are very much of the period, and highly suitable for a Sunday afternoon program. One has to remember that Thomas appealed to many listeners who would not have tuned in for any other classical singer. The pop classics offered by the orchestra, or the operatic arias occasionally served up by Thomas, offered easy access to classical music for the general public.

Even John Nesbitt's stories are still engaging today. Corporations were subtly inserting a business ideology into broadcasts during these years, and the Westinghouse program was no exception. By 1946, Nesbitt was offering cautionary tales of how inflation hurt the young New Salem shopkeeper, Abe Lincoln, or the disastrous effects of the inflationary tulip bulb craze in sixteenth century Holland. Throughout the series, there was a recurring theme of the individual man of vision resisting the ignorant mob — sometimes the hero was destroyed by the mob, but he was always vindicated by history.

Still, weekly radio broadcasts, even with a first-rate orchestra and chorus, could not maintain the artistic edge of formal concerts. Quite apart from the nature of the material offered over the air, the energy that a live audience gives a performer was missing. The Westinghouse program offered many advantages for Thomas. It was weekend work that allowed him to devote the balance of his time to entertaining, golf, and work on the land. Raising chickens, ducks, turkeys and pheasants, or planting 250 rosebushes for Dorothy was a more pleasant use of his time than catching trains for the next concert.[17] This lowering of artistic standards may have contributed to the one sour note among the show's principals.

The popular fare offered by the Westinghouse program, and Thomas's ever more conservative politics, contributed to the distance that developed between him and Carroll Hollister, who had been a pillar of classical music taste and values in the singer's life for over ten years. Photos from the show's set tell the story. Hollister sits uncomfortably glum, surrounded by grinning associates. The drippy nostalgia that poured out of the King's Men and Nesbitt must have left him starving for adult fare. Then too, it must have become increasingly difficult to hold in his political opinions around Thomas while his Party activities grew in importance. In 1945, the two men, who had formed a brilliant artistic alliance for eleven years, dissolved their association.

The exact circumstances of their break-up are still unclear. Ken Darby tells the story that Thomas learned that Hollister had boasted to the Victor Young Orchestra during a rehearsal that he had cancelled Thomas's vote in the election. Since this violated Thomas's rule against discussing politics on the set of the program, Darby reports that the singer led Hollister to the door and said, "Goodbye, and don't come back." That is consistent with information in the FBI files on Hollister that first appear after the November 1944 elections. But Darby was not personally present at the incident, and interviews with surviving members of the orchestra elicited no recollections of such an incident.

The other story of the break-up was that by 1945, Hollister had had enough of Thomas's reactionary views. The crisis may have been brought to a head by some unkind remarks made by Thomas or his friends at the time of Franklin Roosevelt's death in April 1945. This story is confirmed in Hollister's FBI file, which reports the accompanist submitting his resignation at that time, effective, appropriately enough, on May 1, 1945, the international Labor Day celebrated by communists around the world. Hollister quickly found new employment as accompanist for the tenor James Melton. Later, he was accompanist for Gladys Swarthout. Such breakups are always disappointing, even a little bitter. But Hollister's timing was right. Thomas's artistic decline proved to be irreversible.[18]

In February, 1943, a month after launching the Westinghouse show, Thomas sang his last performances at the Metropolitan and resigned. His explanation to his Los Angeles colleagues was probably 90 percent of the truth. "I'm into chickens, pheasants and farming. It pays about as well as the Met, and I don't have to put on makeup for my hens."[19] Thomas is sometimes criticized for a mercenary approach to his art, but after ten years at the Metropolitan, there was little artistic reward to be found in another season of singing Figaro and Germont père. His last performances included not only the standard *Barber* and *Traviata*, but *Faust* and *Aida* as well.

It is often suggested that Thomas somehow used his contract with the Metropolitan to enlarge his concert career, and left it when he no longer needed its cachet. If anything, it was Thomas who gave the Metropolitan a much-needed boost by joining its roster. Few singers brought his freshness and verve to performances. He did not use tags like "star of the Metropolitan Opera" on his publicity, and since he never appeared on more than one Saturday matinee broadcast a year from 1936 to 1943 (not at all in 1940), it is hard to see how the Metropolitan would have helped build his concert audiences. The majority of his fans were probably less interested in his operatic singing than his more popular repertoire.

The Metropolitan had grown increasingly dull, and would not begin to revive artistically until the Bing era a decade later. Moreover, with the advent of singers like Leonard Warren and other American baritones whose acting and vocal resources were as good or better than Thomas's, there was no reason to stay. By contrast, wartime Los Angeles was full of energy — and paid far better.

Besides the Westinghouse show, Thomas also appeared as a guest on other shows. He was, for example, a popular guest on the Edgar Bergen and Charlie McCarthy program, the *Telephone Hour*, Eddie Cantor's show, and *Amos 'n' Andy*. On October 30, 1943, he made an appearance on a program broadcast from the Hollywood Canteen with Betty Davis, Leopold Stokowski, and other stars. In July and August 1944, during his summer vacation from Westinghouse, he hosted a program featuring an all girl orchestra, the Symphonettes. The format would be briefly resurrected a few years later as a pilot television series.

On May 10, 1944, Thomas appeared on a *Mail Call* program with Judy Garland. Then on October 15, 1944, he was a guest on the *Jack Benny Show* in a skit that made fun of Benny's celebrated miserliness. In the show, Benny is about to ask Thomas to substitute for Dennis Day at a fee of $40 per week when he learns that Thomas pays his butler more than that. Benny is delighted when Thomas agrees to appear for Benny, but loses enthusiasm when Thomas says he might as well take Benny's $40 for the job.

On November 1, 1945, Thomas was featured on KDKA in Pittsburgh on the 25th anniversary of the first commercial radio broadcast in the United States. There were also appearances at the Hollywood Bowl, visits to nearby military camps to entertain the troops, auditioning aspiring talent among the troops, and cooking up some of his famous spaghetti sauce.

Living in Los Angeles brought Thomas into contact with a younger generation of talented singers. One photograph from the forties shows him talking to Frank Sinatra. One wonders whether they were comparing vocal techniques or lifestyles. Young singers launching careers in the movies sought him out for advice. He warned them against straining their voices, told them to practice daily, and not to chase a fortune in the film industry. Few took the advice.

With the end of the war came a lifting of the restrictions on travel that permitted Thomas to return to his concert career. He also returned to light opera, playing the role of Sir Joseph Porter in *H.M.S. Pinafore* in Baltimore and Washington in May, 1946. During intermission, he offered the audience two groups of songs. In Washington, President Truman was in attendance, and for the final scene, Thomas appeared dressed as Winston Churchill in a naval uniform. The following month, on June 30, 1946, Thomas and his team performed on their final Westinghouse program. Darby described the expectant scene:

> Clare [Olmstead], behind his double glass shield, raised his hand in readiness for the cue, looking like Zeus preparing a solemn benediction, or a dispassionate thunderbolt. Victor Young stood expectantly, his baton poised shoulder high over the orchestra... . Only John Charles Thomas moved ... silently turning his head to survey the suspended scene. I saw him write something on the flyleaf of his script, and when he held it up for me to see, I read, "Why must there always be a last time?"

Part of the show was preempted by a news report of an atomic test in the Pacific, but the network returned to the scheduled broadcast in time for the finale, in which the chorus and orchestra joined Thomas in "Auf

With Frank Sinatra, c. 1945. (Courtesy of the Archives of the Peabody Institute of The Johns Hopkins University)

Wiedersehen," the song which the Romany chorus had sung sixteen years earlier as they accompanied Thomas to the train depot in West Palm Beach:

> Calm your fears, dry your tears, hold me closer,
> closer to your breast. I must weep or die dear.
> Love lives ever knowing no word like goodbye.
> Hearts may sever, true love can never die.
> Love will remember when all else shall wane,
> Guiding me on through the years
> Auf Wiedersehen, Auf Wiedersehen.

Thomas then signed off for the last time.

> Dear friends; the engagement which today ends three and a half years with Westinghouse Electric ... and this wonderful group ... has been, in many ways, the most pleasurable association in my career. It is my earnest wish that the ensuing years will serve to cement the friendships made... . And so, to Westinghouse Electric, and to our friends of the radio audience, I sing:
>
> > Oh, thank me not for what I sing thee. Thine are the
> > songs, no gift of mine. Thou gav'st them me, I but return
> > thee, what is and ever shall be thine.[20]

In 1940, Thomas's planned European concert tour had been canceled due to war. After the war, Europe offered little inducement to concert artists, and curiously enough, there is no indication that Thomas ever thought of returning to the Continent, despite the advent of regular commercial flights. Instead, the South Pacific now beckoned. From May through August, 1947, Thomas toured extensively in Australia, New Zealand, and Hawaii. Dorothy was prevented from joining him on tour by the death of "Boss" Dobyne the day before their scheduled flight to Honolulu. While her husband toured the Pacific, with their friends, Mr. and Mrs. Jack McGee, Dorothy drove from Palm Beach to Easton with her invalid mother, who had suffered a stroke some years earlier and now had diabetes. Three nurses and a physician accompanied Dorothy, who initiated court proceedings to be declared her mother's guardian. She was not free to join Thomas again until his return to California after the tour. Thomas performed a series of concerts in Melbourne and Sydney, cities with a population of a million or more at that time, as well as Brisbane, whose population then numbered 300,000, Adelaide and Perth. He was surprised to find a woman seated in his room on the train to Melbourne, and asked the conductor if this was another example of Australian hospitality. The woman, who was the wife of a VIP on her way to Thomas's concert, turned out to have taken the room by mistake, so he spent the night in the compartment that had been reserved for her and wired Dorothy the next day that he had slept the previous night in the bedroom of an attractive woman.

In New Zealand, Thomas offered several concerts to full houses in Wellington and Auckland. Included with the program was a sheet of thirty or forty encore selections which the audience was invited to hand in with their requests circled. It is a remarkable example of the consummate concert artist that Thomas was that he was willing to oblige his audience in this way, completely confident that he could fulfill their requests without special rehearsal of the encore selections.

At one concert in Auckland, a dog wandered through an unguarded door and up the center aisle where he sat patiently for a little while before beginning to howl. While ushers herded the dog out of the hall, Thomas told the audience that he never knew what reaction he would get from canines. One dog at home didn't like his singing, but this dog wanted to sing along. However, he added, he could not accommodate his prospective partner because he was a tenor and — to the post- war audience beginning to grow impatient with labor strikes—"not in my union."

While he was received enthusiastically at these concerts, press reports show that critics asked the same questions Thomas had read at home for years: "Why do you include so much popular material in your programs?"

A full house at an Auckland, New Zealand, concert in 1947. (Courtesy of the Archives of the Peabody Institute of The Johns Hopkins University)

By this stage in his career, the answer was well rehearsed. "I want to sing what the public wants to hear." And they did want to hear it. Thomas netted approximately $100,000 from his 24-concert tour of the South Pacific.

As successful as this tour was, it did not open up a lucrative new summer market for Thomas. When he suggested scheduling a return visit, Marcks Levine, who had worked with Thomas for nearly twenty-five years, advised his client that from past experience, second tours in the Pacific were seldom as successful as the first. It was better to leave them cheering. What finally killed the possibility of a return tour was currency controls and restrictions that had been introduced in both Australia and New Zealand by 1950. Foreign performers were only allowed to take £1,000 from either country, and that would include fees for his management. Thomas was willing to consider investing his earnings in each country in order to remove his profits over a longer period, but was told that there were no good investment opportunities. The best investment to be made in those countries in 1950 would be land and sheep, for the advent of the Korean War brought high prices for products like lamb and wool. Both countries, however, discouraged foreign ownership of land.

Behind this letter, one can already hear the manager suggesting that the time was approaching when Thomas would have to bow off the concert stage. As popular as he had been for the past quarter century, Thomas, like all singers, had only so many notes to sing. There was no particularly marked vocal deterioration, though critics at a Hollywood Bowl *Traviata* in 1949 noted that he no longer had his top tones. By 1947 and 1948, the smoothness of the voice that one heard in 1938 was gone. Even allowing for the unreliable witness of transcriptions subject to variable recording speeds, recordings from Thomas's appearances at the Hollywood Bowl from these years show the base of the voice beginning to erode. One hears a darker voice, huskier and heavier, a voice overconfident of the audience's favor, still capable of delivering his trademark character songs with fun and relish, but no longer with the supple flexibility of old.

Though he may not have known it, Thomas's recording career was effectively over. His last commercial recording session with RCA came in March 1945, when he recorded "The Army Air Corps Song" and "Rodger Young," a nondescript Frank Loesser composition about a war hero. A recording of the old McCormack favorite, "Somewhere a Voice Is Calling," from that session, as well as two recordings from the following February, "A Spirit Flower" and "Panis Angelicus," were never released. Cambell-Tipton's "A Spirit Flower," sung with the King's Men, was one of Thomas's more interesting recorded art songs. With its somewhat stilted poetic language and allusion to a lover's death, it is textually and musically a difficult piece. It grows stronger on both levels in the final stanza, however, with a particularly effective melodic resolution that suits Thomas's voice quite well. In April, 1946, he used the RCA studios to produce a private recording of "Evening Star" from *Tannhäuser*. This ended his association with major recording studios.[21]

There were still a few good years left, however, for Thomas's concert career. Pausing for a few months' rest after returning from the South Pacific in August, 1947, Thomas began a 50-stop concert tour on January 4, 1948, on the *David Livingston*, a private railcar. On board were Dorothy, his new accompanist Richmond Gale, a maid, an assistant, probably Charlie Parker, and one of Marcks Levine's assistants, Larry Fitzgerald. The tour was intended to hearken back to the early days of the teens and twenties, when such accommodations were routine for the top musical artists. The Pullman Company provided a chef and steward to prepare and serve all meals— on linen tablecloths of course. The railcar, with its dining room, lounge, observation platform, and five sleeping rooms, each with separate baths, served as the party's hotel, and was parked each evening on quiet sidings with flowerbeds, away from the bustle and congestion of the main rail depots.

Starting in Los Angeles, each engagement averaged $2,250 in receipts. However, due to $9,000 in additional unanticipated charges by the railroads, the net proceeds from the tour were only $95,310. Nevertheless, in two back-to-back tours in the 1947–48 season, Thomas had netted approximately $200,000, not counting royalties from recordings, or income from radio broadcasts. His appearances on the *Telephone Hour* for holiday shows in July and December, 1948, and another the following February, paid $3,600 each, and that fee was subsequently raised to $4,000 per appearance. A radio broadcast from Carnegie Hall paid $4,500.

There were extensive discussions with the Shuberts in New York about a revival of *Apple Blossoms* with a three-month run on Broadway to be followed by a national tour. Big numbers were discussed: $50,000 a week, with Thomas getting from 7 to 10 percent or more of the house receipts in addition to his fee, if he put up some money for the production. Sol Hurok was to be the producer, Tyrone Guthrie the director, and Thomas could name any members of the cast he wanted. He was even going to get a block of fifty to a hundred tickets for each performance that he could sell or distribute to friends. But negotiations collapsed, and while Ezio Pinza would be recruited in 1950 to star in the Broadway production of *South Pacific*, and Lawrence Tibbett would be given the lead in *Fannie* on Broadway a few years later when his voice was in tatters, Thomas would never return to Broadway.

Another of Thomas's celebrated radio appearances from this period came on the *Bing Crosby Show* with fellow guest Al Jolson in a mock minstrel show on April 2, 1947. Jolson, who had been an enormous star on Broadway in the '20s, and made the first talking picture, had been in eclipse for a dozen years when the release of *The Jolson Story* in late 1946, followed by a series of radio appearances with Crosby, revived his popularity. Most of the show is taken up with banter between Crosby and Jolson, with Thomas performing "Gwine to Hebbin," a Negro dialect song that he had recorded for Victor in 1931. Thomas breaks up the commercial for Crosby's sponsor, Philco, with a variation on "Largo al factotum" from the *Barber of Seville*, and joins in the finale of "I'm Alabamy Bound." As opera artists go, Thomas's voice was not particularly large, but even in something as trivial as "Alabamy Bound," where he sounds like he is standing at the back of the stage, he easily soars above his partners.

In an odd way, the revival of Al Jolson's career was symbolic of the changing tastes that would make Thomas an anachronism. Interest in Jolson was based on nostalgia. He was a living relic of the now distant Jazz Age. The songs he sang in 1947 were the same songs he had performed twenty years earlier. Twenty years is not a long time. But the cultural dis-

With Al Jolson and Bing Crosby (from right) and an unidentified fourth performer on the Philco radio show, April, 1947. (Courtesy of the Archives of the Peabody Institue of The Johns Hopkins University)

tance between Coolidge and Truman was as great as the distance between Model T's and television; Mary Pickford and Betty Grable. Thomas had found occasion to recall the Jolson style seven years earlier in a great Cavalcade of Music concert in San Francisco on September 24, 1940. A host of stars preceded Thomas that night, from Judy Garland and Sigmund Romberg to Jerome Kern, Hoagie Carmichael, and William C. Handy. Thomas sang "Mighty Lik' a Rose," "Sally," "Old Man River," and "The Lord's Prayer," before Irving Berlin closed the show with "God Bless America." For his second number, Thomas picked a song from a Broadway show of 1928, "Sally from the Alley," and in reprising the verse, broke into a Jolson imitation that the audience loved. In 1940, Jolson was a long forgotten relic of old Broadway, but Thomas was able to evoke the days when Jolson was the king of the Great White Way.[22]

In his way, Thomas too was becoming a relic. He kept his repertoire more current than Jolson's, but audiences were no longer willing to pay to hear "Annie Laurie" or "Danny Deever." At the outset of his career in 1914, Adelin Fermin had told Thomas that you could not stand still in music, but must always go forward. By 1949-50, Thomas was deeply rooted in his repertoire and audiences were less willing to come to his concerts to hear the old songs. To a great extent, they were not willing to sit in a concert hall for *any* classical singer. They now found their entertainment on the radio or television. For a few more years, Big Bands would still have an audience, but by the mid–1950s, popular audience interest would shift to a new generation of crooners or rock and roll. By that time, the long tradition of major artists appearing in community concert series was dying. Today, concert artists might appear as guests on a symphonic program, but a full evening concert by a single artist, even in major cities, has become very rare.

Other colleagues from Thomas's years at the Met found new careers in the movies. Pinza, Melchior, and Helen Traubel all had brief film careers. Thomas, as we have seen, showed no interest in the movie opportunities that were offered him, and once, in a conversation with Darby, criticized Melchior for marketing himself as an entertainer. Thomas did keep up an active interest in the California Light Opera Company, for which he had long served as an artistic advisor. His last appearance with the company was in a San Francisco performance of *The Great Waltz* in 1953, with Dorothy Kirsten and a very young Florence Henderson. Each year from 1946 to 1954, he performed at the Easter Sunrise Service at the Actors Home in Hollywood, usually with the King's Men. Thomas also offered vocal lessons at a small studio on San Vincente Boulevard in Santa Monica and became Executive Director of the American Academy of the West in 1951. To deter idle auditions by those curious to meet a celebrity, Thomas charged a fifty-dollar audition fee that was credited toward the student's lessons if they were accepted for further study.

In an effort to open up a new market, Thomas teamed up in 1949 with the friends he had made during the Westinghouse program to record a series of hymns accompanied by Ken Darby and the King's Men, who were by now regulars on the very popular *Fibber McGee and Molly* radio show. Roy Urseth provided organ accompaniment. The company met each Tuesday and Thursday for three hours at the RCA studios, and despite Darby's recommendation that they record on tape, Thomas settled for the less expensive disc format. The sessions continued for nineteen-and-a-half weeks, though Darby noticed almost at once that there was no longer the same happy, cheerful spirit that had prevailed on the Westinghouse program.

At first he thought it might simply be the solemn nature of the music that was depressing spirits, but he came to see that Thomas was upset with their producer, Clare Olmstead. And the cause? Olmstead had declined to accept a job offer prior to this project, preferring to devote his energies to the recordings and then begin his retirement. Thomas was doing a kind of slow burn over a man of Olmstead's comparative youth choosing to retire rather than throw himself into new projects.

These hymns, over 250 packaged in groups of four, were designed to be sold to radio stations, and represent the largest group of recordings Thomas made in his career, far more than the total recorded for Brunswick and Victor together. The voice was still intact. It was larger, fuller, and heavier, but still capable of remarkably high tessitura in "Onward Christian Soldiers" or "A Mighty Fortress Is Our God." Unfortunately, the voice is poorly served by the heavy gray curtain of organ accompaniment, and, ultimately, by the mundane nature of the material itself. The recordings demonstrate why the purists were disappointed with Thomas the artist. Given the opportunity and resources to make long-playing recordings, he chose material that might bring a good financial return rather than music that would show his voice in the repertoire that had been largely ignored by Victor. During the war years, Thomas could have hired the Victor Young Orchestra for three-and-a-half hours of rehearsal and two hours of recording time for $2,000, which would have otherwise gone to the taxman. Now at the end of his career, he was content to settle into the mold the commercial world had made for him — as a performer of hymns, humorous songs, and Negro dialect songs— rather than preserving the legacy of the bel canto repertoire he had acquired from de Reszke and Fermin.[23]

The motive in producing the hymn recordings was clear — profit. But once again, timing and perhaps marketing conditions were unfavorable. By the time a distributor for these recordings was found, not a major label but a small-time operation in Texas, television was challenging radio's hold on the mass audience. Singers, from the operatic world to crooners, had been a staple of radio for years, but they were too static for the visual medium of television. It was several years before Clare Olmstead and Thomas recovered the investment they had made in the project, and the King's Men made almost nothing. Rather than facing the facts about the risks in this project, Thomas held a grudge against Olmstead for failing to market the project successfully. After Thomas's death, Dorothy asked Ken Darby's help in locating the master tapes of the recordings. Darby was able to track the tapes through Olmstead, to the Texas distributor, and right back to Dorothy's garage, where they had been resting safely for over a decade.

The early fifties saw the introduction of television, a medium that had little appeal for Thomas. He was invited to host *Visions in Music*, with an all girl orchestra, a reprise of the *Symphonettes* venture on the radio, but the project was mercifully abandoned after the pilot. Several other projects were developed, but Thomas hesitated to commit to the three days or more a week it would take for rehearsal and live performance in a television series. He preferred to keep his time free for recreation. What he was interested in was a program like the Westinghouse show, where he could walk into the studio for a brief rehearsal, show up for the live broadcast, and spend the rest of his time golfing. Despite a few appearances in 1950 on Ed Wynn's show, with his old friend from vaudeville and Broadway days, Thomas stuck to his familiar career as a concert artist.

By 1950, when he was in his early '60s, that career could be expected to be drawing to a close. Many of his younger contemporaries—Ponselle, Tibbett, Richard Crooks—had already left the concert stage. Melchior would soon be forced out of the Metropolitan, and Flagstad's performing years were also numbered. For Thomas, however, forces other than vocal decline were working to bring an end to his career. Tastes were changing.

A signal of this shift in popular taste came at a Town Hall concert in New York on November 17, 1950. For the first time in decades, a John Charles Thomas concert did not fill the house. It did not come close to filling the house. In fact, it lost money. Ticket receipts were $1,063, while costs for rental of the hall, advertising, program printing, and tickets were $1,172. Thomas split the loss with his management, and in a friendly, but frank business letter, Marcks Levine attributed the disappointing house to the outbreak of the Korean War. Between the lines, however, one reads the manager's understanding that Thomas's audience appeal was waning fast. This was effectively the end of his annual concert tours. Just as his Metropolitan career had ended abruptly, with no gala farewell, and his recording career concluded with no final album, so a concert career of over thirty years simply died away. Henceforth, Thomas confined himself to performances in Easton for the benefit of a children's wing of the hospital, and a few concerts each year in California and on the West Coast.

There is a desultory correspondence between Levine and Thomas on concert possibilities, but it was clear that Thomas was no longer interested in pursuing an intense concert schedule. No mention is made of the accompanist issue, but the absence of a pillar like Hollister must have contributed to Thomas's loss of interest. He recognized that the shift in musical taste might have long-term consequences. When Merle Armitage first expressed an interest in writing a biography of his old friend in 1951, the baritone was enthusiastic and grateful, admitting that he was afraid he would be entirely forgotten.

As luck would have it, just as Thomas's popularity and earnings were in decline, he became embroiled in a tax dispute with the IRS, in which he was assessed tens of thousands of dollars in fines. Like many other highly paid artists of the time — Abbot and Costello, and Preston Sturgess come to mind — Thomas could have faced public exposure, confiscation of his property, and liens on future earnings. He was able to borrow the funds needed to placate the IRS from his mother, who had carefully saved the money her son had given her during his many years of high earnings. But the sting of this embarrassment added gall to Thomas's bitterness about big government. We do not know the full impact this affair had on his finances then or in subsequent years, though 1949 was one of his best earning years as a result of the very successful tour of Australia and New Zealand and the private rail tour of the United States. While his concert activity gradually diminished, his income was still substantial through at least 1953.

In this period too, Thomas was approached by friends to consider running for the U.S. Senate — it is impossible to say now whether from Maryland or California. Merle Armitage recalled the boost this gave Thomas's ego for a time, until they stopped in a diner one night and watched while the customers listened respectfully to a Thomas recording playing on the radio. "Now wouldn't you rather be admired as a singer than as a politician?" his old friend asked. Thomas agreed. In fact, he had a loathing of politics and politicians that only grew in later years.

In 1952, Thomas sang at the GOP convention in Chicago in July, and was joined by the King's Men in several campaign appearances for Eisenhower throughout California. Recordings of his appearance for the General in Baltimore, where he was joined by Rosa Ponselle in an obviously unrehearsed rendition of "Swanee River," show the voice still intact, but duller.[24] Despite Thomas's fading power as a concert draw, his management was still able to book him for sixty concerts in the 1952–53 season.

As both of their mothers aged, the Thomases' lives began to center less in the East and increasingly in California. In 1945, the Palm Beach estate was sold, although the Dobynes continued to winter in the resort, and it was there that "Boss" Dobyne died. Mother Thomas made extended seasonal visits to her son in California, but kept her home in Towson. She died there on Easter Sunday, 1953, at the age of 85, with John Charles at her bedside. Thereafter, Thomas's ties to Maryland faded.

What was he to do after his singing career? Today, one can imagine his agent pitching the idea of Thomas as host of a gourmet cooking show for television. There was still some allure in the name of a fading celebrity in the 1950s too. In return for the use of his name in promotions, and a small financial investment, Thomas had become involved with Newt Bass and fifteen other investors in promoting the development of a resort community in the high desert community of Apple Valley, northeast of Los Angeles.

John Charles with his mother, Dora Thomas. Thomas was a devoted son who regularly signed off his radio performances with "Good night, mother." (Courtesy of the Archives of the Peabody Institute of The Johns Hopkins University)

Apple Valley had been founded in the 1920s in hopes, as its name suggested, of becoming a successful orchard settlement. That failed, as did several efforts to establish it as a resort. In the aftermath of the Second World War, with the boom in home building throughout southern California, and particularly the recognition of Palm Springs as a getaway and

With Dorothy under a Joshua tree near Apple Valley, California.

resort for the Hollywood elite, Bass, a developer and oilman (unrelated to the Texas Basses), began promoting Apple Valley as a high desert resort with a perfect climate. The community was named in a popular film, *The McConnell Story*, starring Alan Ladd in 1955. In later years, Roy Rogers and Dale Evans would settle there. But it was a hard sell. One man who worked

for Thomas aboard the *Masquereder* was persuaded to come out and help
the Thomases relocate, but turned down a proposition to build a house
in the area for himself. He remembers looking around the stark desert
environment and asking, "Why would I want to give up the Chesapeake
for this?"

Apple Valley's climate may be comfortably cool most of the year, but
it was then little more than a windswept wilderness at the end of what Ken
Darby called "a long jackrabbit road" from Los Angeles. Beyond Apple
Valley was Barstow, desert, and the new gambling resort of Las Vegas, then
just in its infancy.[25] Modern air travel would put Las Vegas near the center of a transportation perimeter that included Phoenix, Los Angeles, and
San Francisco. But for the masses, sunny Los Angeles in the days when
smog was still unknown beckoned far more than the desert.

Each of the Bass partners received three parcels of property drawn by
lots. Thomas drew the only lot that had a building on it. He subsequently
won additional properties in a card game. He sold his Mandeville Canyon
home to June Alyson and Dick Powells' in 1953 or 1954 for a reported
$200,000, and moved into the Powell's home until his new Apple Valley
home was completed. When that took longer than originally planned,
Thomas moved into a more modest home in Apple Valley. After Mrs.
Dobyne died on January 24, 1955, the Thomases sold the Easton property,
again, for a figure reputed to be in the neighborhood of $200,000.

The new house Thomas built, one of the largest in the community,
was complete with a small swimming pool and a wine cellar. It was the
only home he ever built, and he proved to be a demanding and impatient
client. He complained frequently to the architect about delays in construction and the poor quality of workmanship in the house. In fact, it was a
very well constructed home with many fine custom-finished elements that
would not be found in other homes of that period or this. Given the serious labor shortages in California, particularly in the outback where
Thomas had beached himself, he was lucky to acquire the quality home he
did.

"It's funny," Thomas wrote soon after moving to Apple Valley, "after
all the years of living near the sea, I don't want to be anywhere now, but
right here."[26] Although he continued to consider offers that came his way,
he was now happily settled and begrudged the time away from Apple Valley that concerts required. A curious expression of his semi-retired lifestyle
was the "downshifting" that occurred in Thomas's wardrobe. Always a
dapper dresser in his Broadway years, and resplendent in brightly colored
sporty ensembles in the forties, by the time he moved to Apple Valley he
had settled into Western shirts and would eventually relax in bib overalls.

Relaxing at home on Mandeville Canyon Road, 1954. (Courtesy of Jacques Fievez).

On April 28, 1955, John Charles Thomas made his last professional public appearance at Dickinson College in Carlyle, Pennsylvania, near his birthplace and childhood home in the mining country of south central Pennsylvania. Thus, after forty years as a major artist, Thomas closed his career and faded away. After 1955, Thomas confined his public appearances to programs with the Apple Valley Romanies, the third branch of his amateur choral group that he launched in his new home. He made little effort to maintain links with Hollywood celebrities. When Victor Young died suddenly of a heart attack in 1956, neither Thomas nor Darby attended the funeral.

Once settled in Apple Valley, Thomas dabbled in various business ventures, such as promoting Apple Valley in brochures, operating a franchise for the distribution of automobile seatbelts, and managing the local KAVR radio station, in which he had a one-quarter interest. His management skills did not lead to profits for the station, however, and Newt Bass replaced him with another partner, with Thomas retaining a nominal role for a few months. Correspondence with one of the station's staff suggests that Thomas could be a bully in dealing with employees, and did not hesitate to throw

Thomas (far right) with a group of Romanie choristers in the 1950s. The chorus was founded in Palm Beach during the Depression as a way to give experience to aspiring young singers. (Courtesy of the Archives of the Peabody Institute of The Johns Hopkins University)

his weight around. Most of his time, however, was now devoted to golf and the annual gatherings of the Bohemian Club in their redwood grove north of San Francisco.

In 1957, Thomas made a final recording, "Golfer's Lament," written by Albert Hay Mallotte that was released as a 45 rpm single. There is little left of the familiar, full-bodied baritone voice in the recording. While the ditty was fun, it was not a commercial success. Thomas made two appearances on the *Groucho Marx Show* December 2 and 9 that year to plug the record, but made news instead by inveighing against rock and roll. He declared that he would rather crawl over broken glass on his hands and knees than listen to this new music.

Thomas continued to make occasional appearances with the King's Men at country clubs in Los Angeles and southern California, in part to prepare himself for a prospective television series. As late as February 15, 1959, when he was approaching 70, Thomas still offered a full program of classical songs as well as familiar lighter works at a concert in Apple Valley.

With his concert career over, and his Apple Valley investments lying fallow in empty lots, Thomas generated some income through vocal lessons. Among his most famous students were George Beverly Shea. While he did all that he could to advance the careers of his students, appearing with them in concerts, and recommending others to Marcks Levine, there were also annoyances with students who did not pay their tuition, or who wanted to debate the proper technique of breathing through the diaphragm.[27]

During the 1958 Christmas holidays, Dorothy and John Charles took a cruise to Hawaii. Thomas slipped one day on the ship, bruising his hip and injuring his back. A chiropractor in Hawaii got his back in place again so that John Charles and Dorothy were playing golf after a few days on the Islands. On his return to California, however, he decided to have a full physical at the Scripps Clinic in La Jolla.

Thomas entered the clinic in March, and all the tests turned out negative except for suspicious results in the intestine. On March 18, exploratory surgery was performed at the UCLA Medical Center, but within six days an infection had developed which blocked the colon and required the insertion of a temporary colostomy. Thomas became deeply depressed with his condition, and required psychological consultations and medication for a time, but gradually recovered his good spirits. In November, 1959, doctors attempted to restore Thomas's use of his colon, but discovered cancer in the rectum. Thomas remained remarkably self-possessed in a letter he wrote Newt Bass from his hospital bed in the UCLA Medical Center on November 18, 1959. "It isn't all very pretty, and hasn't worked out as we had hoped, but as you said the other day—'We're out here playing golf, aren't we?'"

He looked forward to getting back on the golf course. He noted in other correspondence that in removing his rectal sphincter muscles, the colostomy had made it impossible for him to sing properly, as he used to rely on that muscle to provide a base for his diaphragm's control of his breathing. Sometime after the operation, Darby joined him once at the Los Angeles Country Club where Thomas sang his signature "I Love Life" and "Marcheta." Unable to sustain his breath line, Thomas began to perspire during the second song, and dropped to a soft-voiced version of the phrases he used to roll out in full voice. The audience applauded enthusiastically, and Thomas wondered later to Darby whether he might have been singing the song the wrong way all these years.[28]

The operation caused him to lose weight, and photographs from his final months show an older, frailer looking man, his hair, now quite white, close cropped in a crewcut. On a visit to Apple Valley in June, 1960, Darby, who had retrieved many discs of the Westinghouse rehearsal sessions, offered to give Thomas a tape recorder and copies of recordings from the show, but Thomas's deterioration was progressing too fast for him to complete the process of making the tapes. As the end approached, a few friends came to Apple Valley to bid him farewell. "It's been fun" were his parting words to the Budds of San Francisco, who saw him when he was bedridden. On December 11, 1960, Thomas fell into a coma and was pronounced dead thirty hours later, at 6:30 P.M., December 13, at the UCLA Medical Center.

It had been a bad year for baritones. Leonard Warren (1911–1960) had collapsed on stage during a performance at the Metropolitan in March. Lawrence Tibbett had died in July after a fall at his home, possibly due to intoxication. The operatic world lost tenor Jussi Bjoerling as well in September. Although Thomas was already fading from public memory, obituaries were duly saddened that his vibrant personality had passed from the scene.

At the funeral service in St. Timothy's Episcopal Church in Apple Valley, Albert Hay Malotte played "The Lord's Prayer" on the organ. The body was cremated and privately interred at Mt. View cemetery in San Bernadino.

Within a few months, Thomas's wine cellar was sold to a local restaurant. In 1962 his papers and music library were transferred to the Peabody in Baltimore.

As wrenching as her husband's final months were for Dorothy, another unpleasant surprise lay in store for her as she tried to organize her finances after her husband's death. After decades of high living, she found that John Charles had "lived it up." Their bank account statement showed a balance of just $1,000. How Thomas spent the money is a mystery. True, everyone who knew him commented on his lavish spending. But he was also a savvy investor with relatively frugal habits. For most of his life he had lived with his in-laws. He made $3 bets on golf games. He and Dorothy did not have a large retinue of servants, and the buying power of his income, $300,000 a year or more during the Depression, was enormous. It may have been his knowledge of the penury he was about to leave Dorothy in that caused Thomas's depression in the last months of his life.

Dorothy's only other assets were the Apple Valley lots, which were not particularly marketable. She had an income from a trust set up after her father's death, but that income had inexplicably begun to decline, even as the stock market began to rise through the late fifties.

What happened to Dorothy's money? When Henry Koehler died, Dorothy's mother had permitted George Dobyne to establish a trust for the brewer's fortune. Besides his wife and stepdaughter, "Boss" had included his own children as beneficiaries of the trust, and this act alone had cost Dorothy and her mother millions over the years. After Boss's death in 1947, management of her trust, as well as her mother's funds, passed to Dorothy's stepbrother, Robert Dobyne. Over the years, payments from Dorothy's trust declined from quarterly payments to just three annual payments, and then even these grew smaller and smaller. An investigation of Robert Dobyne's financial management revealed that for thirty years he had been systematically siphoning money from the trust funds into his own Swiss bank account. When the embezzlement was discovered, Dobyne committed suicide. After a lifetime of good living in Beverly, Massachusetts, Palm Beach and Easton, and after discovering that her husband of 35 years had left her with nothing, Dorothy now found that she had no money left. Hence her interest within a year or two of her husband's death in locating the master recordings of the hymns, in hopes of generating some income. In 1970, she told Ken Darby that she did not have the money to re-carpet the house. Like her mother and grandmother before her, she had been betrayed by men she trusted.

There were reissues of some Thomas recordings on LP by RCA, and Darby managed to get an LP released with some twenty hymns from the 1948 sessions. By now, however, Thomas's recordings were confined to the historical bins in record stores. Most reissues contained his popular material like "Home on the Range," "The Lord's Prayer," and "Boots and Saddles." To this day, the great operatic recordings have never been widely reissued, and the surviving recordings from radio broadcasts, notably those with Victor Young's orchestra for the Westinghouse show, are unavailable for domestic commercial release because they were produced for the Armed Services.

Ultimately, there is no reasoning with history, and no retort. But it is still curious to find Thomas neglected at the beginning of a new century when recordings of contemporaries like John McCormack, Lawrence Tibbett, Richard Crooks, or even more obscure figures are reissued in abundance.

Charlie Parker did not long survive his lifelong friend. Dorothy died in August, 1981. Carroll Hollister survived John Charles Thomas by 23 years, and passed away in 1983. After leaving Los Angeles in 1945, Hollister accompanied Tenor James Melton and mezzo-soprano Gladys Swarthout, before falling victim to the blacklist. From the early fifties, he supported himself as a teacher for aspiring piano accompanists and as a vocal coach from his apartment on West 78th Street in Manhattan. He remained active in a number of front organizations, and supported Paul Robeson's efforts to get his passport restored. Hollister hosted a party for Robeson at his New York apartment in May of 1958. The FBI kept notes on the hundred or more people in attendance, as they did on all of Hollister's vocal students. That was two years after the suppression of the Hungarian uprising by Soviet troops, but Hollister was still loyal to the Party. He was asked to testify before the House Un-American Activities Committee in 1953, 1958, and again in 1962, but invoked his rights under the First and Fifth Amendments, and refused. In May of 1967, he traveled to Bulgaria and the Soviet Union with his second wife on a concert tour. The following summer, the Soviet Union sent its tanks into Czechoslovakia to crush the effort to reform communism in that country.

In all those years, as the dream of communism turned into a grim parade of aging dictators, the accompanist may sometimes have recalled the words of Gérard's monologue, "Nemico della patria," from *Andrea Chenier*, which he had so often heard Thomas sing in concerts. In it, the revolutionary reflects cynically about the way the Revolution had betrayed its ideals:

> How have I fallen from my glorious pathway
> Once like a line of radiant light it lay before me!
> To convert the hearts of all my fellow comrades...
> Make this world a Paradise where men should be as
> Gods divine. To bind all comrades in one vast
> embrace

Ken Darby, the last keeper of the flame, died in 1992.

One is reluctant to say that there was a tragic element in Thomas's career since he enjoyed enormous popularity and success throughout his career. Popular taste turned away from his style of singing just at the time his vocal decline would have brought a natural end to his career. But it is disappointing that so fine a singer was never able to find an audience or a medium that fulfilled his artistic potential. There is little evidence that he felt any sense of underachievement. He certainly did not dwell on it. Beneath the buoyant bravado of his persona, however, was a deeper disappointment. It came through at the death of Herbert Witherspoon, in his frustration when he finally retired from the Metropolitan, and in his break with Hollister. Those who knew him well during the '40s and '50s recall that he was quite happy singing the popular material he was associated with rather than the art songs and French bel canto repertoire in which he excelled. He never hesitated to take up a light opera role for a good fee. He would not have recorded 156 hymns unless he really enjoyed it.

Ironically, Thomas's career was eroded by prosperity. Tastes changed in the early and mid–1950s when Americans, and particularly young Americans, began spending their entertainment dollars on new popular singers, from Frank Sinatra to Perry Como and Tennessee Ernie Ford. The singing style was different, and so was the music. Composers stopped trying to write art songs when they could make better money writing splashy popular hits for the bobby-soxer audience that now controlled the popular music market.

The career of John Charles Thomas is a metaphor for American entertainment culture. With all the trappings of sophistication and high artistic standards surrounding classical music, a great part of the enterprise is, in the end, just business. It is hard to argue, certainly during the Depression years but even earlier, that RCA Victor was making an effort to record the best music by the best artists. One can listen to vintage recordings from the acoustic or early electric era, such as the Kreisler and Zimbalist recordings of Bach, the Caruso-Homer duet "Gia sacerdoti" from *Aida*, any number of McCormack or Ponselle recordings, and recognize that these are real masterpieces. Ultimately, however, the enterprise was purely commercial — hence Caruso's recording of "Over There," and McCormack's many popular songs.

As a recording artist, Thomas had the potential to cross the classical-popular music barrier, as he did in recordings of "Home on the Range," "Green Eyed Dragon," and Jerome Kern standards. But this is material that can only be elevated so far — the range of unrecorded material in his repertoire, from the bel canto operatic arias to American art songs, remained largely untested for simple lack of commercial promise. The disappointment is that in the end, Thomas accepted these rules of the game. He never attempted to leave more of a mark with operatic recordings. Instead he accepted engagements in *Apple Blossoms*, or Gilbert and Sullivan, and finally chose to record hymns, simply to collect high fees. Ultimately, it is impossible to say whether he was a classical singer trying to reach a popular audience, or a popular singer trying to keep one foot in the world of classical music. To Thomas, this was a false issue, and, to a degree, a distinction that would not even have been drawn prior to the invention of amplified sound. He was a singer who worked hard at his craft and tried to adapt to most musical tastes within his range. That he did so, and brought so much of his personality to whatever he sang, is the mark of his special talent. He believed in his music. Listeners who find his music today or in the future will always hear that authenticity in his recordings.

Thomas certainly brought a great deal to opera. His irrepressible

Figaro was inimitable. His Germont was a model of conflicted parent-hood, his Tonio and Iago appropriately malicious. He brought an American character and humanity to these roles, and made them so accessible that he could easily move from one to another and carry the audience with him because they could identify the Thomas personality in the aria as easily as in the popular song.

It is that personality that is so intriguing in his recordings. He is one of those rare artists of whom listeners are always curious to hear how he will interpret a role or song. There are few surprises in a Caruso or Pavarotti recording, but Thomas's recordings always have his individual stamp. No one else growls as gruffly in the "Prologue" from *I Pagliacci*, or in the opening of the Nile scene in *Aida*. Has another Figaro ever whistled so invitingly in the "Largo al factotum"?

When Thomas began his career, the two great stars of the musical world were Enrico Caruso at the Metropolitan and Al Jolson on Broadway. Thomas tried very hard, and almost succeeded, in matching the fame of both men in his own career, in being recognized as both a great opera star and a leading popular entertainer. It is a role that sounds bizarre to us today, when the barriers between both performers and audiences in popular and classical music have become so pronounced. In the America of the 1930s and '40s, however, composers, performers, and audiences wanted to move comfortably from one style to another.

To some degree, almost all major musical figures of the period straddled the popular and classical world. Leopold Stokowski and Sergei Prokofiev collaborated with Walt Disney; Benny Goodman performed Mozart and Weber; Hollywood produced films for a popular market with Deanna Durbin, Nelson Eddy, Jeanette MacDonald, and Rise Stevens singing "classical" music. Vincent Youmanns, Ferde Grofé, and, above all, George Gershwin succeeded in writing music for both styles. The life and recordings of John Charles Thomas demonstrate how well one artist satisfied both audiences.

Appendix A: Discography

The following discography includes only the identifying number of the recording's initial issue, not subsequent reissues. It is also arranged by date within categories, such as 12-inch and 10-inch. Only the one Edison recording of Thomas in song is listed, not his six other "explanatory talks" on the recordings of other singers.

A more comprehensive discography, including many LP reissues of Thomas's records, was published by Charles A. Morgan in *The Record Collector*, March, 1979, pp. 15-31.

Edison Diamond Disc
By the Dreamy Susquehanna Shore serial no. 3254 August 26, 1914, unpublished

Rex Records
5373A Somewhere a Voice Is Calling 1915

Lyric Records
7016A *Forza del Destino* Sollenne in quest ora Mario Rodolfi (Chamlee) and Enrico Martini (Thomas) 1916

Victor Trial Pressings
Until
Chorus of Thy Heart My Prize November 11, 1915
Invictus
Pagliacci Prologue November 19, 1919
The Broken Heart listed as recorded by John F. Thomas, November 8, 1921

Vocalion

12 inch Acoustics

6510	Danny Deever	November, 1920
7691	*Elijah:* It Is Enough	June, 1921
8142	The Lost Chord	October, 1921

12 inch Acoustics

8709	*Pagliacci:* Prologo	January, 1922
8956	The Holy City	May, 1922
10806	Les Rameaux-The Palms	January, 1923

10 inch Acoustics

5959	*Apple Blossoms—* Little Girls Goodbye	May 1920
5961	*Apple Blossoms—* You Are Free w. Lucille Rene sop.	May 1920
6043	In the Gloaming	June, November, 1920
6532	Little Mother of Mine	November, 1920
6535	Sweetest Story Ever Told	November, 1920
6551	Out Where the West Begins	November, 1920
6552	Abide with Me	November, 1920
6611	Mother o' Mine	December,1920
7734	Tommy Lad	June, 1921
7736	On the Road to Mandalay	June, 1921
8111	The Love Letter	November, 1921
8601	Maytime: Will You Remember	December, 1921
8955	Vale-Farewell	May, 1922
10108	Absent	October, 1922
10110	My Message	October, 1922
10133	Passing By	October, 1922
10184	Tally Ho	November, 1922
10843	Nichavo-Nothing Matters	February, 1923
11701	Where Is My Wandering Boy Tonight	July, 1923

12 inch Electrics

N-12476	Nocturne-Song of Love	December, 1923
N-12519	*Bohemian Girl:* The Heart Bowed Down	January, 1924

10 inch electrics

N-11700	Trees (Tours)	July, 1923
N-11711	Love's Old Sweet Song	July, 1923
N-11714	If You Only Knew	August, 1923
N-12517	Marcheta	January, 1924
N-12678	At Dawning	February, 1924
N-11681	Uncle Rome the Old Boatman	July, 1923
N-11703	One Sweetly Solemn Thought	August, 1923
N-11701	Where Is My Wandering Boy Tonight	August, 1923
N-13201	Darling Nellie Gray	May 1924
N-13871	*The Fortune Teller:* Gypsy Love Song	October, 1924

Brunswick

10 inch

Undated, possibly 1924

X 15483	*Ballo in Maschera:* Eri tu
X 15526	*Herodiade:* Vision fugitive
X 15591	*Forza del Destino:* Solenne in quest ora with Chamlee unpub.
X 15640	*Forza del Destino:* Solenne in quest ora with Chamlee unpublished
10151	Mother o' Mine
10151	Smilin' Through
10157	Rose Marie: Rose Marie
10157	My Dream Girl
10167	At Dawning
10167	In the Gloaming
10208	Little Mother of Mine
10208	Daddy

electrics

Undated 1925–1929

10218	The Lost Chord
10218	The Crucifix
15722	Smilin' Through
15724	Mother o' Mine
15720	Roses of Picardy
15737	Your Smiling Eyes
15789	Falling in Love with You
15791	Calling Me Back to You
15832	Abide with Me
15854	Where Is My Wandering Boy Tonight
15715	My Message
15740	Nocturne — A Song of Love
15167	Duna
15748	The Fortune Teller: Gypsy Love Song
28125	At Dawning
25300	In the Gloaming
14085	Nichavo — Nothing Matters
14053	Rolling Down to Rio

RCA Victor

May 26, 1931 New York, Studio 1 N. Shilkret, orch.

B or C as first or second letter signifies 10 or 12 inch recording respectively

BRC 69654-1	Trees (Rasbach)
BRC 69655-1	Home on the Range

Oct 7, 1931 New York, Studio 1 Lester Hodges, Piano

BRC 70273-1	Mah Lindy Lou
BRC 70274-1	Gwine to Hebb'in

February 6, 1932 New York, Studio 1 N. Shilkret, orch.

CRC 71822-2	*Tannhäuser:* O du mein holder abendstern
CSHQ 71823-1	*Tannhäuser:* O du mein holder abendstern unpub.
CRC 71824-1	*La Traviata:* Di Provenza
CRC 71825-1	*La Traviata:* Di Provenza unpub.

May 19, 1932 New York Studio 2 N. Shilkret orch.

BSHQ 72806-1	Sylvia
BSHQ 72807-1	Showboat: Ol' Man River
CSHQ 71825-3	La Traviata: Di Provenza

July 25, 1933 Hollywood W. Garroway piano

PBS 68501-1	The Trumpeter
PBS 68502-1	Sheila
PBS 68503-1	Mattinata (Leoncavallo)
PBS 68503-2	Mattinata unpublished
PBS 68504-1	My Message (d'Hardelot)

November 23, 1933 New York studio 2 C. Hollister piano

BS 78581-1 2&2A	The Green Eyed Dragon
BS 78582-1 2&2A	Steal Away

January 12, 1934 Hollywood C. Hollister piano

PBS 68695-1 2&3	Curly Locks
PBS 68696-1 2&3	Down to de Rivah unpublished

January 14, 1934 Hollywood N. Finton orch.

PBS 68697-1 &2	*Herodiade:* Vision Fugitive
PBS 68698-1 &2	*Hamlet:* O Vin Dissipe la Tristesse

March 26, 1934 New York Studio 2 C. Hollister piano

BS 81979-1 &2	Sailormen
BS 81980-1 &2	Down to de Rivah

October 31, 1934 New York C. Hollister piano

BS 95686-1 1A&2	Just for Today
BS 95687-1 1A&2	The Farmer's Pride

October 31, 1934 New York C. Hollister piano

BS 95688-1 &1A	Take Me Back to My Boots and Saddles
BS 95689-1 1A&2	The Lord's Prayer

May 26, 1938 Hollywood C. Hollister piano

PBS 019287-1 2&3	Children of Men
PBS 019288-1 &2	My Homeland
PBS 019289-3 1&2	Annie Laurie
PBS 019290-2 &1	I Love Life
PBS 019291-2 &1	I Heard a Forest Praying

May 27, 1938 Hollywood C. Hollister piano

PBS 019294-1 &2	Ein Schwan (Grieg) unpublished
PBS 019295-1	Sing a Song of Sixpence
PCS 019296-3 1&2	Requiem du Coeur
PCS 019297-1	Non e Ver (Mattei) unpublished

May 31, 1938 Hollywood C. Hollister piano

PBS 01929801 &2	Mattinata (Tosti)
PBS 019299-2 &1	To My Mother
PCS 019300-	David and Goliath

June 2, 1938 Hollywood C. Hollister piano

PCS 019309-2 &1	Au Pays

November 30, 1938

BS 030512-1	Ruhe meine Seele (R. Strauss) unpublished
BS 030513-1 &2	Gebet (J. Marx) unpublished
BS 030514-1 2&3	Der Ton (J. Marx) unpublished
CS 030515-1 &2	Lord Randall

March 26, 1939 Philadelphia, Academy of Music, E. Ormandy Philadelphia Orchestra

BS 035410-1 &1A	In Questa Tomba Oscura unpublished
BS 035411-1 &1A	O Del Mio Amato Ben unpublished
BS 035412-1 &1A	*La Traviata:* Di Provenza unpublished
BS 035413-1 1A,2&2A	*Zaza:* Piccola Zingara unpublished
CS 035414-1 &1A	*Barbiere de Siviglia:* Largo al Factotum unpublished
CS 035415-1 &1A	*Herodiade:* C'en est fait ... Salomé demande unpublished

August 17, 1939 Hollywood, Victor Symphony, F. Tours

PCS 036424-2 &1   O del mio amato ben
PCS 036425-2 &1   Chanson Triste

August 18, 1939 Hollywood, Victor Symphony, F. Tours

PCS 036426-1 2&3   In questa tomba oscura
PCS 036427-5 3&4   *Zaza:* Zaza piccola zingara
PCS 036426-6 4&5   In questa tomba oscura
PCS 036429-1   *La Traviata:* Di Provenza
PCS 036430-3   *Herodiade:* Cen est fait.
                          .Salomé demande

August 19, 1939 Hollywood, Victor Symphony, F. Tours

PCS 036432-3 4&5   *Andrea Chenier:* Nemico della Patria
PCS 035422-2 &1   My Journey's End
PCS 036434-3   *Barbiere de Siviglia:* Largo al Factotum

August 21, 1939 Hollywood, C. Hollister piano

PBS 036435-2 &1   When Children Pray
PBS 036436-2 &1   Your Presence

August 22, 1939 Hollywood, C. Hollister piano

PBS 036438-1   Come to Me in My Dreams
PBS 036439-1   Comus: Preach Not Me Your Musty Rules/
                          A Little Song of Life (Malotte)
PBS 036440-1   Drink to Me Only with Thine Eyes
PBS 036441-3   O Men from the Fields

August 23, 1939 Hollywood, Victor Symphony, F. Tours

PCS 036446-2   *Otello:* Credo in un Dio crudel
PCS 036447-2   Non e ver
PCS 036448-1&2   Beau Soir unpublished
PCS 036449-1&2   *Pagliacci:* Prologo unpublished

August 24, 1939 Hollywood, Victor Symphony, F. Tours

PCS 036451-3 1&2   *Gypsy Baron:* Love Can Be
                          Dreamed / Mine Alone
PCS 036452-1&2   Bendemeer's Stream
PCS 036453-1   *Gypsy Baron:* Open Road

March 23, 1940 New York studio 2 N. Shilkret orch.

CS 048417-1 2&2A   *Iolanthe:* Love Unrequited unpublished
CS 048414-1 1A,2&2A   *Iolanthe:* None Shall Part Us from

March 23, 1940 New York studio 2 N. Shilkret orch.

	Each Other, If We're Weak Enough to Tarry both unpublished
CS 048415-1,1A	*HMS Pinafore:* Fair Noon to Thee unpublished
CS 048416-1 1A&2	*HMS Pinafore:* When I Was a Lad unpublished
BS 048418-1,1A	Dedication unpublished

March 18, 1941 New York, Lotus Club 110 W. 57th St. N. Shilkret and Lady Garment Workers Union chorus dir. S. Rey

CS 062575-1,1A	I Hear America Singing
CS 062576-1,1A,2&2A	I Hear America Singing
CS 062577-1,1A,2&2A	I Hear America Singing
CS 062578-1,1A,2,2A	I Hear America Singing

March 19, 1941 New York, Lotus Club N. Shilkret orch.

BS 062579-1,2&2A	Swing Low, Sweet Chariot
BS 062580-2,1,1A&2A	Bluebird of Happiness
BS 062581-1	The Last Time I Saw Paris
BS 062582-1,1A,2&2A	Ev'ry Time I Feel de Spirit

March 20, 1941 New York, Lotus Club C. Hollister organ

BS 060986-1,1A,2&2A	Tell Me the Story of Jesus
BS 060987-1,1A,2&2A	Softly and Tenderly

April 28, 1941

PCS 161201-1&2	*The Chocolate Soldier:* My Hero
PCS 161202-1	*The Chocolate Soldier:* Sympathy, That Would Be Lovely, Forgive w. Hope Manning unpublished

August 8, 1941 New York, Lotus Club Victor Symphony Orchestra C. O'Connell

CS 066737-2	There Is No Death
CS 066738-2	*HMS Pinafore:* When I Was a Lad

January 8, 1942 Hollywood C. Hollister piano

PBS 072010-1	Fulfillment
PBS 072011-1	Christmas Candle

January 8, 1942 Hollywood C. Hollister piano

PCS 072012-	E'en as a Lovely Flower unpublished
PCS 072013-1	Among the Living unpublished
PCS 072014-1	Shallow Brown unpublished
PCS 072015-1	Blow Me Eyes unpublished

January 13, 1942 Hollywood C. Hollister piano

PBS 072029-1	Where My Caravan Has Rested
PBS 072030-1	Gentle Annie
PBS 072031-1	In the Gloaming
PBS 072032-1	I Passed by Your Window unpublished

January 14, 1942 Hollywood

PCS 072033-1&2	Music in the Air: The Song Is You
PCS 072037-1	*Blossom Time:* Once to Every Heart
PCS 072038-1	*Chocolate Soldier:* Song in My Heart
PCS 072041-1	*Very Warm for May:* All the Things You Are

December 13, 1944 Hollywood, V. Young orch. K. Darby chorus

| D4-RB-1059-1 | *Oklahoma:* O What a Beautiful Morning |
| D4-RB-1060-1 | *Oklahoma:* Kansas City |

March 26, 1945 Hollywood, V. Young orch. K. Darby chorus

D5-RB-1042-1	Rodger Young
D5-RB-1043-2	The Army Air Corps
D5-RB-1044-1&2	Somewhere a Voice Is Calling unpublished

February 8, 1946 Hollywood, V. Young orch. K. Darby chorus

D6-RC-5502-1&1A	A Spirit Flower unpublished
D6-RC-5503-1&1A	Panis Angelicus unpublished
VP-D3-MC173-1C	Home on the Range & Boots & Saddles V disc
VP-D487-D4-7C-52-1A	Going Home (Dvořák) V disc

1945 NBC Hollywood, V. Young orch. K. Darby chorus

| HD5-MC-6154-1E | Ave Maria (Schubert) private printing |

Apple Valley Music Co.

April 13, 1946

HD6-MC-523   Evening Star (Olmstead) unpublished
Golfer's Lament (Malotte)

Rockhill Recording Company

1957

undated   One World (O'Hara)

Appendix B:
Operatic Appearances at
La Monnaie, Brussels,
1925–1930

The year is followed by Thomas's number of appearances in that season. He always played the same role, which is listed in the left-hand column with the first occurrence of that opera; the number of times he performed a role at La Monnaie follows in parentheses. Thomas often performed in different operas on consecutive dates, an impressive feat by any measure. These are marked with an asterisk (*) on the second date.

1925 (13)

Saturday, August 1, 1925	Herod in *Herodiade* Debut (8)
Friday, September 4, 1925	Amonosoro in *Aida* (7)
Saturday, September 26,	*Aida*
Saturday, October 31	*Aida*
Thursday, November 19	Amfortas in *Parsifal* (16)
Sunday, November 22 matinee	*Aida*
*Monday November 23	*Parsifal*
Thursday, November 26	*Parsifal*
Wed December 2	*Parsifal*
Monday, December 7	*Parsifal*
Friday December 11	*Aida*
Wednesday, December 16	*Parsifal*
Monday, December 21	*Parsifal*

1926 (71)

Sunday, January 3, 1926	*Aida*
Monday, February 1	*Aida*
Thursday, February 11	Harold in *Gwendoline* (15)
Wednesday, February 17	*Gwendoline*
Tuesday, February 23	*Gwendoline*
Saturday, February 27	*Gwendoline*
Thursday, March 4	*Gwendoline*
Monday, March 8	*Gwendoline*
Friday, March 12	*Gwendoline*
Sunday, March 21, matinee	*Gwendoline*
Wednesday, March 31	*Gwendoline*
Thursday, April 1	*Parsifal*
Tuesday, April 6	*Parsifal*
Thursday, April 8	*Gwendoline*
Friday, April 16	*Parsifal*
*Saturday, April 17	*Gwendoline*
Monday, April 19	*Parsifal*
Sunday, April 25	*Parsifal*
Thursday, April 29	*Gwendoline*
Friday, May 7	Orpheus in *Les Malheurs d'Orpheé* (7)
Sunday, May 9	*Parsifal*
Wednesday, May 12	*Les Malheurs d'Orpheé*
Saturday, May 15	*Parsifal*
Monday, May 17	*Les Malheurs d'Orpheé*
Wednesday, May 19	*Gwendoline*
Tuesday, May 25	*Les Malheurs d'Orpheé*
Friday, May 28	Zurga in *Les Pecheurs de Perles* (29)
Monday, May 31	*Parsifal*
Wednesday June 2	*Les Pecheurs de Perles*
Wednesday June 9	*Les Pecheurs de Pperles*
Saturday June 12	*Les Malheurs d'Orpheé*
Thursday June 17	*Les Pecheurs de Perles*
Saturday June 19	*Gwendoline*
Monday June 21	*Parsifal*
Saturday June 26	*Les Pecheurs de Perles*
Thursday August 5	Athanaël *in Thais* (10)
Friday August 13	*Thais*
Saturday August 21	*Thais*
*Sunday August 22	*Gwendoline*
Tuesday August 31	*Thais*
Monday September 6	*Les Pecheurs de Perles*
Saturday September 11	*Herodiade*
Tuesday September 14	*Les Pecheurs de Perles*
Friday September 17	Rigoletto in *Rigoletto* (9)
Sunday September 19	*Thais*

1926 (71)

Friday September 24	Les Pecheurs de Perles
Sunday September 26	*Herodiade*
Wednesday September 29	*Rigoletto*
Sunday, October 3 matinee	*Les Pecheurs de Perles*
Thursday, October 7	*Rigoletto*
Saturday, October 9	*Thais*
Tuesday, October 12	*Les Pecheurs de Perles*
Friday, October 15	*Herodiade*
Sunday, October 17	*Rigoletto*
Sunday, October 24	matinee *Thais*
*Monday, October 25	*Herodiade*
Thursday, October 28	*Rigoletto*
Monday, Nov. 1	*Thais*
Tuesday, November 2	*Les Pecheurs de Perles*
*Wednesday, November 3	*Les Malheurs d'Orpheé*
Wednesday, November 10	*Thais*
*Thursday, November 11	*Rigoletto*
Sunday, November 14	*Les Pecheurs de Perles*
Tuesday, November 23	Tonio in *I Pagliacci* (*Paillasse*) (9)
Thursday, November 25	*Les Pecheurs de Perles*
*Friday, November 26	*Thais*
Monday, November 29	*Les Malheurs d'Orpheé*
Sunday, December 5	matinee *Herodiade*
Tuesday, December 7	*I Pagliacci*
Friday, December 10	*Les Pecheurs de Perles*
Sunday, December 12	*Rigoletto* season farewell

1927 (35)

Wednesday, April 13	*I Pagliacci*
Saturday, April 16	*Les Pecheurs de Perles*
Tuesday, April 19	*Les Pecheurs de Perles*
Friday, April 22	*Rigoletto*
Tuesday, April 26	*Les Pecheurs de Perles*
Saturday, May 7	*Herodiade*
Thursday, May 12	*Les Pecheurs de Perles*
Friday, May 20	Don Giovanni in *Don Giovanni* (*Don Juan*) (7)
Tuesday, May 24	*Don Giovanni*
Thursday, May 26	*Herodiade*
Friday, May 27	*Les Pecheurs de Perles*
Sunday, May 29 matinee	*Don Giovanni*

1928 (25)

Sunday, March 11	*I Pagliacci*
Tuesday, March 13	*Rigoletto*

1928 (25)

Saturday, March 24	Gala
Monday, April 2	*Les Pecheurs de Perles*
Thursday, April 5	*I Pagliacci*
Monday, April 9	*Les Pecheurs de Perles*
Wednesday, April 11	Count di Luna in *Trovatore* (4)
Friday, April 13	*I Pagliacci*
Sunday, April 15 matinee	*Les Pecheurs de Perles*
Tuesday, April 17	*I Pagliacci*
Wednesday, April 25	*Trovatore*
Monday, April 30	*Don Giovanni*
Wednesday May 2,	*Don Giovanni*
Friday, May 4,	*Il Trovatore*
Saturday, May,	*Don Giovanni*
Thursday, May 17	*Il Trovatore*
Sunday, May 27	*Don Giovanni*
Saturday, June 2	John the Baptist in *Salomé* (4)
Monday, June 4	*Les Pecheurs de Perles*
Thursday, June 7	*Salomé*
Tuesday, June 12	*Salomé*
Friday, June 15	Hamlet in *Hamlet* (8)
Sunday, June 17	*Hamlet*
Tuesday, June 19	*Salomé*
Wednesday, June 20	*Hamlet*
Sunday, June 24	*I Pagliacci*
Wednesday, June 27	*Hamlet*

1930 (8)

Monday, June 2	*I Pagliacci*
Friday, June 6,	*Hamlet*
Sunday, June 8 matinee	*Hamlet*
Thursday, June 12	*Hamlet*
Monday, June 16	*Les Pecheurs de Perles*
Saturday, June 21	*Les Pecheurs de Perles*
Tuesday, June 24	*Les Pecheurs de Perles*
Thursday, June 26	*Hamlet*

1931 (4)

Friday, June 12	*Les Pecheurs de Perles*
Tuesday, June 16	*Les Pecheurs de Perles*
Friday, June 19	*Les Pecheurs de Perles*
Tuesday, June 23	*Les Pecheurs de Perles*

Appendix C:
Operatic Appearances
in the United States

With the listing of his initial Metropolitan Opera appearance in each opera, Thomas's total number of Metropolitan performances in that role follows in parentheses.

March 3, 1925   Amonosoro in *Aida* Washington, D.C.

December 8, 1927   Athanaël in *Thais* Washington

December 10, 1927   *Aida*, Washington

September 12, 1930   Giorgio Germont in *La Traviata* San Francisco probably with Clairbert, Gigli

September 15, 1930   *La Traviata* San Francisco probably with Clairbert, Gigli

October 3, 1930   *La Traviata*, Los Angeles Clairbert, Gigli

October 7, 1930   Wolfram in *Tannhäuser*, Los Angeles Jeritza, S. Rayner, Pinza (Hermann)

November 6, 1930   Tonio in *I Pagliacci* Chicago Marshall, Burke

November 9, 1930   *I Pagliacci* Chicago same cast as Nov. 6

November 15, 1930   Renato in *Un Ballo in Maschera* Chicago Raisa, Marshall

November 17, 1930   *I Pagiacci* Chicago same cast as Nov. 6

November 5, 1931   Rigoletto in *Rigoletto*, Chicago N. Eadie (Gilda) J. Kiepura, Lazzari

November 18, 1931   *Rigoletto*, Chicago same cast as Nov. 5

November 26, 1931   Herod in *Herodiade* Chicago Maison, Baromeo

November 28, 1931   *Traviata* Chicago Muzio, Hackett

December 7, 1931   *Rigoletto*, Chicago same cast as Nov. 5

December 12, 1931   Herodiade Chicago matinee same cast as Nov. 26

January 7, 1932   Scarpia in *Tosca* Philadelphia B. Saroya, D. Onofrei

January 14, 1932	*Thais*, Philadelphia B. Saroya (Jepson as Crobyle, Bampton as Myrtale)
February 4, 1932	Zurga in *Pearlfishers*, Philadelphia J. Lucchese, N. Martini
October 22, 1933	*Tannhauser*, Philadelphia
February 2, 1934	*La Traviata* Metropolitan Opera (total performances in this role at the Metropolitan 12) Ponselle, Schipa
February 10, 1934	*I Pagliacci* Chicago A. Roselle, G. Radaelli
February 17, 1934	*Aida* Chicago
March 1, 1934	*La Traviata* Metropolitan Opera Bori, Jagel
March 11, 1934	Gala for the 50th anniversary of the Metropolitan Opera
April 14, 1934	*I Pagliacci* Metropolitan Opera (5) E. Fleischer, Jagel
November 17, 1934	*I Pagliacci* Chicago H. Burke, Martinelli
November 19, 1934	*La Traviata* Chicago E. Mason, G. Bentonelli
November 11, 1935	*Thais* Chicago Jepson
November 16, 1935	*Rigoletto* Chicago M. Kocova (Gilda) G. Bentonelli
November 19, 1935	Rigoletto Chicago same cast as Nov. 16
November 23, 1935	*Gale* Chicago Frank Forest, Helen Bartuch, Julia Peters
December 17, 1935	*Tosca* Philadelphia for Metropolitan Opera (2) Lehmann, Crooks
December 20, 1935	*Aida* Metropolitan Opera (9) Rethberg, Wettergren, Martinelli
January 5, 1936	Metropolitan Opera concert "Eri tu" from *Ballo in Maschera*
January 21, 1936	*La Traviata* Metropolitan Opera in Brooklyn Mason, Martinelli
January 25, 1936	*Aida* Metropolitan Opera Rethberg, Wettergren, Jagel
March 9, 1936	*Rigoletto* Metropolitan Opera (1) J. Antoine, Castagna, Jagel
March 17, 1936	*Aida* Metropolitan Opera Giannini, Castagna, Jagel
November 2, 1936	*Thais* Chicago Jepson, Wm. Martin
November 7, 1936	*La Traviata* Chicago D. Giannini, Castagna, Jagel
January 4, 1937	*La Traviata* Metropolitan Opera Bovy, Crooks
January 13, 1937	*I Pagliacci* Metropolitan Opera Queena Mario, Carron
January 20, 1937	*Aida* Metropolitan Opera Giannini,Wettergren, Martinelli
March 15, 1937	*Aida* Metropolitan Opera Giannini, Bampton, Carron
March 25, 1937	*I Pagliacci* Metropolitan Opera S. Fisher (Nedda), Carron
November 6, 1937	Figaro in *Barber of Seville* Chicago E. Sack (American debut), C. Hackett, V. Lazzari
November 8, 1937	*La Traviata* Chicago Jepson, André Burdino
November 12, 1937	*Thais* Chicago Jepson

December 11, 1937	*La Traviata* Metropolitan Opera Bovy, Martini
December 14, 1937	*La Traviata* Metropolitan Opera in Philadelphia Bovy, Martini
December 17, 1937	*La Traviata* Chicago same cast as Nov. 8
January 22, 1938	*Barber of Seville* Metropolitan Opera (15) matinee Pons, Landi, Pinza
February 11, 1938	*Barber of Seville* Metropolitan Opera Pons, Landi, Pinza
April 4, 1938	*La Traviata* in Cleveland Metropolitan Opera Jepson, Martini
January 17, 1939	*Barber of Seville* Metropolitan Opera Sayao, Martini, Pinza
February 7, 1939	*Barber of Seville* Metropolitan Opera, Newark Sayao, Martini, Pinza
February 10, 1939	*Thais* Metropolitan Opera (6) Jepson, Tokatyan
February 11, 1939	*Barber of Seville* Metropolitan Opera Sayao, Martini, Pinza
February 16, 1939	*I Pagliacci* Metropolitan Opera Burke, Martinelli
February 22, 1939	*Barber of Seville* Metropolitan Opera Pons, Martini, Pinza
February 24, 1939	*Thais* Metropolitan Opera matinee Jepson, Tokatyan
February 28, 1939	*Barber of Seville* Metropolitan Opera, Philadelphia Pons, Martini, Lazzari, Pinza,
March 2, 1939	*Thais* Metropolitan Opera Marjorie Lawrence, Tokatyan
March 5, 1939	Metropolitan Opera concert
March 8, 1939	*Tosca* Metropolitan Opera I. Jessner, Martinelli
March 15, 1939	*Thais* Metropolitan Opera Jepson, Tokatyan
March 22, 1939	*Aida* Metropolitan Opera Rethberg, Castagna, Pinza
March 30, 1939	*Thais* Metropolitan Opera Jepson, Tokatyan
November 1, 1939	*La Traviata* Chicago Jepson, Schipa
November 3, 1939	*Barber of Seville* Chicago H. Reggianni, Schipa, Malatesta, Lazarri
November 10, 1939	*La Traviata* Chicago H. Reggianni, Tokatyan
November 18, 1939	*I Pagliacci* Chicago V. Della Chiesa, Carron
February 16, 1940	*Barber of Seville* Metropolitan Opera H. Reggiani (Rosina,) Tokatyan, Lazzari
March 25, 1940	*Barber of Seville* Metropolitan Opera in Baltimore Sayao, Martini, Pinza, D'Angelo
November 2, 1940	*Aida* Chicago Milanov, K. Branzell, Martinelli, Lazzari
November 5, 1940	*La Traviata*, Chicago Jepson, Melton
November 9, 1940	*Falstaff* Chicago mat. D. Giannini, M. Harrell (Ford), S. Sharnova
November 11, 1940	*I Pagliacci* Chicago Jepson, Martinelli
November 13, 1940	*Aida* Chicago Milanov, K. Branzell, Martinelli, Lazzari
November 22, 1940	*Falstaff* Chicago same cast as Nov. 9
December 4, 1940	*Falstaff* Chicago same cast as Nov. 9

December 7, 1940	*Tosca* Chicago Rose Pauly, Kiepura
February 19, 1941	*Barber of Seville* Metropolitan Opera Tuminia, Landi, Pinza, Baccaloni
March 1, 1941	*Barber of Seville* Metropolitan Opera matinee Tuminia, Landi, Pinza, Baccaloni
April 5, 1941	*Barber of Seville* Metropolitan Opera Tuminia, Schipa, Pinza, Baccaloni
November 10, 1941	*Falstaff* St. Louis
November 14, 1941	*La Traviata* Chicago Jepson, Bartlett
November 19, 1941	*Aida* Chicago M. Lushanya, K. Branzell, K. Brown, Lazzari
November 24, 1941	*Falstaff* Chicago D. Giannini, H. Thompson, S. Sharnova
November 29, 1941	Escamillo in *Carmen* Chicago, Castagna, Turner, Kiepura
December 1, 1941	*Tosca* Chicago Moore, Jagel
February 5, 1942	*Masked Ball* Metropolitan Opera Roman, Martinelli
February 16, 1942	*La Traviata* Metropolitan Opera Novatna, Peerce
February 20, 1942	*I Pagliacci* Metropolitan Opera Albanese, Carron
February 21, 1942	*Aida* Metropolitan Opera matinee Greco, Castagna, Jagel
April 10, 1942	*La Traviata* Metropolitan Opera Jepson, Peerce
April 18, 1942	*Barber of Seville* Metropolitan Opera, Dallas, Sayao, Landi, Pinza, Baccaloni
October 17, 1942	*Barber of Seville* Montreal
November 9, 1942	*Rigoletto* Chicago Antoine (Gilda), Kiepura
November 14, 1942	*Faust* Chicago Albanese, Crooks
November 20, 1942	*Barber of Seville* Chicago Tuminia, Martini, Lazzari
November 30, 1942	*I Pagliacci* Chicago Martinelli, Kirsten
December 12, 1942	*La Traviata* Chicago Jepson, Tokatyan
January 30, 1943	Valentin in *Faust* (2) Metropolitan Opera Albanese, Jobin, Pinza
February 2, 1943	*La Traviata* Philadelphia with Metropolitan Opera Sayao, Peerce
February 8, 1943	*La Traviata* Metropolitan Opera Sayao, Melton
February 12, 1943	*Barber of Seville* Metropolitan Opera Reggiani, Landi
February 17, 1943	*Aida* Metropolitan Opera Milanov, Castagna, Carron, Pinza
February 22, 1943	*Faust* Metropolitan Opera Albanese, Kullman, Cordon (Mephisto)
February 25, 1943	*La Traviata* Metropolitan Opera final appearance Albanese, Melton

Appendix D: Radio Appearances and Programs, 1934–1943

The broadcast date and program (left) are followed by the songs performed by Thomas and their composer when known.

1934

March 21, Vince

Prologue from *Pagliacci*, Leoncavallo; Trees, unidentified, probably Tours; I Love Life, Mana-Zucca; Green Eyed Dragon, Charles; Just A Wearyin' for You, Bond; You are Free/I Love the Girls, Jacobi

March 28, Vince

Toreador Song from *Carmen*, Bizet; Ah! Love But a Day, H.H. A. Beach; The Farmer's Pride, Kennedy Russell; Smilin' Thru, Arthur Penn; Gwine to Hebbn-Jacques Wolfe; Home on the Range, David Guion

April 4, Vince

Time for Making Songs Has Come, Michael Head; My Message, Guy D'Hardelot

April 4, Vince

Sailormen, Jacques Wolfe; Di Provenza from *Traviata*, Verdi; Brown October Ale, De Koven; In the Gloaming, Harrison

April 11, Vince

Tommy Lad, Margetson; Vision Fugitive from *Herodiade*, Massenet; Bird Songs at Eventide, Coates; Three for Jack, Squire; Oh Dry Those Tears, Del Riego; Nichavo, Mana-Zucca

April 18, Vince

The Minstrel Boy, Moore; Erlkönig, Schubert; Sweetest Story Ever Told, Stults; Pale Hands I Love, Woodforde-Finden; Old Black Mare, Squire; Where Is My Wandering Boy Tonight, Baron

April 24, Vince

Annie Laurie, Scott; Drinking Song from *Hamlet*, Thomas; Nocturne, Pearl Curran; Ride, Cowboy, Ride, David Guion; Ringers of St. Mary, Lohr; Little Mother o' Mine, Burleigh

May 2, Vince

Homing, Del Riego; Largo Al Factotum from *Barber of Seville*, Rossini; The Trumpeter, Dix; Big Brown Bear, Mana-Zucca; At Dawning, Cadman; Ol' Man River, Kern

November 13, Vince

Toreador Song from *Carmen*, Bizet; The Devout Lover, White; My Homeland, Hurley

November 13, Vince

Sailormen, Wolfe; Beautiful Isle of Somewhere, Fearis; When I Think Upon the Maidens, Head

November 21, Vince

Zaza, Piccolo Zingara from *Zaza*, Leoncavallo; Vale, Russell; There Is a Ladye, Bury; The Stuttering Lovers, Hughes; Steal Away, Johnson; Mother o' Mine, Tours; Honor, Johnson

November 28, Vince

Danny Deever, Damrosch; O Del Mio Amato Ben, Danaudy; I Think of Thee, Thomas; Trottin' to the Fair, Villiers— Stanford; Land of the Sky Blue Water, Cadman; Hame, Walford Davies; Requiem, Homer

December 5, Vince

Absent; Tally-Ho, Leoni; My Shadder, Nesbit; I Love Life, Mana-Zucca; Three for Jack, Squire; Just a Wearyin' for You, Bond

December 12, Vince

Di Provenza from *Traviata*, Verdi; Mah Lindy Lou, Strickland; Roll Along Home, Easthope Martin; Come to the Fair, Geehl; Nichavo, Mana-Zucca; Annie Laurie, Lady Scott

December 19, Vince

Life of a Rover from *Fortunio*, De Koven; Erlkönig, Schubert; My Message, Guy D'Hardelot; Land of Degradashun, MacGimsey; Green Eyed Dragon, Wolseley Charles; O Dry Those Tears, Del Riego

December 26, Vince

Border Ballad, F.H. Cowen; Sylvia, Oley Speaks; That's Why Darkies Were Born, Brown & Henderson; Bird Songs at Eventide, Eric Coates; Old Black Mare, W.H. Squire; Marcheta, Schertzinger; Adeste Fideles, Latin Hymn

1935

January 2, Vince

Ring Out Wild Bells, Gounod; Evening Song, H.B. MacPherson; Prologue to *Pagliacci,* Leoncavallo; Farmer's Pride, Kennedy Russell; Old Man River, Jerome Kern; Home on the Range, David Guion

February 13, Vince

Vision Fugitive from *Herodiade,* Massenet; Curley Locks, Earl Behnha; Invictus, Bruno Huhn; Brown Bird Singing, Haydn Wood; The Ringers (piano), Hermann Lohr; Forgotten, Eugene Cowles

February 20, Vince

Evening Star from *Tannhauser,* Wagner; Gypsy John, Frederic Clay; My Old Kentucky Home, Stephen Foster

February 20, Vince

The Crying of Water, Campbell Tipton; Major General's Song from *Pirates of Penzance*, Arthur Sullivan; Because, Guy D'Hardelot

February 27, Vince

The Time for Making Songs Has Come, James H. Rogers; Ride, Cowboy Ride, David Guion; It Is Enough from *Elijah,* Mendelssohn; I'll Sing the Songs of Araby, Frederic Clay; Tally-Ho, Franco Leoni; Sweetest Story Ever Told, R.M. Stults

March 6, Vince

Tu Lo Sai, Guiseppe Torelli; Life Here with a Smile, Sir Landon Ronald; Cavatine from *Faust,* Gounod; Big Brown Bear, Mana-Zucca; Rose Marie, Friml; Throw Out the Life Line, Hymn

April 24, Vince

On Wings of Song, Mendelssohn; Mighty Lak a Rose, Nevins; Largo al Factotum from *Barber of Seville*, Rossini; Trees, unidentified, probably Tours; Twickenham Ferry, Marzials; Beautiful Isle of Somewhere, Fearis

May 1, Vince

I Love Life, Mana-Zucca; Massa's in de Cold Cold Ground, Stepehn Foster; Promesse de Mon Avenir from *Le Roi de Lahore,* Massenet; Smilin' Thru, Arthur Penn; Green Eyed Dragon, Wolseley Charles; Gentlemen Good Night, Ernest Longstaffe

May 8, Vince

Nichavo, Mana-Zucca; Absent, Metcalf; Eri Tu from *Masked Ball*, Verdi; Sailormen, Jacques Wolfe; Old Man River, Jerome Kern

May 15, Vince

Flow Gently Sweet Afton, Folk Song; Song of the Road, Albert Hay Malotte; Credo from *Otello*, Verdi; Dreams of Long Ago, Enrico Caruso; Contrary Mary (piano), Malotte; Mother, J.C. Thomas; Deep in Your Heart

May 22, Vince

Danny Deever, Walter Damrosch; None but the Lonely Heart, Tchaikovsky; Salomé from *Herodiade*, Massenet; Long Ago in Alcala, Messager; In the Gloaming, Harrison; Maytime, Romberg

May 29, Vince

The Trumpeter, A.J. Dix; Beautiful Dreamer, Stephen Foster; Au Pays, Augusta Holmes; Trees, Frank Tours; Old Mother Hubbard, Herbert Hughes; The Lord's Prayer, Malotte; Abschied Dir Vogel, Eugen Hildach

June 5, Vince

Minstrel Boy, Wm. Arms Fisher; Beautiful Mother, Henry Hadley; Some Day I'll Find You, Coward; Di Provenza from *Traviata*, Verdi; Leetle Bateese, Geoffrey O'Hara; Nocturne, Pearl Curran; Land of Degradashun, NacGimsey

June 12, Vince

Drei Wanderer, Hans Hermann; Ah Love but a Day, H.H.A. Beach; Tell Me That You Love Me, Bixio; Air "O Nadir" from *Pearlfishers*, Bizet; When You're Lying Awake from *Iolanthe*, Arthur Sullivan; The Song Is You, Kern; When I Think Upon the Maidens, Michael Head; Where Is My Wandering Boy Tonight, Hymn

June 19, Vince

Camerado, James H. Rogers; Just a Wearin' for You Carrie, Jacobs Bond; Air from Comus, Dr. Arne; Music When Soft Voices Die, Alice Bartlett; Babes in Woods, unidentified; Uncle Rome, Sidney Homer; Didn't It Rain?, Harry T. Burleigh; Hold Thou My Hand, C.S. Briggs

June 26, Vince

Love Went a Riding, Frank Bridge; Angus MacDonald, Joseph Roeckel; Venetian Vision, Brogi; Evening Star, from *Tanhauser* Wagner; Love's Roundalay, unidentified; When I Was A Lad, Gilbert & Sullivan; Gwine to Hebb'n, Jacques Wolfe; I Must Go Down to the Sea, John Densmore; Thy Beaming Eyes, Edward McDowell; Il Balen from *Trovatore*, Verdi; The Wedding of Miss Duck, Marshall Bartholomew; I'm Falling in Love with Someone, Victor Herbert; Won't You Buy Sir?, unidentified; Sing Me to Sleep, Edwin Greene

July 10, Vince

As Ever I Saw, Peter Warlock; Verborgenheit, Hugo Wolf; The Heart Bow'd Down, M. Balfe

July 10, Vince

Bob-White, Jacques Wolfe; A Perfect Day, Carrie Jacobs-Bond; The Lost Chord, Arthur Sullivan; Only a Rose, Friml

July 17, Vince

Care Selve, Handel; Song of Songs, Moya; Steal Away, Hall Johnson; Drinking Song From *Hamlet*, Ambroise Thomas; Baigne D'eau Mes Mains From *Thais*, Massenet; Banjo Song, Sidney Homer; Honor, Honor, Hall Johnson; The Lord's Prayer, Albert Malotte;

July 24, Vince

Prologue from *Pagliacci*, Leoncavallo; Annie Laurie, Lady Scott; My Message, Guy D'Hardelot; The Rosary, Ethelbert Nevin; Sweethearts From *Maytime*, Romberg; O Dry Those Tears, Del Riego; Green Eyed Dragon, Wolseley Charles; O Love That Will Not Let Me Go, Hymn

July 31, Vince

Over the Steppe, Gretchaninoff; By the Bend of the River, Clara Edwards; Elegie, Massenet; Le Veau D'or from *Faust*, Gounod; I'll See You Again, Noel Coward; Tally-Ho, Francesco Leoni; Sheila, Arthur Kellogg

August 7, Vince

She Dwelt Among the Untrodden Ways, Lawrence Kellie; Pari Siamo from *Rigoletto*, Verdi; Song of Steel, Meredith Wilson

August 7, Vince

Song of the Night, Uda Waldrop; You Are Free, Jacobi; Kitty My Love, Herbert Hughes; My Darling Nellie Gray, B.R. Hanby

August 14, Vince

The Sea, Edward MacDowell; How Like a Rose, Martin Broones; Per Me Giunto from *Don Carlo*, Verdi; The Vagabond, James Molloy; Blue Skies, unidentified; Song of the Flea, Mousorgsky; Think on Me, Lady Jane Scott

August 21, Vince

Pinafore, Arthur Sullivan; (John Charles Thomas, Willie Morris Quartette)

August 28, Vince

Traume, Richard Wagner; I Know of Two Bright Eyes, Geo. H. Clutsam; Toreador Song from *Carmen*, Bizet; On the Road to Mandalay, Oley Speaks; Whispering Hope, A. Hawthorne; Three for Jack, W.H. Squire; Abide with Me, Monk

September 4, Vince

The Mikado, Arthur Sullivan

September 11, Vince

Do You Fear the Wind?, Geoffrey O'Hara; The Sleep that Flits on Baby's Eyes, John Alden Carpenter; Flower of My Heart, My Rose; Leo Edwards

September 11, Vince

The Life of a Rover, DeKoven; Hope the Hornblower, John Ireland; Brindisi *Hamlet,* A. Thomas; Sweetest Story Ever Told, R.M. Stults

September 18, Vince

My Old Kentucky Home, Foster; Jeannie with the Light Brown Hair, Foster; Beautiful Dreamer, Foster; Old Dog Tray, Foster; Massa's in de Cold Cold Ground, Foster

September 25, Vince

At Parting, James H. Rogers; Give Me Your Hands, Frank Tours; Largo Al Factotum from *Barber of Seville,* Rossini; I'm Going Home to the Blue Hills, Wendell Keeney; Mother, John Charles Thomas

October 2, Vince

Yeoman's Wedding Song, Prince Poniatowski; Mattinata, F. Paolo Tosti; Mattinata, Leoncavallo; Homing, Teresa Del Riego; Broken Toys, Earl Benham; The Sleigh, Richard Kountz; The Lord's Prayer, Albert Malotte

October 9, Vince

Do Not Go, My Love, Richard Hageman; Erlkönig, Schubert; Vision Fugitive from Massenet *Herodiade,* Boats of Mine; Ann Stratton Miller, Mia Carlotta; Carl Oberbrunner, Music of the Night; Eric Coates, Boots and Saddle; T. Powell

October 16, Vince

Trial by Jury, Arthur Sullivan

October 23, Vince

Bonnie George Campbell, F. Kell; Trees, Frank Tours; Big Brown Bear, Mana-Zucca; I Love Life, Mana-Zucca; Eri Tu from *Masked Ball,* Verdi; Tommy Lad, Margetson; Stuttering Lovers, Herbert Hughes; In the Gloaming, Annie Harrison

October 30, Vince

From the Victor Herbert Program: Neapolitan Love Song from *Princess Pat;* I Want What I Want When I Want It *Mlle. Modiste;* I'm Falling in Love *Naughty Marietta;* Serenade of Alvarado *Natoma;* Gypsy Love Song *Fortune Teller;* Ze English Language; Ah, Sweet Mystery of Life

November 6, Vince

Mr. Belloc's Fancy, Peter Warlock; Ich Liebe Dich, Beethoven; Ich Liebe Dich, Grieg; In the Time of Roses, Reichardt; One Last Love Song, Martin Broones; Nichavo, Mana-Zucca; My Message, Guy D'Hardelot; Because, Guy D'Hardelot

November 13, Vince

Invictus, Bruno Huhn; Forgotten, Eugene Cowles; Curly Locks, Earl Benham; Brown Bird Singing, Hayden Wood; Danny Deever, Waler Damrosch

November 13, Vince
Old Man River, Jerome Kern; Boots and Saddle, Samuels etc.

November 20, Vince
Children of Men, Sydney King Russell; Turn Ye to Me, Malcolm Lawson; Toreador Song from Bizet *Carmen;* Little Boy Blue, Ethelbert Nevin; Charming Chloe Edward German, Contrary Mary; Albert Malotte, Come Unto Me, William Coenen

November 27, Vince
Ombra Mai Fu from Handel *Xerxes;* Minstrel Boy Drink to Me Only with Thine Eyes; Wm. Fisher, Old English; Promesse de Mon Avenir from *Le Roi de Lahore,* Massenet; Moon Melody, Martin Broones; The Ringers, Hermann Lohr; We Thank Thee, Malcolm Fitzgerald

December 4, Vince
By the Bend of the River, Clara Edwards; Air from *Comus,* S. Endicott; Autumn Dream, Leonard Thomas; Di Provenza from *Traviata,* Verdi; The Blind Ploughman, R. Coningsby Clarke; Gwine to Hebb'n, Jacques Wolfe; Home to My Blue Hills, Colin Wendell

December 11, Vince
Bonnie Earl o' Moray, F. Kreisler; In an Old English Garden, Amber Roobenian; When I Think Upon the Michael Head Maidens

December 11, Vince
Drinking Song from *Hamlet,* Ambroise Thomas; Swannee River, Stephen Foster; The Farmer's Pride, Kennedy Russell; The Lost Chord, Sullivan

December 18, Vince
As Ever I Saw, Peter Warlock; Bendemeer's Stream, Alfred Scotty Gatty; Do You Fear the Wind?, Geoffrey O'Hara; Credo from *Otello,* Verdi; None But the Lonely Heart, Tchaikovsky; Tally-Ho, Leoni; Smilin' Thru, Arthur A. Penn

December 25, Vince
Adeste Fideles, J. Reading; Sailormen, Jacques Wolfe; The Little Tin Soldiers, Mana-Zucca; My Sore Thumb, Mana-Zucca; Evening Song, Helen B. MacPherson; A Christmas Folk Song, William Lindsay; Boats of Mine, Anne Stratton Miller; Green-Eyed Dragon, Wolseley Charles; Christmas Carol, B. Gagliano

December 29, General Motors
Evening Star from *Tannhauser,* Wagner; Vision Fugitive from *Herodiade,* Massenet; Prologue from *Pagliacci,* Leoncavallo

1936

January 1, Vince
I Love Life, Mana-Zucca; Green Pastures, Wilfred Sanderson; Largo Al Factotum from *Barber of Seville,* Rossini; Elsie Janie; Boots and Saddle, Samuels, etc.

January 1, Vince

Leetle Bateese, Geoffrey O'Hara; Lord's Prayer, Albert Malotte

January 15, Vince

The Trumpeter, J. Airlie Dix; Litanei, Schubert; Il Balen from *Trovatore,* Verdi; Dreams of Long Ago, Caruso; Susan Is Her Name, O!, G.W. Sanderson; Red River Valley, Jacques Wolfe

January 22, Vince

Lead Kindly Light, Dykes; She Delft Among Untrodden Ways, Lawrence Kellie; E me ne Voglio Andar, Alberto Bimboni; Thais Duet, M.W. Balfe; Song of Steel, Meredith Willson; Darling Nellie Gray, B.R. Hanby

January 25

Aida Metropolitan Opera matinee

January 29, Vince

The Time for Making Songs Has Come, James H. Rogers; Your Presence, Meta Schumann; Love Went A-Riding, Frank Bridge; Prologue from *Pagliacci,* Leoncavallo; Annie Laurie, Lady Jane Scott; Fishing, Harvey Enders; Beautiful Isle of Somewhere, Fearis

February 5, Vince

My Homeland, Oley Speaks; Oh, Didn't It Rain?, H.T. Burleigh; The Devout Lover, Maude V. White; Cavatine from *Faust,* Gounod; Flow, Gently, Sweet Afton, Spilman

February 5, Vince

Rolling Down to Rio, Edward German; Little Mother o' Mine, H.T. Burleigh

February 12, Vince

Tu Lo Sai, Torelli; Land of Sky Blue Water, Charles W. Cadman; Beau Soir, Debussy; Border Ballad, Frederic H. Cowen; Vision Fugitive from Massenet *Herodiade;* Pale Hands I Love, Amy Woodford-Finden; Big Brown Bear, Mana-Zucca; Song of the Road, Albert Malotte

February 19, Vince

On Wings of Song, Mendelssohn; For You Alone, Henry E. Geehl; Per Me Giunto from *Don Carlos,* Verdi; Marcheta, Victor Schertzinger; Long Ago in Alcala, Messager; Just for Today, Blanche Seaver

February 26, Vince

Just You, H.T. Burleigh; Mattinata (Piano), Leoncavallo; It Is Enough from *Elijah,* Mendelssohn; Sheila, Arthur Kellogg; The Flea (Piano), Moussorgsky; Steal Away, Hall Johnson

March 4, Vince

Sylvia, Oley Speaks; Moon Melody, Martin Broones; Until, Wilfred Sanderson; Toreador Song from *Carmen,* Bizet; The Road Is Calling, Serge Walter; Gwine to Hebb'n (piano), Jacques Wolfe; Love's Old Sweet Song, J.L. Molloy

March 11, Vince

I know a Lovely Garden, Guy D'Hardelot; Song of India from *Sadko,* Rimsky-Korsakoff; Homing, Del Riego; Nemico della Patria *Andrea Chenier,* Giordano; Banjo Song, Sidney Homer; My Old Shako (piano), H. Trotere; Danny Boy, Fred Weatherly

March 18, Vince

The Bonnie Earl o' Moray, F. Kreisler; She Moved Thro' the Fair Herbert (piano), Hughes; Der Ton, Joseph Marx; Cortigianni from *Rigoletto,* Verdi; Nocturne, Pearl Curran; Danny Deever, Walter Damrosch; In the Gloaming, Annie F. Harrison

March 25, Vince

All From Oley Speaks: Morning; Oley Speaks; To You; On the Road to Mandalay; My Homeland; The Lane to Ballybree (piano); Sylvia; When the Boys Come Home;

April 1, Vince

When, Earl Benham; Come to the Fair, Easthope Martin; Di Provenza from *Traviata,* Verdi; The Little Irish Girl (Piano), Hermann Lohr; The Ninety and Nine (organ), Edward Campion; Song of Sleep, Kenneth Walton

April 8, Vince

Deep River, Harry T. Burleigh; Honor (Piano), Hall Johnson; The Donkey, Richard Hageman; The Holy City, Stephen Adams

April 8, Vince

At Dawning, Charles Wakefield Cadman; Sailormen (piano), Jacques Wolfe; The Lords Prayer, Albert Hay Malotte

April 15, Vince

I Love Life, Mana-Zucca; Annie Laurie, Lady Jane Scott; Texas Star, Peter De Rose; Prologue from *Pagliacci,* Leoncavallo; Mother o' Mine, Frank E. Tours; Green Eyed Dragon, Wolseley Charles; May Day Carol, Deems Taylor

May 10, Mother's Day Program from Baltimore

Mother, John Charles Thomas; May Day Carol, Deems Taylor

Sunday, September 20, Ford

Evening Star from *Tannhauser,* Wagner; Drinking Song from *Hamlet,* Thomas; Danny Deever, Damrosch; Long Ago in Alcala, Messager; Old Folks at Home, Foster

Sunday, November 15, General Motors

Credo from *Otello,* Verdi; Toreador Song from Carmen, Bizet; Green Pastures, Wilfred Sanderson; Song of the Road, Albert Malotte; Sailormen (piano), Jacques Wolfe

1937

January 17, Ford

Vision Fugitive from *Herodiade*, Massenet; Largo al Factotum from *Barber of Seville*, Rossini; Nocturne, Pearl Curran; Green Eyed Dragon (piano), Wolseley Charles; Goin' Home, Dvorák

May 9, Mother's Day Program Golden Rule

My Homeland, Oley Speaks; The Lord's Prayer, Albert Malotte

May 9, General Motors

Major General's Song from *Pirates of Penzance*, Arthur Sullivan; All in All Since That Fond Meeting from *Iolanthe*, Arthur Sullivan; For He Is an Englishman from *Pinafore*, Arthur Sullivan; Toreador Song from *Carmen*, Bizet; Mother, John Charles Thomas; On the Road to Mandalay, Oley Speaks

June 20, RCA Magic Key

Nemico della Patria *Andrea Chenier*, Giordano; Mah Little Banjo, Dichmont; Prayer of Fr. Serra from Fiesta Music, Charles Hart

September 12, Ford

Prologue to *Pagliacci*, Leoncavallo; The Trumpeter, J. Airlie Dix; Chancellor's Song from *Iolanthe*, Arthur Sullivan; Lost Chord with Chorus, Sullivan

Wednesday September 29, Chesterfield

Largo al Factotum from *Barber of Seville*, Rossini; I Love the Girls from *Apple Blossoms*, Jacobi; Home on the Range, Guion

October 3, RCA Magic Key

Salomé from *Herodiade*, Massenet; Rhymes of a Rover (piano), Hollister; To My Mother, MacGimsey; David and Goliath (piano), Albert Malotte

December 5, Vick's Open House

For You Alone, Henry Geehl; Promesse de Mon Avenir from *Le Roi De Lahore*, Massenet; Mah Little Banjo, Dischmont; David and Goliath, Albert Hay Malotte; In the Gloaming, Annie F. Harrison

December 26, Vick's Open House

Come to the Fair, Easthope Martin; Di Provenza from *Traviata*, Verdi; Darling Nellie Gray, B.R. Hanby; Green Eyed Dragon, Wolseley Charles; Home on the Range, David Guion

1938

April 24, Ford

Monologue from *Andrea Chenier*, Giordano; May Day Carol, Deems Taylor; I Heard a Forest Praying, Peter De Rose; When I Think Upon the Maidens, Michael Head; The Ninety and Nine, Edward Campion

May 1, RCA

Danny Deever, Walter Damrosch; Jeannie With the Light Brown Hair, Stephen Foster; Land of the Sky Blue Water, C.W. Cadman; Sing a While Longer, Geoffrey O'Hara; Steal Away, Hall Johnson; Ol' Man River, Jerome Kern

May 8, Mother's Day Program California

My Homeland, Oley Speaks; To My Mother, MacGimsey; A Little Song of Life, Albert Hay Malotte

September 11, Ford

Evening Star from *Tannhauser,* Richard Wagner; Salomé from *Herodiade,* Massenet

September 11, Ford

I Heard a Forest Praying, Peter De Rose; On the Road to Mandalay, Oley Speaks

December 18, RCA

Per Me Giunto from *Don* Carlos, Verdi; Serenade from *Don Giovanni,* Mozart; Traume, Wagner; Daniel in the Lion's Den, MacGimsey; Fountain Mingles with the River, Gounod; Into the Night, Edwards

1939

February 26, Ford

Romanza Di Cascart from *Zaza,* Leoncavallo; Serenade De Mephistopheles from, *Damnation of Faust;* Berlioz, Eventide; Davis, Sing a Song of Sixpence (piano); Malotte, My Journey's End; Foster, Old Folks at Home, Stephen Foster

April 16, RCA

Air from *Comus,* Dr. Arne; Beau Soir, Debussy; Toreador Song from *Carmen,* Bizet; When Children Pray, Beatrice Fenner; Green Eyed Dragon, Wolseley Charles; Journey's End, Fay Foster

May 14, Mother's Day

When Children Pray, Beatrice Fenner; Sons, Robert Huntington Terry; For My Mother, Albert Hay Malotte

October 8, Ford

La Procession, Cesar Franck; Ye Banks and Braes, J.A. Murray

October 8, Ford

The Ballynure Ballad, Herbert Hughes; Bendemeer's Stream, Alfred Scott Gatty; Toreador Song from *Carmen,* Bizet

November 11, Red Cross from Detroit

I Heard a Forest Praying, Peter De Rose; A Little Song of Life, Albert Malotte

November 12, Ford
Per Me Giunto from *Don Carlos,* Verdi; Mother o' Mine, Tours; Yarmouth Fair, Peter Warlock; Ode to Music, Uda Waldrop

November 19, Screen Actors' Guild
Someone Like You, William Worthington; Ol' Man River, Jerome Kern

December 31, Curtain Calls of
In the Gloaming, Annie F. Harrison; Good Will to Men, Geoffrey O'Hara

1940

February 18, Ford
Ombra Mai Fu from *Xerxes,* Handel; Jean, My Jean, Burleigh; Conscientious Deacon, Buzzi-Peccia; A Little Song of Life, Malotte; Old Man River, Kern

March 10, 1940 Ford
Vien Leonora from *La Favorita,* Donizetti; The Lost Chord, Arthur Sullivan; Flow Gently, Sweet Afton, Scotch Air; The Old Black Mare, W.H. Squire

May 12, Mother's Day
Mother of Mine, Tours; I Love Life, Mana-Zucca

September 9, Cavalcade of Music Concert S.F.

December 1, Coca Cola
Sylvia, Oley Speaks; Home on the Range, Guion

December 12, Westinghouse, Musical Americana
Ol' Man River, Jerome Kern; In the Gloaming, Harrison

December 21, British War Relief
Christmas Candle, Elinor Remick Warren; Farmer's Pride, Kennedy Russell

December 22, Coca Cola
Adeste Fideles, Latin Hymn; Silent Night, Gruber; Lord's Prayer, Malotte

1941

January 12, Coca Cola
Steal Away, Hall Johnson; Drink to Me Only with Thine Eyes, Old English

February 16, Coca Cola
Swing Low, Sweet Chariot, Johnson; Irish Medley; In the Gloaming, Harrison

March 9, Coca Cola

Come Where My Love Lies Dreaming, Foster; Ev'ry Time I Feel De Spirit, Johnson; None but the Lonely Heart, Tchaikowsky

March 30, Coca Cola

Low Bridge, Bacon; Evening Star *Tannhauser*, Wagner; Cowboy Songs, Annie Laurie; Lady Scott

May 9, War Savings Feature Canada

John Charles Thomas and Frank Black

May 11, Coca Cola

All I Desire; Believe Me If All Those Endearing Young Charms, Moore; Evening Song, Wagner; The Old Refrain, Kreisler; El Caminito

May 11, Mother's Day Golden Rule

Songs My Mother Taught Me, Dvořák; Softly and Tenderly, W. Thompson

May 25, Coca Cola

Steal Away, H. Johnson; Someone Like You, W. Worthington; Gentle Annie, S. Foster

August 26, For America We Sing

To My Mother (Through the Years), MacGimsey

1942

April 1, Time to Smile Eddie Cantor

Song of the Open Road, Albert Malotte; Dialogue, Berners

April 10, Mother's Day Golden Rule

Mother o' Mine, Burleigh

June 29, Bell Telephone Hour NYC

Prologue from *Pagliacci*, Leoncavallo; Green Eyed Dragon, E. Charles; Steal Away, Johnson; Medley of Army Songs

August 17, Bell Telephone Hour NYC

I Love Life, Mana-Zucca; My Message, Del Riego; Vision Fugitive, Massenet; Gwine to Hebben Wolfe

October 26, Bell Telephone Hour

Carmen Torreador Song, Bizet; I Heard a Forest Praying, De Rose; The Farmer's Pride, Kennedy Russell

December 21, Bell Telephone Hour

Largo al factotum, Rossini; Annie Laurie, Lady Scott; Sailormen, Wolfe

1943

March 20, Command Performance
With Judy Garland and Kenny Baker

May 1, Command Performance
With Kate Smith

October 16, Command Performance
With Bette Davis and Gary Moore

Appendix E:
Westinghouse Radio Series,
1943–1946

John Charles Thomas Westinghouse Broadcasts relayed through the Armed Forces Radio Series. The broadcast's series number precedes each entry. There are two sides to most of the recordings; a two in parentheses (2) marks the beginning of the second side.

JCT = John Charles Thomas VYO = Victor Young Orchestra KDC= Ken Darby Chorus or more commonly, the King's Men Quartet Dean Whitman, Clare Olmstead producers. The guide was taken from the collection in the Library of Congress. Missing programs may exist in other collections. Programs are dated when possible. Although the Westinghouse Program ran from January, 1943, the early AFRS recordings date from late 1943.

Victor Young's Papers at the Boston Public Library, Music Department, contain an index of musical selections performed by Thomas, the chorus, and the orchestra, but no dates are given for the pieces, and of course many were repeated over the course of three years.

3

Hame, Hame, Hame (My ain country) (JCT) ... Ignace Hilsberg pianist Salute to Poland Chopin Polonaise in A and Minute Waltz medley (VYO), ... Requiem (Under the Wide and Starry Skies) JCT ... medley from *HiJinks* by Friml (VYO) ... Brown Bird Singing JCT.... (2) I Love You Truly (VYO) ... Marching Along Together / In God We Trust (KDC) ..... America I Love You (VYO) ... The Marching Song of Freedom by C. Hollister (JCT & Chorus)

4 Wedding Theme

Ding Dong Wedding Morning (JCT).... You'll Be So Nice to Come Home To (VYO Cole Porter) ... O Promise Me (JCT) ... Goodbye Boys I'm Going to Be Married

Tomorrow / If There Is Someone Lovelier Than You (KDC JCT joins in the chorus) ... (2) Wedding of the Painted Doll (VYO) ... Abide with Me (JCT).... Fulfillment (JCT) ... Halleluja Chorus from Messiah (KDC) ... Stars & Stripes Forever (VYO)

6 January 6, 1944

Home on the Range Prelude to Cycle of Life (JCT, KDC) ... Dream Lover (VYO) Sweet and Low (JCT) Roll On to Victory (KDC) ... Camptown Races (VYO) ... House That Jack Built (KDC) ... Perfidia (VYO) ... Tramp, Tramp, Tramp (JCT) (2) Replacement for Telephone Hour: David and Goliath (JCT) ... Why Do I Love You (VYO) ... Brown Bird Singing (JCT) By the Light of the Silvery Moon / Me & Marie (KDC) ... Rudolf Friml medley (VYO) ... Home on the Range (JCT) Camptown Races (VYO) ... (KDC) ... When I Was a Lad (JCT *Pinafore*)

8

Give Me Your Hands to Hold (JCT) ... Starry Night (VYO) ... The Last Time I Saw Paris (JCT).... Marseilles / Twinkle, Twinkle Little Star medley (KDC) (2) A Pretty Girl Is Like a Melody (VYO) ... Abendstern *Tannhäuser* (JCT) ... Dancing Tambourines (VYO) ... You Are Free / I Love the Girls, Girls (JCT from *Apple Blossoms*)

12 US Navy February 13, 1944

The Bird of the Wilderness (JCT) ... I Love You (VYO) ... In the Gloaming (JCT) Bombs, Bombs, Bombs for the Bombadiers (KDC) ... John Nesbitt ... The Girl I Left Behind Me (VYO) ... I Want What I Want When I Want It (JCT)

13 February 20, 1944

Green Pastures (JCT) Tambourin Chinois (VYO) ... Forgotten (JCT) ... Love Nest / Margie (KDC) ... Ragging the Scale (VYO) ... Through the Years (JCT) ... Tramp,Tramp, Tramp (JCT / KDC) Wedding of the Painted Doll (VYO) ... Abide with Me (JCT / KDC)

16 March 12, 1944

Nemico della Patria (JCT) Lady of the Evening (VYO) ... My Message (JCT) Balalaika (KDC) ... A Pretty Girl Is Like a Melody (VYO) ... Evening Star *Tannhäuser* (JCT) ... España (VYO) ... The Riff Song, *Desert Song* (JCT) ... *Showboat* Melody (VYO)

17

I Must Down to the Seas Again (JCT) ... Wild Rose from Sally (VYO) ... Honey Lamb (JCT) ... Buckle Down Winsocki / What If Tomorrow Brings Sorrow (KDC) ... Hame, Hame My Ain Country (JCT) (2) Overture to *Secret of Suzanne* (VYO).... The Year of Jubilee Kingdom Come, by Henry Clay Wirth (VYO) ... Faith of Our Fathers (JCT & KDC) ... Ode to Music (JCT & KDC)

18 US Navy March 26, 1944

Bonnie George Campbell (JCT) More Than You Know (VYO) I Cannot Sing the Old Songs (JCT) Goodbye Boys / If There Is Someone Lovelier Than You (KDC).... (2)Nesbitt ... When You're Away(JCT) Pop Goes the Weasel (VYO) ... Major General's Song, *Pirates of Penzance* (JCT)

19 April 2, 1944

Let Us Sing a While Longer (JCT) ... With a Song in My Heart (VYO) ... Green Eyed Dragon (JCT) The Sunshine of Virginia / Indiana (KDC) ... America I Love You (VYO) ... Requiem (Under the Wide & Starry Skies) (JCT) ... Chopsticks (VYO) ... Shaller Brown (JCT / KDC) Swanee (VYO) ... On Wings of Song (JCT)

20 April 9, 1944

Yarmouth Fair (JCT) ... Blue Skies (VYO) ... Passing By (JCT) I Got Plenty o' Nothin' (KDC) ... Liebesfreud (VYO) ... Just for Today (JCT) ... Cheer Up Mary / For Me and My gal (KDC) ... Nola (VYO) ... The Lord's Prayer (JCT / KDC)

21

Love Me and the World Is Mine (JCT) ... Someday I'll Find You (by N. Coward VYO) ... Eventide (JCT) ... Sky Anchors Away (Navy Air song KDC) ... Nemico della Patria (JCT) ... (2) Ain't Gonna Rain No More (VYO) ... My Message (JCT) ... Lady of the Evening (VYO) ... Balalaika (KDC)

22 Southern Theme Program

Mattinata (JCT Tosti) ... Shardark? (VYO) ... Jean (JCT Harold Burleigh comp.) ... When the Midnight Choo-choo Leaves for Alabam / Lindy by the Watermelon Vine (KDC) ... Kitten on the Keys (VYO) Sheila (JCT) ... Crinolin Days (VYO) ... Sunshine of Your Smile (JCT) ... Ain't Gonna Rain No More (VYO) ... Brown October Ale (JCT

23

Twickenham Ferry (JCT) ... Sympathy (from *Firefly* by Friml VYO) ... When Children Pray (JCT by Fenner) ... Marine Hymn (KDC) ... (2) None but the Lonely Heart (JCT) ... A Kiss in the Dark (VYO from *Sweethearts* by Herbert) ... Ballynure Ballad, A Little Song of Life (JCT) ... Midsummer Night's Dream (Mendelssohn VYO) ... Meadowland (Russian Army Song in English, JCT KDC)

25 Mark Warnow Orchestra and Lyn Murray Singers

Gypsy John (JCT) ... Villia, *Merry Widow* (orch.) ... Beautiful Dreamer (JCT) Brahm's Hungarian Dance #6 (orch.) ... Tramp, Tramp, Tramp *Naughty Marietta* (JCT) ... instrumental (VYO).... We Gather Together (JCT)

26 Mark Warnow Orchestra and Lyn Murray Singers

Blow Me Eyes (JCT) ... My Heart Stood Still *Connecticut Yankee* Rodgers & Hart (orch.) ... Bluebird of Happiness, ... Until (JCT) ... (2) Instrumental (VYO)..... The Lost Chord (JCT) ... Guitars (orch. Mussorgsky) ... Landsighting (JCT Grieg)

27 Spring 1944 ? Mark Warnow Orchestra and Lyn Murray Singers

The Song of the Road (JCT) ... Siren Song (orch. Kern) ... E'en As a Lovely Flower *Du bist die Blume Bridge* (JCT).... Row, Row, Row / Down Where the River Rolls Along (KDC) (2) O Promise Me (JCT) ... Let Joy to Heaven Ascend ... O Me O My (orch. Youmans comp.).... What Did You See Soldier (JCT, KDC)

28 Mark Warnow Orchestra and Lyn Murray Singers

Preach Not Me Your Musty Rules (JCT) ... Serenata (orch. Muskovsky) ... By the Bend of the River (JCT saving his high notes Clara Edwards comp.).... Joshua / My Last Love (orch. medley from *What's Up*, Broadway show composed by M. Warnow) ... C'mon Get Happy (orch.) (2) Glory of Home (JCT).... Someone to Watch Over Me (orch.) Passing By (JCT setting by Bury) ... Oh By Jingo (orch.) (JCT sings two phrases from Take Me Out to the Ball Game and another song by this composer) ... The Ashgrove (JCT Welsh song)

29 Mark Warnow Orchestra and Lyn Murray Singers

Largo al factotum *Barber of Seville* (JCT) ... Yankee Doodle (MWO á la Beethoven) ... A Dream (JCT Bartlett) ... So Long Mary (chorus joined briefly by JCT) Spanish theme (orch.) ... Kashmiri Love Song (Pale Hands I Love JCT) ... Daisy, Daisy / Good Old Summer Time (chorus) ... Rancho Grande (orch.).... Once to Every Heart (JCT)

30

Green Pastures (JCT) ... Snowfall (VYO Claude Thornhill comp.) ... Sailormen (JCT) ... Margie / Love Nest (KDC) ... Raggin' the Scale (VYO) (2) Prelude to Cycle of Life (JCT, KDC Sir Landon Ronald comp.) ... Dream Lover (VYO by Scherzinger comp. of Marcheta) ... Sweet and Low (JCT) ... Spanish theme (VYO).... The Marching Song of Freedon by C. Hollister (JCT & Chorus)

31

Home on the Range Invictus (JCT) Easy to Love (VYO) ... Dedication (*Widmung* Franz comp.) (JCT) ... When Good Fellows Get Together / I Love You Truly (KDC) ... Haystraw (VYO) ... Green Pastures (JCT) Fiddle solos (VYO) ... Forgotten (JCT) Raggin' the Scale (VYO) ... Through the Years (JCT / KDC)

32

Prelude to Cycle of Life (JCT, KDC) ... Kashmiri Love Song (Pale Hands I Loved JCT) ... There Is a Tavern in the Town / Mr. Jefferson Long (KDC) ... Blue Skies (VYO) (2) Margie / Love Nest (KDC) ... Sunshine of Your Smile (JCT) ... Mimi (VYO) ... Shaller Brown (JCT)

33

Ah, Love but a Day (JCT) ... Goodbye Girls, I'm Through (VYO).... Mr. Jim (JCT Robinson / Malotte) ... Oklahoma / Oh What a Beautiful Morning (KDC) ... Love Me and the World Is Mine (JCT) (2) Some Day I'll Find You (VYO) ... Eventide (JCT) ... Arenski Waltz (VYO 2 pianos) ... My Hero (JCT, KDC) ...

34

Home on the Range As Ever I saw (JCT) Oh Lady Be Good (VYO) ... Buckle Down Winsocki (2) (KDC) ... Boats of Mine (JCT) ... Way Up Yonder (King's Men) Wild Rose (VYO) ... España (VYO) ... Riff Song *Desert Song* (JCT) ... (KDC) ... Ooh That Kiss (VYO) ... One Sweetly Solemn Thought (JCT)

35

Home on the Range Border Ballad (JCT), Love for Sale (VYO), Thy Beaming Eyes (JCT), Three Blind Mice (KDC) (2) Czardas (VYO) Jean (JCT comp. Burleigh), By the Watermelon Vine (KDC), S'Wonderful (VYO), Every Time I Feel de Spirit (JCT)

36

Home on the Range Lend Me Thy Fillet Love (JTC), I Heard You Cried Last Night (VYO), Flow Gently Sweet Afton (JCT) Saskatchewan (KDC) instrumental (VYO) (2) Danny Boy (JCT lyric by Dorothy Thomas) I'm an Old Cowhand (KDC) Die Fledermaus Waltz (VYO) Pinafore: I Am the Captain of the Pinafore / For He Is an Englishman (JCT and KDC)

37

Home on the Range Ah Sweet Mystery of Life (JCT) Dearly Beloved (VYO) Ye Banks and Braes o' Bonnie Doon (JCT) Simple Simon (KDC) (2) Nesbit A. Lincoln Flow Gently Sweet Afton (JCT) Gypsy Rondo (Hayden VYO) I Hear America Singing (JCT)

38

Home on the Range The Bird of the Wilderness (JCT) I Love You (Porter VYO) In the Gloaming (JCT) Bombs for the Bombadier (KDC) (2) Nesbit Nazi War Story Medley of French songs (KDC) The Girl I Left Behind Me (VYO) I Want What I Want When I Want It (JCT)

39

Avant de quitter ces lieux *Faust* (JCT) ... Embraceable You (VYO Gershwin).... When You're Away *The Only Girl* by Herbert (JCT) (2) Nesbitt.... You Are Free / I Love the Girls, Girls *Apple Blossoms* (JCT) ... Row, Row Your Boat (VYO) ... Heigh Ho, Come to the Fair (JCT)

42

Three for Jack (JCT) ... One Touch of Venus *Speak Low* by Weill / Nash (VYO) ... The Song Is You.... Patter of Rain on the Roof / Somewhere Over the Rainbow (KDC) (2) Every Time I Feel the Spirit (JCT, KDC) ... La Cuccaracha (VYO) ... Great Day (JCT, KDC) ... Nesbitt

43 Same as 18

44

O Swallow, Flying South (JCT) My Sweet Love (VYO) Think on Me (JCT) Russian Prayer (KDC) (2) Nesbit ... Mimi (VYO) Shaller Brown (JCT) Homing (JCT

46 April 1944

Because (JCT) ... Dreamlover *Love Parade* (VYO) ... Nocturne (JCT) ... Hayride / Moonlight Bay (KDC) (2) Nesbitt on Ignace Semmelweiss, and hospital hygiene ... Sing Me to Sleep (JCT) ... Raggin' the Scale (VYO) ... Spirit Flower (JCT Stanton Campbell–Tipton comp.)

53 June 4, 1944

Home on the Range, Because (JCT) ... It Could Happen to You (VYO) ... A Brown Bird Singing (JCT) ... Swanee (VYO) ... No, No Nora / Dearly Beloved (KDC) ... John Nesbitt ... Ye Banks and Braes O' Bonnie Dune (JCT) Arkansas Traveler (VYO) You Are Free / I Love the Girls, Girls, Girls (JCT / KDC)

54

Home on the Range, Over the Mountains (JCT) ... Underneath the Stars (VYO).... Bendermere Stream (JCT) ... On Our Way (KDC) ... John Nesbitt ... Four Waltzes (VYO) ... A Mighty Fortress Is Our God (JCT)

55

Ombra mai fu Largo from Handel's *Xerxes* (JCT) ... Long Ago and Far Away (VYO) ... Sailormen (JCT) ... Kerry Dances / Ashgrove (KDC) (2) Nesbitt Skyline of Tomorrow ... Tiger Rag (VYO) ... Marching Song of Freedom (JCT best version) ... La Cuccaracha (VYO)

56 June 25, 1944

Song of the Road (JCT) ... Beautiful Love (VYO) ... Swing Low, Sweet Chariot (JCT) ... Bicycle Built for Two / Good Old Summer Time (2) Nesbitt Adventure of Grandma.... Nocturne (JCT) ... Sing Something Simple (VYO) ... Thine Alone *Eileen* by V. Herbert (JCT)

57 July 2, 1944

Home on the Range, The Minstrel Boy (JCT) ... Waltz (VYO) ... Gentle Annie (JCT) You're a Grand Old Flag / America the Beautiful (KDC) ... Speak Low (VYO).... (2) Nesbitt ... Stars & Stripes Forever ... (VYO) ... Faith of Our Fathers (JCT)

58 July 9, 1944?

Home on the Range, All the Things You Are (JCT) Birth of the Blues (VYO) ... I Heard a Forest Praying (JCT) Trolley Song / Sweet Genevieve (KDC) ... In the Time of Roses (JCT) ... Nesbitt ... Down Diddle Down (VYO) ... Men of Harlech (JCT)

59 July 16, 1944

Home on the Range, Fury of the Sea (JCT) ... Besame Mucho (VYO) ... In the Garden of Tomorrow (JCT) ... They Go Wild Over Me / My Melancholy Baby (KDC) (2) Nesbitt ... Begin the Beguine (JCT) ... El Relicario (VYO) ... I'll See You Again (JCT)

60–63 July 23–August 13, 1944

Lee Sweetland substitutes for JCT

64

O What a Beautiful Morning (JCT) ... The Swan (VYO Saint-Saens) ... When My Boy Comes Home (JCT) ... Little David Play on Your Harp (KDC) Mary Had a Little Lamb (arr. Leo Schucken á la Ravel, Shostakovich et al.) ... I Am the Captain of the Pinafore / He Is an Englishman *Pinafore* (JCT, KDC)

65 August 27, 1944?

Ombra mai fu Largo from Handel's *Xerxes* (JCT) ... 'S Wonderful (VYO) ... Onward Christian Soldiers (JCT) (2) Home on the Range, Border Ballad (JCT) ... Yesterdays (VYO).... Can't You Hear Me Calling Caroline (JCT) ... Patriotic Medley (KDC) ... John Nesbitt...

66

I am Thy Heart (JCT) ... If I Love Again (VYO) ... Nocturne (JCT).... Nellie Gray (JCT) (2) Sky Anchors Away (KDC) ... Nesbitt ... The Bee (VYO) ... Torreador Song *Carmen* (JCT)

68 September 1944 ?

Home on the Range Invictus (JCT) ... I've Got You Under My Skin (VYO) A Child's Prayer (JCT) ... There's a Long, Long Trail a Winding (KDC) ... Waltz (VYO) ... Bicycle Built for Two / In the Good Old Summertime (KDC) ... Swing Low, Sweet Chariot (JCT) ... Put on Your Old Grey Bonnet (VYO) Frére Jacques (JCT / KDC) ... Instrumental

70

Il Neige / The Sleigh (JCT) ... La Cinqotin (VYO Marie Gabriel comp.) ... Clouds (JCT, E. Charles comp.) ... The Most Beautiful Girl in the World / Sweet Sue (KDC) (2) Nesbitt.... Tico, Tico (samba VYO) ... One Alone *Desert Song* (JCT)

71 Summer 1944?

Diaphenia (JCT) ... Frenscita (VYO Lehar) ... Love Can Be Dreamed / Mine Alone *Gypsy Baron* (JCT) (2) Long Ago and Far Away (JCT) ... Nesbitt ... Joy of Life and Love Waltz (VYO Jos. Strauss) ... The Lord's Prayer (JCT)

72

Igor's Song (JCT Madeleine Phillips comp.) ... Air for G String (VYO Bach).... The Heart Bowed Down *Bohemian Girl* (JCT) ... Sourwood Mountain (KDC) orchestral piece (VYO) ... Nesbitt Old Town ... Minute Waltz (VYO Chopin) ... Brown October Ale *Robin Hood* by De Koven (JCT)

73

Ah, Sweet Mystery of Life (JCT) ... Scottish Rhaphsody (Adolph Deutsch) ... Silver Ring (JCT Cecile Chaminade comp.) ... I've Been Working on the Railroad (KDC) (2) When You're Away, Herbert, *The Only Girl* (JCT) ... Nesbitt ... Haystraw (VYO Youmans).... Major General's Song *Pirates of Penzance*(JCT)

76

Home on the Range, Road to Mandalay (JCT) ... Stella by Starlight (VYO).... The Crying of Waters (JCT) ... Buckle Down Winsocky (KDC) ... Mexican song (VYO).... (2) Nesbitt ... The Girl I Left Behind Me (VYO) ... Louisiana Hayride / Moonlight Bay (KDC) ... Bless Us Oh Lord (JCT)

77

I Love Life (JCT Mana-Zucca) ... String Serenade Waltz (VYO Tchaikowsky) ... Smilin' Through (JCT) Nesbitt ... Perfect Day (JCT Carrie Bond comp.) ... Nola (VYO)

79

Home on the Range, Thine Is My Heart Alone (JCT) ... The Shardark (VYO) ... Trees (JCT) ... Enchilada Man / La Golondrina (KDC) ... two waltzes (VYO) ... John Nesbitt ... I Want My Mama (VYO) ... Throw Out the Lifeline (JCT)

80

Little Song of Life (JCT Malotte) ... When I Grow Too Old to Dream (VYO Romberg) ... Il Balen *Trovatore* (JCT) ... Little Liza Jane (KDC) (2) By the Sea / Avalon (KDC) ... instrumental (VYO) ... A Child's Prayer (JCT)

81

Open Road *Gypsy Baron* (JCT) ... Thine Alone, *Eileen* V. Herbert (VYO) ... Dream Valley (JCT R.Quilter comp. W. Blake poem) ... Blow the Man Down / Lorelei (KDC) (2) Nesbitt Mayo Clinic ... Torreador Song(JCT) ... The Bee (VYO) ... He's Got the Whole World in His Hands (JCT, KDC)

82

On the Road to Mandalay (JCT) My Heart Tells Me (VYO from *Sweet Rosie O'Grady*) ... The Sweetest Story Ever Told (JCT) ... Semper paratus (KDC Coast Guard Anthem) (2) Ye Banks and Braes O Bonnie Dune (JCT) ... Dream Lover (VYO from film *Love Parade*).... The Song Is You (JCT) ... orch.... Through the Years (JCT, KDC Youmans)

87

All the Things You Are (JCT, Kern) ... You're Everywhere (VYO, Youmans) ... Lindy Lou (JCT) ... Louisiana Hayride / Moonlight Bay (KDC) (2) Nesbitt Pony Express ... London Bridge Is Falling Down (VYO George Parish arr.) ... Funny Old House (JCT Kern / Hammerstein)

89

Sing a While Longer (JCT) ... This Heart of Mine (VYO form *Ziegfeld Follies*) ... Swanee River (JCT with W.C. Fields imitation in intro.) ... Battle Hymn of the Republic (KDC) (2) Nesbitt Temperature Control.... The Continental (VYO from *Gay Divorcé*) ... Victory Anthem / Hymn (JCT unidentified title) ... instrumental (VYO).

90

Give Me Your Hands to Hold (JCT) ... Blue Is the Night (VYO) ... Irish Lullaby (JCT) ... Maybe (VYO from *OK*) (2) When I Grow Too Old to Dream (VYO JCT says "let's get the words to that, Victor," see 117) ... Nesbitt Superstition ... Yankee Doodle (VYO) ... American Flag (JCT F. Kuphal comp., Joseph Redman Duke poet)

92 March 4, 1945

Dedication (*Widmung*) (JCT) ... Where or When (VYO).... By the Bend of the River (JCT) ... Instrumental (VYO) ... Little David Play on Your Harp (KDC) ... Nesbitt ... Somewhere a Voice Is Calling (JCT) ... Swanee (VYO) ... Toreador Song (JCT)

93

Until (JCT) ... The Way You Look Tonight (VYO Kern) ... The Stars Look Down (JCT Hayden Wood)

94 March 18, 1945

Prelude to Cycle of Life (JCT, Sir Landon Ronald comp.) ... Easy to Love (VYO C. Porter from *Love to Dance*) ... My Wild Irish Rose (JCT) ... Phil the Fluter's Ball Irish medley (KDC) (2) Nesbitt Transportation ... You Know That I Know (VYO Youmanns) ... Rodger Young (JCT F. Loessor)

95

West of the Sun (JCT F. Tours & wife) ... Moonlight Madonna (VYO) ... Annie Laurie (JCT) (2) Nesbitt Xrays ... Rondo Capricioso (VYO, Mendelssohn) ... Spirit Flower (JCT)

96 Easter

Johnny Appleseed Program written by Nesbitt, JCT sings Christ the Lord Is Risen Today and Green Pastures

97 April 1945

Someone Like You (JCT W. Worthington) ... If There Is Someone Lovelier Than You (VYO) ... Green Eyed Dragon (JCT) (2) Nesbitt ... Tambourin Chinois (VYO F. Kreisler) ... Begin the Beguine (JCT, KDC)

99 April 1945 Tribute to Many Nations

Sweet Land of Home (JCT very good, Clarence Humphrey comp.) ... Malagueña (VYO) ... La Maison Grise (JCT, Messager comp.) ... Meadowlands (KDC) (2) Nesbitt ... Air on G String (VYO, Bach) ... America the Beautiful (JCT)

100

Where the Long Trail Winds (JCT CW Cadman comp.) ... This Heart of Mine (VYO from *Ziegfeld Follies* movie) ... I Love You *Mexican Hayride*, C. Porter (JCT) ... Keep the Home Fires Burning (KDC) (2) Nesbitt Titanic and Radar ... Sing Me to Sleep (JCT) ... La Cuccaracha (VYO) ... Faniculi, Fanicula (JCT, KDC Italian / English)

101

Road to Mandalay (JCT), May Day Carol (JCT arr. Deems Taylor) ... Underneath the Stars (VYO) ... Pretty Sally Lives in Our Alley (JCT) ... *Wizard of Oz* medley (KDC) (2) Nesbitt Automated Light Houses ... Anetra's Dance (Grieg *Peer Gynt*) ... La Marseilles (JCT, KDC)

102 April FDR program

Recessional (JCT, Kipling) ... Brahm's Lullaby (VYO) ... Farewell (JCT for E. Pyle) ... Halleluja Chorus from *Messiah* (KDC) (2) Nesbitt on Accidents ... Stars & Stripes Forever (VYO) ... Onward Christian Soldiers (JCT, KDC)

103

Because (JCT in French) ... Minute Waltz (VYO) ... None but the Lonely Heart (JCT) ... Casey Jones medley (KDC) (2) Nesbitt on Salmon ... O That Kiss (VYO) ... Villia *Merry Widow* (JCT Lehar)

104 Winter 1944?

Danny Deever (JCT) ... Ol' Black Joe (VYO Foster) ... Sailormen (JCT) (2) Nesbitt on Vitamins ... My Lovely Celia (JCT) ... Peter's Theme *Peter and the Wolf*, Prokofiev (VYO) ... Holy, Holy, Holy (JCT)

105

O What a Beautiful Morning (JCT) ... Maybe (VYO from *OK* by Gershwin) ... Brown Bird Singing (JCT) ... Midnight Choo Choo / By Watermelon vine medley (KDC) (2) Serenade (JCT, KDC *Student Prince*) ... The Continental (VYO from *Gay Divorcé*) ... I'm an Ol' Cowhand / Lazy Rolls the Rio Grande medley(KDC) ... Blue Skies (VYO)

106

Lindy Lou (JCT) ... Too Ra Loo Ra Loo Ra (VYO) ... Per me giunto (JCT *Don Carlos*) ... Old Ark's a Movin' (KDC) (2) Swing Low Sweet Chariot (JCT) ... Nesbitt on Patents ... Lady of Spain (VYO) ... God of Battle (JCT lyrics by Gen. Patton)

107

Tommy Lad (JCT) ... To Spring (VYO Grieg comp.) ... Flow Gently Sweet Afton (JCT, R. Burns) ... Enchilada Man / La Golondrina (KDC) (2) Nesbitt Invention ... Overture to *Secret of Suzanne*, Wolf-Ferrari (VYO) ... Lost Chord (JCT)

108

Me and Marie / By the Light of Silvery Moon (KDC) ... Open Road *Gypsy Baron* (JCT substitutes line "what's to stop me and the wife") ... While You're Away *Reputation* Max Steiner comp (VYO) ... Just for Today (JCT) ... Daisy, Daisy / Good Old Summer Time (KDC) (2) Nesbitt on paper ... Perpetual Motion Paganini (VYO) ... The Sailor's Life (JCT)

109 July 1, 1945

Hail to the US of A (JCT) ... To a Wild Rose (VYO).... Walk Through Jerusalem Just Like John (KDC) ... (2) Nesbitt ... Nellie Gray (JCT) ... Kingdom Come (VYO) ... Battle Hymn of the Republic (JCT)

110 July 8, 1945

Barber of Turin (JCT) ... My Romance *Jumbo*, Rodgers & Hart (VYO) ... Smilin' Thro' (JCT) ... Skylark Carmichael (KDC) (2) Nesbitt on Old Cars ... Bambalina Youmans (VYO) ... Shaller Brown (JCT)

111–113 JCT replaced by Richard Tucker during pneumonia bout

117

O What a Beautiful Morning (JCT) ... When I Grow Too Old to Dream Romberg / Hammerstein (JCT) ... Melody in F(VYO) ... Tumbling Tumbleweed (KDC) Nesbitt Compass Iron Ore ... Wedding of the Painted Doll (VYO) ... One Alone *Desert Song* (JCT)

118 (after V-J Day?)

The Time for Making Songs Has Come (JCT) ... Paspié Delibes (VYO) ... If I Forget You I. Caesar, comp. (JCT) ... Bouilla from Disney's *Three Caballeros* (KDC) (2) Nesbitt Clara Barton ... Haystraw, Youmanns (VYO) ... Guide Me O Thou Great Jehova (JCT)

119

Amor (JCT G. Ruiz comp.) ... Love Letters (KDC) ... This Heart of Mine (VYO) ... Little Mother o' Mine (JCT) Per me giunto *Don Carlos* (JCT) (2) Nesbitt Perkin Warbeck. . Polonaise in A Chopin (VYO) ... O Dry Those Tears Del Riego comp. (JCT)

120

Nemico della Patria (JCT) ... Pop Goes the Weasel (VYO V. Young arr.) ... In the Time of Roses (JCT) ... Schooldays / Songs My Mother Taught Me (KDC) (2) Lindy Lou (JCT) Nesbitt Selenium and Television ... Jamaican Rhumba (VYO) ... Great Day (JCT)

121

Someday (JCT from *Vagabond King*) ... Dream Lover (VYO) ... Got a Lover There (JCT MacGimsey comp.) ... Enchilada Man / La Colandrina (KDC) (2) Nesbitt Lost Canyon Mine ... Jahora Stacatto (VYO violin instrumental) ... When Day Is Done (JCT, KDC)

122

Prelude to the Cycle of Life (JCT) ... Traumerei (VYO) ... Marcheta (JCT) ... Tumbling Tumbleweed (KDC) (2) Nesbitt Ghost Ships ... Waltzes from Faust (VYO) ... Rancho Grande (JCT, KDC)

123

Tally Ho (JCT) ... I've Got You Under My Skin Porter (VYO) ... Annie Laurie (JCT) ... Grandfather Clock (KDC) (2) Nesbitt Run-away Train ... Prelude E Major (VYO Bach) ... 'Neath a Southern Moon (JCT)

124

I Love Life Mana-Zucca comp. (JCT) All Through the Night *Anything Goes* (VYO) ... My Wonderful One Paul Whiteman comp.(JCT) ... O Mary Don't Grow Up (KDC) (2) Nesbitt Rocket Travel in Future ... Pearls on Velvet (VYO piano solo) ... O Worship the King Hayden (JCT)

125

For You Alone (JCT) ... Softly as in the Morning Sunrise (VYO New Moon) ... Hold Thou My Hand (JCT) ... Evaline (KDC) (2) Nesbitt Midget Story ... Brigadoon (VYO Kreisler) ... When the Boys Come Home (JCT Speaks) ... Little Mother o' Mine (JCT) ... Loveletters (KDC)

126

The Rosary (JCT) ... My Silent Love Dana Suss (VYO) ... Sing a Song of Sixpence (JCT great sound) ... orchestral selection (VYO) ... Anchors Aweigh (KDC) (2) Moonlight Madonna (VYO) Nesbitt Billy the Kid ... Gypsy Rondo (VYO Hayden) ... Auf Wiedersehen *Blue Paradise* (JCT)

127

Invictus (JCT Henley) ... Tristesse Chopin Etude in A major arr. from *Song to Remember* (VYO) ... The Sweetest Story Ever Told (JCT) ... Paspié (VYO Delibes) Nesbitt on Broadcasting ... Harikati (VYO Hungarian music) ... Bayiea (KDC) ... The Hills of Home (JCT)

128

When Johnny Comes Marching Home (JCT) ... Stardust (VYO) ... My Lovely Celia (JCT) ... Old Joe Clark (KDC) (2) Nesbitt Hippocrates ... Dance of the Buffoons (VYO Rimsky Korsakov) ... Tally Ho (JCT)

129 Thanksgiving

Bless This House (JCT) Bess, You Is My Woman Now *Porgy & Bess* (VYO) ... Homing, Diego comp. (JCT) ... If There Is Someone Lovelier Than You (KDC) (2) Camptown Races (VYO) ... Schooldays / Songs My Mother Taught Me (KDC) ... Keep the Home Fires Burning / I'm Home for a Little While (KDC) ... America the Beautiful (JCT) We Gather Together (JCT)

130

I Love Life (JCT Mana-Zucca) ... If I Loved You Rodgers & Hammerstein from *Carousel* (VYO) ... Boots & Saddles (JCT) ... Buckle Down Winsocki (KDC) (2) Nesbitt Emperor Norton ... Skip to Ma Lou (VYO) ... One World Jeffrey O'Hara comp. (JCT)

131

Until Wilfred Sanderson (JCT) ... Romance, Grieg (VYO) ... Promesse de mon avenir *Le Roi de Lahore*, Massenet (JCT) (2) Nesbitt Pellagra ... March (VYO Rossini) ... Sing a Song of Sixpence (JCT) ... Guide Me O Thou Great Jehovah (JCT / KDC)

132 Dec. 9, 1945

Home on the Range, Tell Me That You Love Me (Parlami d'Amore) (JCT) ... Noel Coward song (VYO) ... Sails (JCT) ... Chopin Nocturne (VYO) ... Nesbitt ... Through the Years (JCT)

133

I'm Dreaming of a White Christmas (JCT) ... As Long as I Live (VYO) ... Strange Music *Song of Norway* Grieg (JCT) ... Nesbitt, Mt. Palomar (2) Per me giunto *Don Carlos* (JCT) The Sweetest Story Ever Told (JCT) The Bells of St. Mary's (JCT) ... Skater's Waltz (VYO)

135 New Year's Eve

Spacious Firmament on High (JCT) ... Love Letters (VYO) ... Home Sweet Home (JCT) ... Auld Lang Syne (KDC) (2) Nesbitt Prophecies ... El Reliqario (VYO) ... Ring Out Wild Bells (JCT) ... orchestral number (VYO)

137

All the Things You Are (JCT Kern / Hammerstein) ... Rachmaninoff 2nd piano concerto (VYO excerpt Ed Rebner pianist) ... Weary Cowboy (JCT) ... Nesbitt Antibiotics (2) Nesbitt concludes ... Saskatchawan / Winter, I. Caesar comp. (KDC) ... Simple Simon (KDC) ... Arkansas Traveller (VYO) ... Fairest Lord Jesus (JCT / KDC).... (VYO)

138

Roll Along Home (JCT) ... This Is Madness (VYO from film *Calcutta*) ... When Song Is Sweet Gertrude Sans Souci comp. (JCT) ... Nesbitt (2) Blue Tailed Fly (KDC) ... Sails Newell & Anthony, comp. (JCT) ... Bambalina, Youmans comp. (VYO) ... Rose Marie (JCT / KDC "all star number") ... Among My Souvenirs / Get Out and Get Under (KDC)

139 Jan. 27, 1946

Home on the Range ... Dedication *Widmung* Franz comp. (JCT) ... You'll Never Walk Alone (VYO) ... Credo *Otello* (JCT) ... (2) Nesbitt ... Sweet Leilani (KDC) ... Fiddle instrumentals (VYO) ... Little Brown Jug (VYO) ... Our God, Our Help in Ages Past (JCT)

140 February — Victor Herbert Memorial

Ah, Sweet Mystery of Life (JCT) ... Dagger Dance *Natoma* (VYO) ... When You're Away *The Only Girl* (JCT) 'Neath a Southern Moon *Naughty Marietta* (JCT) ... Just Because You're You *Red Mill* (KDC) (2) Nesbitt on Victor Herbert ... My Little Gypsy Sweetheart *Fortune Teller* (JCT)

141

I Heard a Forest Praying Peter deRose comp. (JCT) Rose Marie (JCT) ... Stella by Starlight (VYO) ... Tristesse Eternelle Chopin (JCT) ... Peanut Vendor (KDC) Nesbitt Levi Plessner ... Sing a Song of Sixpence (JCT) ... Minute Waltz (VYO) ... You'll Never Walk Alone *Carousel,* Rodgers / Hammerstein (JCT / KDC)

142

Sheila (JCT) O Dry Those Tears del Riego (JCT / KDC) ... Gratitude, Grieg (VYO strings) ... Fulfillment (JCT) ... This Heart of Mine (VYO) (2) Nesbitt, Mascani *Cavalleria* intermezzo (VYO) ... Cindy (KDC) ... Begin the Beguine (JCT)

143 Jerome Kern Memorial

The Song Is You *Music in the Air* (JCT) This Is Madness (VYO) ... Yesterday *Roberta* (VYO) ... Smoke Gets in Your Eyes (JCT) ... Long Ago and Far Away (KDC) (2) Nesbitt Westinghouse centenary.... She Didn't Say Yes (VYO) ... All the Things You Are (JCT)

144

Sing a While Longer (JCT Jeff O'Hara comp.) ... Warsaw Concerto excerpt (VYO) ... All Through the Night (JCT) ... Minute Waltz (VYO Chopin) ... Vive l'amour / Speak to Me of Love (KDC) (2) Land of Sky Blue Waters (VYO) ... Nesbitt Physicist at Football Game.... Guitars (VYO Moskoski) ... Great Day (JCT)

145

Children of Men (JCT) ... Stella By Starlight (VYO) Spanish Dances, Granadas Comp. (VYO) ... Guitars, Moskoski, comp. (VYO) ... Sweet Molly Malone (JCT) Nesbitt Omar Khayyam joined by KDC Ah Moon of My Delight and Myself When Young (JCT) Less Than the Dust Beneath My Chariot Wheel (JCT)

146 St. Patrick's Day, 1946

The Minstrel Boy (JCT) Annie Laurie (JCT) ... Irish Lullaby (VYO).... A Little Bit of Heaven (JCT with brogue) ... Don't Tread on the Tails o' Me Coat (KDC) Little Mother o' Mine (JCT) ... Nesbitt Phillipe Pinelle Mental Illness ... Irish Washerwoman (VYO) ... Thine Alone *Eileen* V. Herbert (JCT / KDC)

147

My Homeland (JCT O. Speaks) ... Great Day (JCT / KDC) ... As Long as I Live (VYO) ... Cindy (KDC) ... Smilin' Through (JCT) ... Do You Ken John Peel / Wert Thou in the Cold Blast? (KDC) (2) Nesbitt John McClaren Golden Gate Park ... Little March Rossini, B. Britten arr (VYO) ... Torreador Song (JCT)

148

Come to the Fair E. Hope Martin comp (JCT) ... Peanut Vendor (KDC) ... Strange Love Miklos Roszn comp. (VYO) ... Moon Melody Broones comp. (JCT) ... Make Mine Music, title song from Disney film (KDC) (2) Because You're You (KDC) ... Nesbitt Paganini . . Perpetual Motion Paganini (VYO) ... Rodger Young (JCT)

149

Because (JCT) This Is Madness (VYO) ... When Day Is Done (JCT / KDC) When Children Pray (JCT) ... Tumblin' Tumbleweed (KDC) (2) Nesbitt Westinghouse ... Gypsy violin number (VYO) ... Finlandia, Dear Land of Home (JCT / KDC)

150 Easter?

Faith of Our Fathers (JCT) I Heard a Forest Praying (JCT) ... With the Wind and the Rain in Your Hair (VYO) ... Evening Song (JCT) ... Big Rock Candy Mountain (KDC) (2) Nesbitt Architect and Farmer ... Marcheta (JCT) ... Camptown Races (VYO) ... My Journey's End (JCT / KDC)

152

Roving Gambler (JCT) A Little Bit of Heaven Ernie Ball comp. (JCT) ... To Each His Own (VYO) ... Someone Like You Wm. Worthington comp. (JCT) ... Who Is Sylvia (KDC) (2) Nesbitt Queen Elizabeth I ... William Tell Overture (VYO) ... Battle Hymn of the Republic (JCT) ... O Dry Those Tears (JCT)

153

May Day Carol (JCT Deems Taylor arr.) Tristesse Eternelle (JCT) ... To Spring Grieg (VYO) ... My Message (JCT) ... Carminia (VYO) (2) Nesbitt Tulip Bulbs 1559 Conrad Gestner Inflation ... Ora Staccato (VYO) ... Road to Mandalay (JCT / KDC)

154 Mother's Day

Thine Is My Heart Alone (JCT) ... Could I Be in Love from film *Champagne Waltz*, Wm. Daley comp. (VYO) ... Mother (JCT comp.) Roving Gambler ... Songs My Mother Taught Me Dvorák (KDC) (2) Nesbitt Great Pyramid ... Brigadoon, Kreisler(VYO) ... Spirit Flower, Campbell-Tipton (JCT)

155

Someday (JCT from Vagabond King by Friml) ... All Through the Night (VYO from *Anything Goes* C. Porter) ... Forgotten (JCT) Fulfillment (JCT) ... Blue Tailed Fly (KDC) (2) Nesbitt Mary Reed, Pirate ... Instrumental, Indian theme (VYO) ... Classical Symphony (VYO Prokofiev comp.) ... He's Got the Whole World in His Hands (JCT / KDC)

156–158 Sweetland substitutes for JCT vacation

159

Give Me Your Hand to Hold (JCT F. Tours comp.) ... strings instrumental (VYO) ... Prelude in C minor (VYO Young arr.) ... Sing a Song of Sixpence (JCT) ... Old Joe Clark (KDC) (2) Nesbitt Lincoln Storekeeper Importance of Business ... My Message (JCT), Tarantella (VYO Tchaikovsky from *Caprice Italien*) ... Lord's Prayer (JCT)

160

My Lovely Celia (JCT) Ah, Sweet Mystery of Life (JCT) ... Strange Love (VYO Nicholas Rozsca comp.) ... Nemico della Patria (JCT) ... Out California Way (KDC) (2) Nesbitt One Minute Without Power ... When Children Pray (JCT) ... Faust waltzes (VYO, JCT) ... Every Time I Feel the Spirit (JCT / KDC)

161 June 30, 1946

Love I Have Won You (JCT Landon-Ronald comp.) Smilin' Through (JCT) ... Make Mine Music (VYO) ... Annie Laurie (JCT) ... Margie / Love Nest (KDC) Nesbitt Tom Paine ... instrumental (VYO) ... Auf Wiedersehen (JCT / KDC)

Chapter Notes

Preface

1. *New York Herald Tribune*, November 27, 1940.
2. Ken Darby, "On the Toss of a Coin: The Jubilant Life of John Charles Thomas," 1986, unpublished.
3. Rosa Ponselle and James A. Drake, *Ponselle, a Singer's Life*, Garden City, NJ: Doubleday, 1982, p. 137. Ponselle praised Thomas's wonderful vocal tone, but found his technique insufficient to achieve the exquisite softness that Tibbett could bring to an aria, and his acting insufficient to create believable characters.
4. Robert Merrill, *Once More from the Beginning*, New York: Macmillan, 1965, p. 137. See also *Between Acts: An Irreverent Look at Opera and Other Madness*, New York: McGraw Hill, 1970, p. 64.
5. Richard T. Soper, *Belgian Opera Houses and Singers*, Spartanburg, S.C.: Reprint Co. Publishers, 1999.

Chapter 1

1. Darby, p. 6.
2. In a 1937 program of the Palm Beach Romanies chorus, Thomas took his fudging on age a step further. His bio read that he was born "when the Gay 90s were about to give way to a new century." The piece then went on to accurately record that he attended the Peabody from 1910 to 1913, which would have made the youngster quite a prodigy.
3. Satia Saleno, columnist, in the *New York Times*, June 16, 1916.
4. Although there are few recorded examples of it, Thomas's Latin diction was excel-

lent. His pronunciation of diphthongs and vowels is a delight to hear. The final syllable of "mirabilis" is pronounced "ees"; the "u" in "humilis" is "yu," not "oo."
5. During his Broadway years in the teens, Thomas told a reporter that his voice never had changed, that he was not an alto as a boy, but always a baritone. Darby, p. 24.
6. In a letter to the author, Ken Darby recalled Charlie Parker as an "amanuensis, beloved pal, gofer, gardener, pig fancier, dog bather, sandwich maker, often living in the same house, or in a place nearby. Sometimes (rarely) he went with John on tour, more often stayed at home as company and guardian of Dorothy when she remained behind, overseer of the property when she joined JCT on tour. He was a good conversationalist, story teller, alter ego ... best friend ... a self-effacing gentle man ... a bright, nimble wit, it was always a pleasure to be in his company." Parker was also a keeper of secrets, and declined to open up to Darby about private aspects of his friend's life.

Chapter 2

1. Mathilde Marchesi (1821–1913) was probably the most renowned singing teacher of the late 19th century. She was herself a pupil of Manuel Garcia the Second, and a colleague of the greatest divas of the middle 19th century. She served as the link between the long established Italian bel canto method and the beginning of the 20th century. Early in her career her work was praised by Rossini, and toward the end of her career she prepared such superstars as Nellie Melba, Emma Calvé, Emma Eames, and Frances Alda.
2. In 1943, Thomas discussed "Color in

Singing" in an article written by Rose Heyl-butt.

3. An article in the *New York Times*, March 14, 1915, made this suggestion.

4. Darby, p. 107.

5. Thomas de Koven may have been related to Reginald de Koven (1859–1920), a major figure on Broadway in these years, playwrite and composer of such songs as "O Promise Me" and "Brown October Ale," which Thomas frequently performed.

6. One of Hopper's six wives would become the famous Hearst columnist Hedda Hopper. Thomas would appear on her radio show in March of 1951.

7. Darby, p. 50.

8. While Thomas was on tour with *Naughty Marietta* in Canada, the theater burned down, and Thomas was stranded for a time with nothing to wear but his costume.

9. Thomas performed a duet, "Will You Remember," from Sigmund Romberg's *Maytime* in his Broadway costume; "Danny Deever" in morning coat; and the "Pro-logue" from *Pagliacci*.

10. Chamlee remained one of Thomas's closest friends for many years.

11. Pickford and Chaplain were earning approximately $650,000 per year in the teens, but Broadway had far more cachet for a performer than Hollywood, and, at three or four days distance from New York by train, impossibly remote from the center of the entertainment industry. Al Jolson was probably the biggest entertainer on Broad-way in the early twenties. We do not know his income then, but in 1913 he had been signed to a five-year contract by the Shu-berts at $1,000 per week for 35 weeks plus 10 percent of the house receipts.

12. Merle Armitage, *Accent on America*, New York, E. Weyhe, 1944, p. 267. Armitage was able to reassure the manager of the San Francisco Opera that Thomas was a serious artist, not a vaudevillian.

Thomas was not the only opera star who graced vaudeville stages. The great Russian bass Feodor Chaliapin also appeared in vaude-ville on rare occasions, and enjoyed it immensely. Soprano Rosa Ponselle was dis-covered by Caruso in her vaudeville act with her sister Carmella, but she never returned to vaudeville once she joined the Metropolitan.

13. This is not to say opera singers or composers did not earn handsome fees for their work. Caruso was paid $2,500 for each

of his fifty or more performances during the Metropolitan season, and made a still greater fortune from recordings, as did John McCormack, Galli-Curci, and a handful of other stars. Yet the number of highly paid opera singers was minuscule compared to those who succeeded on Broadway.

14. In 1916 a news reporter found Thomas ready to sell his four-cylinder Overland since he was about to depart for a tour of some months with a show in Boston and beyond. Thomas told the reporter the car had a loose oilpan and a bad sparkplug, then took him for a test drive up Broadway to Harlem. The reporter could detect no rattle in the oilpan, despite the bumpy pavement, nor any broken rhythm due to spark plugs, and bought the car.

15. Thomas also declared that he began to save money during his Broadway years, and was a millionaire by age 32, a fact confirmed by his banker. It was this nest egg that financed his European training in the twen-ties. In Europe too, however, he continued to spend money extravagantly. See pp. 65–67 and 72 ff. below.

16. Darby, p. 102. Victor Herbert had a regular corner table at the restaurant, and is reputed to have called the meeting that led to the founding of ASCAP at Luchow's.

17. Income tax rates soared to 12 percent during the First World War, with a sur-charge of 52 percent on incomes over $100,000, then gradually declined in the 1920s to a base rate of 5 percent, with sur-charges of 20 percent on high incomes.

18. London, Ontario, was the site of Thomas's debut as a leading man five years earlier. One suspects there was an element of superstition in Thomas, at least when it came to professional matters. A newspaper reported this concert was in Philadelphia, but a program exists for the London, Ontario, performance.

19. Armitage erred in recalling this per-formance to be at the Globe. Thomas did not perform the role in that theater.

Chapter 3

1. Three charges of cruelty were alleged by the plaintiff: that her husband had dropped her cat out of a window, that he had bitten her on the shoulder and drawn blood, and that he had torn off a gown she was wearing in the presence of another man. The

other man could have been Charlie Parker, and this story is indicative of the temper Thomas could display on occasion.

2. The film was remade with sound in 1937, with Conrad Veidt playing the role of de Berault and Raymond Massey as Cardinal Richelieu.

3. See Georges Cunelli, *Voice No Mystery*, London, Stainer & Bell, 1973. Cunelli was a baritone whose voice de Reszke tried to place in the tenor range. See also, Voytek Matushevski, "Jean de Reszke as Pedagogue," *The Opera Quarterly*, 1995, 12(1):47–70, and "Bidu Sayao, the Last Pupil of Jean de Reszke," *The Opera Quarterly*, 1995, 12(2):65–87.

4. Thomas had three records of Batistini in his small phonograph collection: "Ah, non mi ridestar" from *Werther*, "Per me giunto" from *Don Carlos*, and "Vien Leonora" from *La Favorita*. The Werther selection is the most intriguing. Massenet rearranged this tenor aria for baritone, and one wonders if Thomas was ever tempted to perform it in concert.

5. See Appendix B for a list of Thomas's appearances at La Monnaie. This list was compiled by Jacques Fievez of Brussels.

6. Dorothy changed the spelling of her maiden name from Koehler to Kaehler to make its pronunciation and spelling easier to the American ear.

7. See Darby, p. 69, for a description of Armitage's negotiations.

Thomas's reticence in accepting Armitage's offer is puzzling since it is not clear what his career plans could have been apart from concerts. He repeatedly expressed his restlessness with the musical theater, and even told reporters that he hoped to go to Europe to pursue operatic training. But even the greatest operatic stars of the time could not have supported their grand lifestyle without record royalties and concert receipts.

8. Darby, p. 70.

9. Op. cit, p. 213.

10. What Smith probably did not know was that Dorothy was the beneficiary of a trust from her father's estate. We do not know the amount of her income, but given Mr. Koehler's wealth, it would have been substantial, perhaps in the range of $75–100,000 a year or more, perhaps a great deal more.

11. Other portraits were Escamillo, from *Carmen*, Harold in Chabrier's *Gwendolyn*,

Hamlet, Athanael in *Thais*, Count di Luna in *Trovatore*, Zurga in *Pearlfishers*, and Don Giovanni.

12. Thomas was disturbed in later years to find that a music teacher and aspiring composer who sometimes served as his accompanist at his summer home in Easton, Maryland, had no running water in her home. Thomas paid for its installation. This does not reflect a fixation about plumbing, but he did like to have the latest gadgets, from cars to kitchen appliances, and although he opposed the idea of government handouts, he often intervened financially in cases of personal need that came to his attention.

13. The author is indebted to Jacques Fievez of Brussels for information, correspondence, and photographs of Thomas and Van Obbergh. The two men re-established correspondence after the Second World War, and the Van Obberghs visited the Thomases in the 1950s.

For more information on La Monnaie and the Belgian music scene, see Richard T. Soper's *Belgian Opera Houses and Singers*, Spartanburg, S. C., Reprint Company Publishers, 1999.

14. Dorothy Thomas, *Diary*, July 18, 1928, at Vichy. The remnants of Dorothy's *Diary* is in the Thomas Papers at the Peabody Archive.

15. Some stories say the chorus rode in the back of a hay truck, but the mule wagon has more charm.

16. Today the Omni Berkshire Place Hotel.

17. While the principal motive for Thomas's move to Easton was no doubt his wish to be closer to his parents, the fact that Maryland's Governor Ritchie was an opponent of federal enforcement of Prohibition would also have been a recommendation. Besides local distillers, local rumrunners on the Chesapeake did a steady business supplying quality labeled imports to Washington's thirsty market. See Eric Mills, *Chesapeake Rumrunners of the Roaring Twenties*, Centreville, Maryland: Tidewater Publishers, 2000.

18. Edwin MacArthur, who subsequently served as the long-time accompanist of Kirsten Flagstad, accompanied Thomas for at least one engagement. Thomas offered to hire MacArthur on a permanent basis, but wanted an exclusive commitment, which MacArthur was unwilling to make.

19. One of the stranger endorsement deals

his management arranged was a role in inaugurating American Airlines' air service between Chicago and New Orleans on November 9, 1931. Thomas dressed as the explorer LaSalle and flew from Chicago to New Orleans, with stops in Springfield, Illinois, St. Louis, Memphis, and Jackson, Mississippi. Another example of the lengths his management was willing to go to get publicity for Thomas is a photo distributed to the press with Thomas sitting on the wing of an airplane throwing records on the ground. The caption read that he had "broken a record" in flying time between two concert sites.

20. Arthur Atwater Kent, who manufactured radios in Philadelphia, was a regular in Palm Beach, and the first sponsor of regular classical music programming on radio. The show ran from 1925 to 1931.

21. Darby, p. 125. Other sources give 1936 as the beginning of this ongoing conflict.

22. Darby, pp. 136–37. There is no question that Thomas lived lavishly. While this suited his personal taste, in many ways it was a lifestyle imposed upon him by the times. There were few opportunities for rewarding investments during the Depression and war when his career was at its peak. The stock market would not return to its 1929 high until 1958. Moreover, tax policies under the New Deal heavily penalized savings, investment, and capital formation in favor of consumption.

Chapter 4

1. The Met Archive website shows that in the 1932–33 season, Lawrence Tibbett earned only $562 per performance, and Ponselle $1,900. Beniamino Gigli quit the Met rather than take a reduction in his fee of $2,250 per performance. By 1940, salaries were capped at $1,000 per performance, for Kirsten Flagstad, Lauritz Melchior, Lilly Pons, and Tibbett. Thomas received $700 at a time when his concert fee was at least $2,500, along with a percentage of the house in larger cities. Jussi Bjoerling was paid $650, Ezio Pinza $500, and Bidu Sayao $400. See www.metopera.org. There was no allowance for the cost of costumes, so the leading performers were required to pay for their own costumes, including custom made footwear.

2. See Paul Jackson, Saturday Afternoons at the Old Met: The Metropolitan Opera Broad-

casts 1931–1950, Portland, Or.: Amadeus Press, 1992.

3. See Ronald L. Davis, Opera in Chicago, NY: Appleton Century, 1966, p. 209. He was similarly neglectful in his preparation for the role of Falstaff on several occasions in Chicago.

4. Thomas had appeared at a concert with Ponselle previously in Toronto in February, 1930.

5. Darby, p. 121. Gilbert adds that Thomas later told him that his show of possibly making a speech was all done to alarm Dorothy, and he was irked that she never even mentioned it. The incident and Gilbert's description of the performance demonstrates nothing so much as Thomas's supreme assurance and relaxed attitude at what for most singers would have been a moment of high tension.

6. In Hollywood, by contrast, the thirties were a period of extraordinary technical innovation, in lighting, set design, sound, choreography, and composition. Most of Thomas's recordings for RCA after 1934 were produced in Hollywood, where he may well have found more artistic vitality than on the East Coast.

7. Virgil Thomson, The Musical Scene, New York: Greenwood Press, 1968 reprint of 1945 edition, pp. 182–183. The column appeared in the Herald Tribune on April 9, 1944.

8. Thomas's roles at the Metropolitan were: Barber of Seville (15 appearances), Traviata (12), Aida (9), Thais (6), Pagliacci (5), Faust (2), Tosca (2), Rigoletto and Ballo in Maschera (1 each). For dates of his performances, see Gerald Fitzgerald, Annals of the Metropolitan Opera, vol. 1, New York: H.W. Wilson, 1947.

9. Paul Jackson, Saturday Afternoons at the Old Met: The Metropolitan Opera Broadcasts, 1931–1950, Portland, Or., Amadeus Press, 1992, pp. 127, 119, and 230. Jackson may be too much the purist on the matter of Thomas's lingering over his consonants. Stanislavsky argued that "Consonants should be sung and savored. Both Chaliapin and Battistini held every consonant to the end. Without consonants there is no bel canto." See Fyodor Chaliapin, Chaliapin, an Autobiography as Told to Maxim Gorky, New York: Stein and Day, 1967, quoting Stanislavsky's My Life in Art and The Actor's Workshop, published by Soviet Theatre, 1936.

It is instructive to compare the singing of

Tibbett and Thomas in this role. In a performance with Rosa Ponselle in January, 1935, Tibbett sings with remarkable economy, scarcely exerting himself before the finale of "Dite alla giovine." One would not say Tibbett is disengaged, but his characterization in the role is done entirely with small modulations in tone, so that he seems more of an accompanist to Violetta than an interlocutor. Thomas, in contrast, is a much more involved partner in recordings of his performances.

10. Behrman's account books for these years are in the manuscript collections of the Huntington Library. They show that Tibbett regularly earned more than Thomas, averaging $3,300–3,400 in appearances from 1933 to 1940, while Thomas earned $2,900–3,300. Jeanette MacDonald could earn $3,700 in a 1940 concert, and Nelson Eddy over $3,400 in 1937. But Kirsten Flagstad took the crown with earnings of $7,600 from just one concert in 1939!

11. It is a mark of Thomas's stamina that he tended to wave the stress of a concert tour aside when Darby pressed him on the topic. He pointed out that his annual pattern was still six months on the road and six months off.

12. He cancelled a Sacramento concert in 1934 when he came down with diverticulitis. In other cases, he made special efforts to maintain his scheduled appearances. A widely publicized story reported Thomas's anger at American Airlines when a scheduled flight left New York without him en route to Syracuse. He complained loudly that 3,000 people were waiting to hear him, and told the American staff that he flew over 100,000 miles a year and would direct his management to cancel all future flights on American. He was able to make his concert appearance by chartering another flight for $124. A ticket on the regularly scheduled flight cost $15.

13. Programs with symphony orchestras were the most important exception to this pattern. In November, 1940, for example, he performed the four songs in Mahler's *Songs of a Wayfarer* cycle with the Minnesota Orchestra in Minneapolis. He had performed the cycle in the Town Hall German concert the previous February, an unusual departure from his standard repertoire.

14. *New York Herald Tribune*, November 27, 1940.

15. Thomas recorded only a small fraction of his repertoire of "character" songs and lighter material. A much better source for them are the transcriptions of his wartime broadcasts for the Westinghouse program.

16. In his biography, *Bing Crosby: A Pocketful of Dreams, the Early Years, 1903–1940*, Boston: Little Brown, 2001, Gary Giddins credits Crosby with introducing "Home on the Range" and making it a national standard. The historical record is clear, however, about Thomas's precedence. Thomas recorded it for RCA Victor in May, 1931, and it was associated with him ever after. Crosby's first recording of the song was made in 1933.

17. See the John Jacob Niles website at http://www.john-jacob-niles.com/John_Jacob_Niles_Gambling_Songs.htm

18. Charles O'Connell, the head of classical recording at Victor in those years, provides some insight into this neglect in his memoirs published in 1947. He cited twin banes of the recording business: artistic egos and miserly executives. By all accounts, Thomas was a complete professional, and very good humored in both rehearsal and performance sessions, so one is inclined to blame the failure on corporate decision-makers. See Charles O'Connell, *The Other Side of the Record*, New York, Knopf, 1947, reprinted Greenwood Press, Westport, Conn., 1970.

19. In July, 1942. See below, p. 159.

20. RCA launched a major campaign to sell Thomas records in California in November, 1943.

For the curious, most of Thomas's recording sessions were scheduled from 10:30 a.m. to 2 p.m. He usually did two takes of a number, but sometimes just one or as many as four. His sessions included some famous sidemen. Spike Jones was the drummer for the January, 1942, session in Hollywood that produced Kern's "All the Things You Are," "The Song Is You," and Oscar Strauss' "A Song in My Heart" from the *Chocolate Soldier*.

21. See Appendix D for a list of songs Thomas performed on his radio broadcasts between 1934 and 1943.

22. The text of the poem is:

Dark brown is the river, golden is the sand
It flows along forever with trees on either
    hand.
Green leaves afloating, castles of the foam.
Boats of mine a boating When will all come
    home?

On goes the river and out past the mill
Away down the valley, away down the
hill.
Away down the river, a hundred miles or
more,
Other little children shall bring my boats
ashore.

23. Thomas recorded an unpublished "E'en as a Lovely Flower" for RCA in 1942 that is beautifully sung. It is an English version of Frank Bridge's setting of Heine's "Du bist wie eine blume," and is probably better rendered in English by Thomas than in German. Similarly, his English language version of the "Abendstern" aria from Wagner's *Tannhäuser* offered on a radio broadcast during the Second World War may have been even better than his recording in German due to his better feel for the English language.

24. The screenplay was by Nunnaly Johnson from a story by Baltimorean James M. Cain (*Double Indemnity*), with Linda Darnell in the major singing role. The climactic scene has Douglas ruining an opera performance and wrecking the sets. A similar scene occurs in a Pinza film, *Strictly Dishonorable*, as well as a Melchior film, but it is difficult to imagine Thomas allowing himself to be used to mock grand opera.

25. Ken Darby attributed the inspiration for this project to Thomas's manager, Marcks Levine, but it is much more likely to have been a suggestion of Carroll Hollister. It is likely that several of Thomas's French and German recordings in 1938 and 1939 were intended for release and sale abroad during this tour.

26. I think I heard Him say, when He was struggling up the hill / I think I heard Him say, take my mother home / Then I'll die easy, take my mother home / I'll die so easy, take my mother home.

I think I heard Him say, when they was raffling off His clothes/ I think I heard Him say, take my mother home /I think I heard Him cry, when they was nailing in the nails /I think I heard Him cry, take my mother home, / Please, take my mother home.

Chapter 5

1. *World Telegram*, January 16, 1936. It is interesting that a man who was otherwise so at ease with a concert audience did not like

to have an audience for recording sessions or broadcasts. He made an exception for Christmas Eve broadcasts in 1932 and 1935 when he invited 300 orphans to the NBC studios for his program, and gave each a gift, usually a book.

2. The date was November, 1942. Darby, p. 51, 177–78.

3. It was Budd who vouched for one of the most improbable stories in the Thomas canon. Leaving a party one evening for some peace and quiet, Budd and Thomas went to the Budds' apartment. Thomas sang a little in the evening before retiring, and was mildly put out the next day when the management reported a complaint about the noise from another tenant on the floor. Thomas joked that people usually paid to hear his "noise," but recalled that the same thing had once happened to Caruso. When the neighbor learned that his complaint had been directed at the famous baritone, he admitted that he was the same man who had once complained about Caruso's singing when he had a room adjoining the tenor's in a hotel!

4. In *Ed Wynn's Son*, New York, Doubleday, 1959, Keenan Wynn recalled how much his father enjoyed dressing the part of captain, having the crew salute him when he came on board, and dining at sea. Wynn made a million dollars in three years on radio in the early thirties (p. 77), which put him in Thomas's income level, and paid $150,000 for his yacht, which is probably close to what Thomas would have paid.

5. Darby, p. 126, for the Hemingway story. See Everett B. Morris, "John Charles Thomas: The Boating Baritone," *Motor Boating*, April 1936, pp. 33, 88–89, for details of the singer's nautical interests.

6. Thomas also had a small boat he and Dorothy used for fishing, the *Half Dot*, as in half Dorothy's. When George Dobyne died, Thomas and his wife inherited his yacht, the *Coconut*, a slower ship that they sold in 1947.

7. Profanity was forbidden in the company of six or more men during Club gatherings, with fines or penalties imposed on transgressors.

8. Darby, pp. 319, ff.

9. At the time of the *Anschluss*, the German acquisition of Austria in 1938, Thomas is reported to have remarked, "That paperhanging Nazi son-of-a-bitch is going to obliterate culture and learning, annihilate millions, and defecate all over my Belgium."

10. Darby, p. 100. *One World* was the title of Willkie's best-selling 1944 report of his round-the-world trip. In it, he reported on his meetings with Allied military and civilian leaders, and painted a hopeful picture of a peaceful and united post-war world.

11. Darby, pp. 169–70. Even in the admiring recollections of Darby it is clear that many friends, who certainly knew of his philandering and his tendency to offer windy opinions on any subject, thought Dorothy was a saint to be able to live with Thomas.

Chapter 6

1. See Kenneth S. Davis, *FDR, the War President, 1940–1943: A History*, New York: Random House, 2000, p. 462. Roosevelt, of course, had inherited wealth that was only taxed at the rate it was converted to income, and, as President, enjoyed a virtually unlimited expense account.

2. Thomas was more vocal than other performers in grumbling about the difficulties he had in simply pursuing his craft. In an interview with the *San Francisco Chronicle* on May 2, 1941, he complained that he had to belong to nine different unions in order to sing on radio. These included the American Guild of Musical Artists for his operatic appearances, the American Federation of Radio Artists, the Screen Actors Guild, Actors Equity, and ASCAP. Once he had even had to change managers because bad feelings between theater owners and his management prevented his being booked into some towns.

3. Darby, p. 173.

4. Darby reports 37 acres. Other sources say as many as 55 acres.

5. Tony Thomas, *Music for the Movies*, New York: A.S. Baumer, 1973, pp. 46–47.

6. For Young, see William Darby and Jack DuBois, *American Film Music*, Jefferson, NC, McFarland, 1990.

7. Hollister had joined the Party in 1934. Copies of the FBI files on him are now housed with the Thomas Papers at the Peabody Archives.

8. There is now a voluminous literature on Communist Party activities in Hollywood, though most of it focuses on screenwriters, who became the focus of Congressional investigations in 1947. The author has found very little on the role of musicians in Party activities.

Most studies of Hollywood communists are sympathetic to blacklisted party members. One of the few books critical of them is Kenneth Lloyd Billingsley's *Hollywood Party: How Communism Seduced the American Film Industry in the 1930s and 1940s*, Rocklin, California: Forum, 1998. Billingsly focuses primarily on the story of Herbert K. Sorrell, leader of the Conference of Studio Unions, and the critical period of labor strikes from April, 1945, through the end of 1946. Readers may also consult Patick McGilligan and Paul Buhle's *Tender Comrades: A Backhistory of the Hollywood Blacklist*, New York: St. Martin's Press, 1997.

9. In 1940, Dalton Trumbo's contributions to the cause included his novel *The Remarkable Andrew*, in which the ghost of Andrew Jackson discourages any Anglo-American alliance against German aggression on the grounds that no one in Europe was attacking the United States. Victor Young scored the music for the film. See Billingsley, *Hollywood Party*, p. 83.

10. See Herbert Romerstein and Eric Breindel, *The Venona Secrets: Exposing Soviet Espionage and America's Traitors*. Washington, D.C.: Regnery, 2000, pp. 212–19.

11. See Harvey Klehr, John Earl Haynes, and Fridriky Igorevich Firsov, editors, *The Secret World of American Communism*, New Haven, Ct.: Yale University Press, 1995, pp. 249–52. Browder's contact was Josephine Truslow Adams, who had taught at Swarthmore College, and had a slight acquaintance with Mrs. Roosevelt. She was mentally unstable and eventually ended up in and out of hospitals for her psychiatric problems.

One author, Thomas Fleming, has estimated that the Roosevelt administration included at least 329 communist agents, the most senior of whom that can be verified was Harry Dexter White in the Treasury Department. See Fleming's *The New Dealers' War: Franklin D. Roosevelt and the War Within World War II*, New York: Basic Books, 2001, p. 459.

12. The joke may have been on Thomas. At least one member of the Bohemian Club, Fred Thompson, the son of one of its founders and early presidents, and brother of novelist Kathleen Norris, was a Communist Party member who appears, from evidence in Soviet files, to have acted as an agent for the Soviets in Europe during the Spanish Civil War. Whether he would have

revealed himself to Hollister at the Club's encampments, however, is a matter of speculation. See Klehr, Haynes, and Firsov, *The Secret World of American Communism,* pp. 303–4.

13. Darby, p. 185.

14. In general, Thomas's performances are remarkably uniform, perhaps from years of repeated practicing and regular performance of his repertoire in concerts.

15. In July 1944, Hollister boasted of having "induced" Thomas to include the "Marching Song of Freedom" on his radio show, and proposed that the song might be sung at Communist Party meetings and rallies.

16. For the best illustration of Thomas's vocal range, readers might listen to "My Hero" from *The Chocolate Soldier,* which shows his high notes to advantage, and "Men from the Field," which shows an unfamiliar darker cast in the voice not found in other recordings.

17. He was ill only once during the three-year run of the Westinghouse show, when he caught pneumonia. A young Richard Tucker substituted for Thomas, but did not host the program. An announcer introduced each selection, and Tucker sang solo.

18. In interviews with at least seven surviving members of the Victor Young orchestra, no one confirmed this incident or claimed ever to have heard of it from other members of the orchestra. Nor did anyone recall that Thomas laid down a strict rule against discussing politics on the set. On the contrary, their recollection was that during the war there was no politics.

19. Darby, p. 189.

20. Darby, p. 229. The lyrics are those of the show's theme song, "Widmung," by Robert Franz.

21. None of the operatic stars of the 1930s or '40s made it to the era of LPs or stereo recording. Gigli, Martinelli, Ponselle, Crooks, Tibbett and Melchior all ended their recording careers at approximately the same time. The only exceptions that come to mind are Flagstad and Bjoerling, though Bjoerling's pre-war experience with the Metropolitan was very brief.

22. Jolson's popularity was such in 1947 and 1948 that Kraft Foods was willing to pay him $7500 per show for his radio program, roughly twice what Thomas was earning for his radio appearances. On the other hand, Thomas was earning about nine or ten times what Dean Martin and Jerry Lewis were making during their first major success at the Copacabana night club in New York. They received $5,000 a week for some 15 or more performances.

23. During the war years.

24. The Baltimore appearance was on September 25, 1952, at the Baltimore Armory, just a few blocks from the Pennsylvania Station. Thomas sang "I Love Life," "Home on Range" and "Old Man River" before inviting Ponselle to join him on "Swanee River." Ponselle then performed "Some Enchanted Evening," and Thomas continued with "Onward Christian Soldiers," "The Sunshine of Your Smile" for Mamie Eisenhower, and "The Caissons Go Rolling Along."

25. Thomas, who criticized the great Wagnerian tenor Lauritz Melchior for stooping to popular entertainment, was booked for a week-long engagement at the Flamingo Hotel in Vegas August 13–20, 1953.

26. Darby, p. 311.

27. Levine declined to represent at least one of these students because "he couldn't be heard beyond the footlights."

28. Darby, pp. 389–90.

Bibliography

Armitage, Merle. *Accent on America*. New York: E. Weyhe, 1944.

_____. *Accent on Life*. Ames: Iowa State University Press, 1965.

_____. "John Charles Thomas: A Biography." Unpublished manuscript. John Charles Thomas Papers. Peabody Conservatory, The Johns Hopkins University.

Bernheim, Alfred L. *The Business of the Theatre: An Economic History of the American Theatre 1750–1932*. New York: Benjamin Blom, 1972.

Billingsley, Kenneth Lloyd. *Hollywood Party: How Communism Seduced the American Film Industry in the 1930s and 1940s*. Rocklin, CA: Forum, 1998.

Bond, Carrie Jacobs. *The Roads of Melody*. New York: Appleton, 1927.

Chapple, Steve, and Reebee Garofalo. *Rock 'n Roll Is Here to Pay: The History and Politics of the Music Industry*. Chicago: Nelson-Hall, 1977.

Churchill, Allen. *The Great White Way: A Re-creation of Broadway's Golden Days of Theatrical Entertainment*. New York: Dutton, 1962.

Cowden, Robert H. *Classical Singers of the Opera and Recital Stages: Bibliography of Biographical Materials*. Westport, CT: Greenwood, 1994.

Cunelli, Georges. *Voice No Mystery*. New York: Galaxy Music Corp., 1973.

Darby, Ken. *On the Toss of a Coin: The Jubilant Life of John Charles Thomas*. 1986, unpublished. John Charles Thomas Papers. Peabody Conservatory, The Johns Hopkins University.

Davis, Ronald L. *Opera in Chicago*. New York: Appleton Century, 1966.

DeLong, Thomas A. *The Mighty Music Box: The Golden Age of Musical Radio*. Los Angeles: Amber Crest, 1980.

Drake, James A. *Rosa Ponselle: A Centenary Biography*. Portland, OR: Amadeus, 1997.

Dunning, John. *Time in Yesterday: The Ultimate Encyclopedia of Old Time Radio 1925–1976*. Englewood Cliffs, NJ: Prentice Hall, 1976.

Farkas, Andrew. *Lawrence Tibbett, Singing Actor*. Portland, OR: Amadeus, 1989.

Freedland, Michael. *Jolson*. New York: Stein and Day, 1972.

Gelatt, Roland. *The Fabulous Phonograph 1877–1977*. New York: Macmillan, 1977.

Gilbert, Douglas. *Lost Chords: The Diverting Story of American Popular Songs*. New York: Cooper Square, 1970.

Goldman, Herbert G. *Jolson: The Legend Comes to Life*. New York: Oxford University Press, 1988.

Jackson, Paul. *Saturday Afternoons at the Old Met: The Metropolitan Opera Broadcasts, 1931–1950*. Portland OR: Amadeus, 1992.

Johnson, E.F. Fenimore. *His Master's Voice Was Eldridge R. Johnson.* Milford DE: Stat Media, 1974.

Lamb, Andrew. *Jerome Kern in Edwardian England.* Brooklyn, NY: Institute for Studies in American Music, 1985.

Leiser, Clara. *Jean de Reszke and the Great Days of Opera.* Freeport, NY: Books for Libraries, 1934.

Levine, Faye. *The Culture Barons: An Analysis of Power and Money in the Arts.* New York: Crowell, 1976.

Levy, Lester M. *Give Me Yesterday: American History in Music 1890–1920.* Norman: University of Oklahoma Press, 1975.

Limbacher, James L., ed. *Film Music from Violins to Video.* Metuchen, NJ: Scarecrow, 1974.

MacDougald, Duncan, Jr. "The Popular Music Industry." In Lazarsfeld, Paul F., and Fran N. Stanton, eds. *Radio Research 1941.* New York: Duell Sloan & Pearce, 1941.

Matushevski, Voytek. "Bidu Sayao, the Last Pupil of Jean de Reszke." *The Opera Quarterly,* 1995 12(2):65–87.

_____. "Jean DeReszke as Pedagogue." *The Opera Quarterly,* 1995 12(1):47–70.

Moore, Jerrold Northrup. *A Matter of Records: Fred Gaisberg and the Golden Era of the Gramophone.* New York: Taplinger, 1977.

O'Connell, Charles. *The Other Side of the Record.* New York: Knopf, 1947; reprint, Westport, CT: Greenwood, 1970.

Pleasants, Henry. *The Great American Popular Singers.* New York: Simon & Schuster, 1974.

_____. *Serious Music and All That Jazz.* New York: Simon & Schuster, 1969.

Reed, Oliver, and Walter L. Welch. *From Tinfoil to Stereo: The Evolution of the Phonograph.* New York: Howard Sams/Bobbs-Merrill, 1959.

Sarlin, Robert. *Turn It Up (I Can't Hear the Words).* New York: Simon & Schuster, 1973.

Schicke, C.A. *Revolution in Sound: A Biography of the Recording Industry.* Boston: Little, Brown, 1974.

Shapiro, Nat, comp. *Popular Music and Annotated Index of American Popular Songs 1920–1969.* 6 vols. New York: Adrian, 1973.

Shubert Archive Staff. *The Shuberts Present: One Hundred Years of American Theater.* New York: Abrams, 2001.

Tommasini, Anthony. *Virgil Thomson: Composer on the Aisle.* New York: Norton, 1997.

Villamil, Victoria Etnier. *From Johnson's Kids to Lemonade Opera: The American Classical Singer Comes of Age.* Boston: Northeastern University Press, 2004.

Walters, Edward N. *Victor Herbert: A Life in Music.* New York: Macmillan, 1955.

Weinstat, Hertzel, and Bert Wechsler. *Dear Rogue: A Biography of the American Baritone Lawrence Tibbett.* Portland OR: Amadeus, 1996.

Wilder, Alec. *American Popular Song: The Great Innovators 1900–1950.* Ed. James T. Maher. New York: Oxford University Press, 1972.

Index